LIVED EXPERIENCES OF ABLEISM IN ACADEMIA

Strategies for Inclusion in Higher Education

Edited by
Nicole Brown

First published in Great Britain in 2021 by

Policy Press, an imprint of
Bristol University Press
University of Bristol
1–9 Old Park Hill
Bristol
BS2 8BB
UK
t: +44 (0)117 954 5940
e: bup-info@bristol.ac.uk

Details of international sales and distribution partners are available at:
policy.bristoluniversitypress.co.uk

British Library Cataloguing in Publication Data
A catalogue record for this book is available from the British Library

ISBN 978-1-4473-5411-6 paperback
ISBN 978-1-4473-5412-3 ePdf
ISBN 978-1-4473-5413-0 ePub

Cover design by Robin Hawes
Image credit: iStock/ifc2
Printed and bound in Great Britain by CMP, Poole
Bristol University Press and Policy Press use environmentally responsible
print partners.

To everyone in academia, who is directly or indirectly affected by disabilities, chronic illness and/or neurodivergence;

And to those who need to learn.

NB

Contents

Contents

List of figures and tables

Figures

Tables

Notes on contributors

Jeanne Barczewska is Programme Leader for the Early Years Foundation Degree and the Graduate Employment Based Route to Initial Teacher Training (Early Years) at the University of Northampton.

Stan Booth is a lecturer and PhD student at the University of Winchester as well as being an Access to Work support partner. Stan worked for many years as a local government manager advising members of the community of a disadvantaged area of London. Seeing the credit crunch coming and the obvious impact it would have, he returned to learning, undertaking an MSc in Health and Disease and from there re-entered academia. His doctoral project explores the discourse of physical paralysis in the eighteenth century with a cultural studies emphasis that allows scope to explore individuals and to go beyond the notion of the typical and the predicted models.

Nicole Brown is a lecturer in Education at UCL Institute of Education and Director of Social Research & Practice and Education. Nicole gained her PhD in Sociology from the University of Kent for her research into the construction of academic identity under the influence of fibromyalgia, which employed participatory and creative approaches to data collection and analysis. Nicole's editorial work includes *Ableism in Academia: Theorising Disabilities and Chronic Illnesses in Higher Education* and *Creativity in Teacher Education: International Perspectives*. Nicole has co-authored *Embodied Inquiry: Research Methods* and is currently authoring *How to Make the Most of Your Research Journal*. Nicole's research interests relate to physical and material representations and metaphors, the generation of knowledge and, more generally, research methods and approaches to explore identity and body work, as well as to advance learning and teaching within higher education. She tweets as @ncjbrown, @FibroIdentity and @AbleismAcademia.

Angharad Butler-Rees is a geography PhD candidate at the University of Southampton. Angharad's current research explores the lives of those involved in disability activism during times of austerity. Through this research, she has sought to uncover both how and why individuals have become involved in activism along with the spaces in which these acts are taking place. Angharad's research interests have largely been driven by her personal experience of having a visual impairment and being aware of the lack of research into disabled people as political actors. Prior to her PhD, Angharad completed a BA (Hons) in Geography at Durham University in 2016.

Bryan C. Clift is Senior Lecturer (Associate Professor) in the Faculty of Humanities and Social Sciences, Department for Health at the University of Bath, where he is Director of the Centre for Qualitative Research. His research is oriented around sport and physical activity in relation to issues of contemporary urbanism, popular cultural practices and representations and qualitative inquiry. He has co-edited two books: *Populism in Sport, Leisure, and Popular Culture* with Alan Tomlinson (2021), and *Temporality in Qualitative Inquiry: Theories, Methods, and Practices* with Julie Gore, Sheree Bekker, Ioannis Costas Batlle, Stefanie Gustafsson and Jenny Hatchard (2021).

Oliver Daddow is Assistant Professor in British Politics and Security at the University of Nottingham. Oliver was educated at Oxford University (Philosophy, Politics and Economics) and the University of Nottingham (MA in International Relations), where he also researched his doctorate in British European policy since 1945. His research, writing and teaching interests are in British foreign policy, Brexit and public policy evaluation. Among his publications he has authored *Britain and Europe since 1945*, *New Labour and the European Union* and a textbook on *International Relations Theory*. He co-edits the textbook

Politics UK. This chapter was written while he was an affiliate researcher at the Bennett Institute for Public Policy, University of Cambridge.

Laura L. Ellingson is the Patrick A. Donohoe, S.J. Professor of Communication and Women's Gender Studies at Santa Clara University. Laura Ellingson's research focuses on gender in extended families, feminist and qualitative methodologies and interdisciplinary collaboration and teamwork in health care organisations. She also publishes extensively in the field of qualitative methodology, on topics such as ethnography, embodiment and envisioning a continuum approach to social science methodologies. Laura is also the author of *Communicating in the Clinic: Negotiating Frontstage and Backstage Teamwork* (2005, Hampton) and *Engaging Crystallization in Qualitative Research* (2009, Sage), and co-author with Patty Sotirin of *Aunting: Cultural Practices that Sustain Family and Community Life* (2010, Baylor University Press) and *Where the Aunts Are: Family, Feminism, and Kinship in Popular Culture* (2013, Baylor University Press).

Chloe Farahar is an Autistic academic whose research interests revolve around her Autistic specialisations (not 'special interests'). Her specialisations include reducing mental health stigma with a neurodiversity script, Stigmaphrenia © (Farahar, 2012); reimagining the spectrum as a three dimension Autistic space; and educating both Autistic and non-autistic learners about Autistic experience in her training courses. Together with Annette Foster, Chloe has co-developed and run a novel eight-week, pre- and post-diagnostic support programme for Autistic students, integrating their expertise in psychology and art. This support programme has highlighted the need to promote Autistic identity, community and culture, and create a shared space for students. They aspire to extend this programme to academic staff. For more information and to contact Chloe, head to SoYoureAutistic.com.

Annette Foster is a multidisciplinary performance and live artist, Autistic self-advocate and PhD researcher. Her autobiographical, multidisciplinary performance work has been informed by feminism, identity, gender, sexuality and difference. She is dyslexic and dyspraxic, and was diagnosed as Autistic seven years ago. This has led her to become an Autistic and neurodivergent self-advocate and to undertake a funded PhD at the University of Kent, starting in 2016. Her ambition is to collaboratively explore creative autistic self-advocacy by producing art with workshop participants that aims to dispel stereotypes, in order to make autistic women, non-binary and trans people more visible. Together with Chloe Farahar, Annette has co-developed and run a novel eight-week, pre- and post-diagnostic support programme for Autistic students, integrating their expertise in psychology and art, respectively. This support programme has highlighted the need to promote Autistic identity, community and culture, and create a shared space for students. They aspire to extend this programme to academic staff. For more information and to contact Annette, head to SoYoureAutistic.com.

Ian P. Gent is a professor at the University of St Andrews. Ian is a British computer scientist working in the area of Artificial Intelligence and specialising in the area of constraint programming.

Jennifer Hiscock is Director of Innovation and Enterprise and Reader in Chemistry at the University of Kent. Jennifer obtained her PhD from University of Southampton under the supervision of Professor Philip A. Gale in 2010. She continued her post-doctoral research within this group until 2015 when she moved to the University of Kent (UK) as the Caldin Research Fellow. In 2016 she was awarded a permanent lectureship position at that institution, which has since been followed by her promotion to Reader in Supramolecular Chemistry and Director of Innovation and Enterprise for the School of Physical Sciences in 2019. Her current research focuses on applying supramolecular chemistry to solve real-world problems. This includes the development of 'frustrated' supramolecular self-associated systems as weapons in the fight against antimicrobial resistance.

Rosalind Janssen is an honorary lecturer in Education at UCL's Institute of Education. Rosalind currently teaches Egyptology at Oxford University's Department of Continuing Education, and at the City Lit in London. Her previous roles were as a curator in UCL's Petrie Museum, followed by a lectureship in Egyptology at its Institute of Archaeology. A wide range of publications in both Egyptology and Education includes her *Growing Up and Getting Old in Ancient Egypt* (2007). Her interest in gerontology led to an MSc in life course studies. Rosalind's most busy and challenging spare time role to date is as an *ouderling* (elder) at the Dutch Church in London. She is the first English member of the *kerkenraad* (church council) since 1570.

Jennifer Leigh is a senior lecturer at the Centre for the Study of Higher Education, University of Kent. Jennifer's research weaves together threads of embodiment, reflective practice, identity, academic practice, ableism and inclusivity, creative research methods and development in higher education. As Senior Lecturer in Higher Education and Academic Practice at the University of Kent, Jennifer works closely with the Graduate School supporting graduate teaching assistants, has instigated a competition to enhance the post-doctoral research environment and opportunities for independent research and undergraduate opportunities, and liaises with the Science Faculty in addition to teaching and leading core MA and PGCHE modules in the Centre for the Study of Higher Education. She has a degree in Chemistry with Analytical Science, and a PGCE in Secondary Science Teaching, an MA in Higher Education and is a senior fellow of the HE Academy (Advance HE).

Clare Lewis is a lecturer (teaching) and PhD candidate at the University College London (UCL). Clare studies at the Institute of Archaeology (UCL), where her research focuses on the development of Egyptology as an academic subject in the UK. In her role as lecturer (teaching), she is the lead personal tutor on the Societies Pathway of the Arts and Science (BASc) degree and co-convenes two core modules, drawing on her eclectic combination of Masters in Engineering, Economics and Management and in Egyptology, plus ten years of experience as an equities analyst in the City. In addition to her teaching and PhD research, she is currently preparing an edited volume with Gabriel Moshenska entitled *Life Writing in the History of Archaeology: Critical Perspectives.*

Ben Lunn is a Mackem composer and an associate artist for Drake Music and Drake Music Scotland. Ben studied at the Royal Welsh College of Music and Drama under the guidance of Peter Reynolds, and at the Lithuanian Academy of Music and Theatre with Marius Baranauskas. He has also received guidance from Param Vir and Stuart MacRae. Since graduating from his Master's degree, Ben now resides in Glasgow, working in various elements including conducting, musicology, teaching and composing. His work has been featured in many leading international festivals and he has had the privilege of working with leading international ensembles and soloists. As a musicologist, his specialities focus around Baltic music, Horațiu Rădulescu and composing and disability. He is also featured in the *British Music Collection* and the British Council's *Disability Arts Online* as a featured artist. His music is published by Orianna Publications.

Robert H. Mann is a PhD candidate in the Children's Health and Exercise Research Centre at the University of Exeter. Robert's PhD is focused on the training practices and injury experiences of adolescent distance runners, funded by the Economic and Social Research Council. His work has recently been published in the *International Journal of Sports Physiology and Performance* and *Journal of Sports Sciences.* Alongside his PhD research, Robert is interested in examining how his stammer influences his capacity to carry out qualitative research.

Nicola Martin is a professor in the Law and Social Sciences School at London South Bank University. Nicola has worked in education for over 35 years and is the author of numerous publications on inclusive education. She is currently Professor of Social Justice and Inclusive Education at London South Bank University. Nicola is a National Teaching Fellow, a fellow of the RSA and a visiting fellow at Cambridge and Sheffield Hallam Universities. Nicola is a disabled leader from a Critical

Disability Studies background. As well as working in academia and research, Nicola has led professional services departments, which focus on the equalities agenda, in three UK universities. She played a leading part in the development of the National Association of Disability Practitioners (NADP) and is an editor of the *Journal of Inclusive Practice in Further and Higher Education*.

Chris Mounsey is a professor of Eighteenth-Century English Literature at the University of Winchester. Chris has special interests in the histories of sexualities and disabilities. In 2014, he won the student-led award for the best taught module in the university for Literature, Sexuality and Morality. Before Chris's vision was impaired, he wrote and directed a number of plays: *Written on Water, And Did Those Feet* and *Love Intrigues*. At the same time, he ran the annual conference for the British Society for Eighteenth-Century Studies and edited their journal, moving it to an online format with John Wiley. On a smaller scale, Chris co-organised the *Queer People* series of conferences at Christ's College, Cambridge and the Variabilities conferences at Emory University, Atlanta and Winchester. Further afield, Chris has been for many years an active member of the American Society for Eighteenth-Century Studies Queer Caucus, and two years ago set up the Disability Studies Caucus.

Emma Sheppard is Lecturer in Sociology at Coventry University, although at the time of writing she was precariously employed elsewhere. Emma's research and teaching falls into Sociology and Disability Studies, depending on who's asking. On good days, she describes herself as an early career academic, and on bad days, her description is unprintable. Her research explores concepts of disability, time, pain and embodied experience.

Sharon Smith is a senior lecturer in Education Studies at the University of Worcester. Sharon's research interests are predominantly in the areas of special education and inclusion. Sharon has an active interest in the development of online tools to support lecturers and trainers and currently manages the Strategies for Creating Inclusive Programmes of Study (SCIPS) website. Sharon has engaged with a number of JISC projects and has undertaken research as part of a team on two European Union Comenius-funded projects, Guidelines for Teachers Working with Students with Medium-light Cognitive Impairment (GUIDE, 2013) and Student-Centred Adult Learning Engagement in Higher Education (SCALE).

Jo Sullivan is a lecturer in the Faculty of Health and Social Care at Chester University; she is also a qualified adult nurse and registered health visitor. Jo spent much of her career working with individuals and their families who have a diagnosis of Asperger's Syndrome and autism, as well as having personal experience of the condition. Jo is a campaigner for change within academia and broader healthcare settings; her experiences of supporting students in both settings and witnessing the inadvertent institutional bias and ableism that exists, compels her to campaign for change within both academic and professional settings. Jo invites all of us to rethink our positioning of autism and to acknowledge and nurture the latent skills and gifts that individuals have to offer any organisation.

Mikael Vejdemo-Johansson is Assistant Professor of Data Science at the CUNY College of Staten Island. Mikael did his PhD in computational group cohomology at the Friedrich-Schiller-Universität Jena, and then continued with a post-doctoral position in Gunnar Carlsson's group at Stanford. After leaving Stanford in 2011, he held post-doctoral positions at the University of St Andrews in the GAP group, at KTH in CAS/CVAP, and at the AI Laboratory of the Jozef Stefan Institute. Since starting at Stanford, Mikael has been active in persistent homology and topological data analysis, and he is on the coordinating committee for the ATMCS series of applied topology conferences.

Acknowledgements

Whenever I start writing up a bigger project, the section I always dread writing most is the Acknowledgements. It goes without saying that an edited book, like the collection on hand, does not develop in a vacuum, but is shaped by many conversations and encounters.

I am lucky to be part of an amazing community. Academic and non-academic acquaintances, peers, colleagues, research participants, friends and family continually inspire me to push myself that little further. There are simply too many people to name, and at the same time I worry that I may forget mentioning someone. So, thank you to everyone.

I would like to thank my family – my husband Craig, my son Stephen and my parents Seppi and Otti – whose unconditional love and unwavering support encouraged me to stick with my ideas and bring to life the vision I had for this edited book.

I would like to thank the many members of staff at Policy Press/ Bristol University Press, in particular Isobel Bainton, Sarah Bird, Philippa Grand, Jade Harris, Shannon Kneis, Amelia Watts-Jones and Laura Vickers-Rendall, who have been part of this journey. Without your professional advice and guidance alongside your belief in my ideas, this book simply would not exist.

Above all, I would like to thank the contributors, whose generous gift of their time and energy made this book possible at all. I am very privileged to have been invited into your lives and to have been part of your journeys. For some of you, this journey included medical treatments, hospital stays and prolonged absences from work. For others, this was a journey of self-discovery and acceptance, an opportunity to explore a new version of yourselves, to negotiate that new-found identity and to come to terms with difficult experiences.

I am forever grateful and indebted.

Introduction:
Being 'different' in academia

Nicole Brown

Introduction

This book is the result of a long process. In November 2017, I spearheaded the organisation of a conference on the theme of ableism in academia held at the UCL Institute of Education in the spring of 2018. My interest in organising the conference came out of fieldwork, which led to me understanding more deeply the sense of failure many academics experience because they cannot meet expectations placed upon them due to their ill health or disabilities. The response to the conference was so overwhelming that I decided straight away there would be two edited books: one would provide the space for theorising experiences and the second would use the lived experiences as a starting point for recommendations to improve attitudes and practices in higher education. After the successful launch of *Ableism in Academia: Theorising Experiences of Disabilities and Chronic Illnesses in Higher Education* (Brown and Leigh, 2020), this is now the second edited book.

In this edited collection, members of academia explore notions of ableism in academia from the viewpoint of their personal and professional experiences and scholarship. The book introduces pressures and challenges faced by disabled, chronically ill and/or neurodivergent academics written from the viewpoint of those working in academia and exploring what can be done to help others like them. Of course, lived experiences of illnesses and disabilities are not uniform, and neither are the circumstances and backgrounds of individuals. As such, the experiences presented in this book are merely a starting point to begin conversations around ableism in academia in earnest. As contributors we are aware of our privileges and the responsibilities that accompany these privileges: to raise awareness, to highlight inequities, to present the reality of struggles, to offer helpful, practical ideas and to further the conversation that began with that conference in March 2018.

Higher education in the 21st century

Academia always had the reputation of privilege, with those working in higher education contexts considering themselves lucky to have the autonomy and flexibility that research and teaching afford and that hardly any other profession or job can offer. At the same time, the public narrative includes a discourse of inclusion, equality and diversity within the academy, which again is unrivalled across sectors and professions. It is true that particular aspects of academic and scholarly work – such as researching in the field, guest lecturing or presenting at conferences and working from home to prepare for these duties – look enticing to outsiders. These are the kinds of tasks that make the roles varied, and that foreground the widely valued autonomy and flexibility. However, when we look more closely at academic employments and working conditions in the 21st century higher education institutions, an image emerges that is quite at odds with that public narrative.

Where students are concerned, within the UK there is a clear increase of students that are Black, Asian, Mixed or from Other ethnic backgrounds, while the number of White students has remained relatively stable during the latter half of the 2010s (HESA, 2020). Additionally, the number of students reporting and recording a disability keeps increasing year on year, so that from the academic year 2003/04 to the academic year 2017/18 the proportion of students with a known disability has more than doubled from 5.4 per cent to 12.9 per cent (Advance HE, 2019a), with many students in the late 2010s disclosing specific learning difficulties and mental health conditions (Advance

HE, 2019a). Yet, the student statistics already cast doubt on the image of equality and inclusion within higher education. The largest proportion of students disclosing disabilities is the student body of first-degree undergraduates, who account for 14.4 per cent of disclosures. This compares with 10.6 per cent of other undergraduate students, 9.3 per cent of taught postgraduate students and 9.0 per cent of research postgraduate students who disclose a disability (Advance HE, 2019a). The real picture behind the façade of inclusion and equality is clarified further when looking at staff within higher education. In the academic year 2017/18 only 0.6 per cent of all professors in the UK were Black and only 3.1 per cent of all heads of institutions in the UK identified as Black, Asian or minority ethnic (BAME), which accounts for fewer than five heads of institutions across the entire UK higher education landscape (Advance HE, 2019b). Institutions may pride themselves for having increased their proportion of BAME staff, and indeed, this is a good trend to observe (Advance HE, 2019b). However, this is and should not be seen as providing equality and inclusion. Considering the statistics for disability disclosure, the picture is equally bleak. Despite the fact that overall disability disclosure rates have more than doubled from 2007/08 to 2017/18, the disclosure rates remain lower among academic staff than among professional and support staff (Advance HE, 2019b). Among the academics, further trends are worrisome: 5.3 per cent of academic staff on teaching-only contracts disclosed as disabled, compared with 3.2 per cent of those on research-only contracts. The disability disclosure rate among academic staff on teaching and research contracts was between the two, at 4.2 per cent (Advance HE, 2019b).

The disclosure rates reported here, as well as the above-mentioned student statistics, suggest that the more 'scholarly' academic work is the more likely it is for individuals not to report a disability. There are two particular factors at play here that explain the drop in disclosure reports: First, disclosure is a cost-benefit analysis between the cost of stigmatisation and discrimination and the benefit of support systems, such as reasonable adjustments (see Brown and Leigh, 2018; Brown, 2020a). The figures quoted suggest that for undergraduate students the benefit from support more likely outweighs the risk of stigmatisation than is the case for postgraduate students or academic staff, for example. Second, the drop of disclosure rates at transition points from undergraduate level through to academic roles and jobs raises the question of whether or not there are disabled and chronically ill students who drop out of the academy. The figures make us ask ourselves whether individuals in research positions are uncomfortable reporting a disability or if they drop out of academic careers. Whatever the precise answer is to both of these questions, the picture painted here is not one of inclusion and equality, but one of an environment where those who are marginalised and vulnerable are not supported in the best possible way. We can see how academia only enables specific kinds of people and favours particular ways of learning and working.

The typical academic is one who is a 'hyperprofessional', a person who remains connected and switched on at all times, who is highly productive, who offers more than what is required, who engages in visible and unseen work and who goes above and beyond (Gornall and Salisbury, 2012). The reality of working in higher education in the 21st century is further compounded by developments of marketisation, globalisation and internationalisation in the neoliberal academy (Molesworth et al, 2010; Brown and Carasso, 2013; Taylor and Lahad, 2018; del Cerro Santamaría, 2020). As a consequence of the trends towards marketisation, institutions compete for excellence in research and teaching, which requires academics to undertake the best possible research, to win the highest amounts of grant funding and to publish in the most reputable journals alongside maintaining the highest quality in teaching and tutorials (Watermeyer, 2015). The institutional drive towards excellence therefore leads to individuals also needing to be better, faster, more productive in order to contribute meaningfully to this excellence discourse (Blackmore, 2015). The lines between work and life become blurred to such an extent that individuals struggle to keep apart the personal, private and the public, and such work, in turn, makes the 'hyperprofessional' (Gornall and Salisbury, 2012) go even further.

Another consequence of neoliberalism is that permanent positions in academia are rarer than ever, with most vacancies being filled on a fixed-term, contractual or hourly paid basis. In

2017/18, the percentages of academics on full-time and open-ended/permanent contracts amounted to 66.4 per cent and 66.5 per cent, respectively (Advance HE, 2019b). Conversely, this means that one third of the academic workforce in the UK was not. Of those, who were working on a part-time basis, 50.4 per cent were on fixed-term contracts. More sobering still is the fact that 66.4 per cent of academics on fixed-term contracts were aged 40 and under (Advance HE, 2019c). These stark facts highlight the result of competition and competitiveness among jobseekers. Under these circumstances, it should be all too easy to step away from the academic workplace. And yet, individuals do compete and continue to run the mills of the academy. As the figures have shown, however, individuals, who do not fit in with the given pace and productivity needed to stand out, will be left behind.

The body enters

Within the discourse of the neoliberal academy and its ways of working, work remains distinctly disembodied, as is common for most of anglophone Euro-Western education overall (Kelan, 2011). Generally, the academic body, the physical body, does not enter the conversation or consciousness. And yet, the precarious and competitive working conditions described result in drastic increases of stress-related illnesses, burnout and mental health conditions among university staff (Taris et al, 2001; Opstrup and Pihl-Thingvad, 2016; Darabi et al, 2017). Thus, irrespective of our collective preference for a disembodied workforce, the body enters. If we are able to ignore our own embodiment under common circumstances, this is only possible because of and due to us not being aware of and ignoring the existence of our bodies. As, however, our bodies start to react to external factors with extreme fatigue, pain or anxiety, for example, they re-enter our awareness and push themselves to the forefront of our minds and experiences (Leder, 1990). In Leder's (1990) terms a healthy body is an absent body, whereas a body that does not function normally 'dys-appears' in that it asks for us to attend to it and at the same time causes us to feel removed from our usual selves.

It is this dys-appearance of the body that disabled, chronically ill and/or neurodivergent individuals experience in academia.

Disability and ableism studies emphasise the social model of disability (Oliver, 1983, 2013), according to which disability is not a personal fault or failure of the disabled individual, but the collective failure of society as a whole to remove barriers preventing the disabled individual from taking part in everyday life. While this is an important basic view to take, the social model does not necessarily consider the individual's emotional, embodied experiences. The experience of disability itself is not dichotomous but lies on a spectrum of more or less 'normal' or 'disabled' depending on the circumstances one finds oneself in (Barnartt, 2010; Deegan, 2010). A physically disabled person will 'feel more disabled' when the limitations are brought to the foreground as a result of societal barriers than say when the environment is so inclusive and welcoming that the physical disability and the body's deviance can return to the state of being 'absent' (Leder, 1990). This striving for the absent body needs to be challenged, as it merely perpetuates the image of particular kinds of workers and workings, and thus the ableism that is so prevalent in academia (Brown, 2020b). Ableism is the thought process that presumes a specific version of a body, an able body that is free from 'faults' (Chouinard, 1997) and that, as a consequence of its focus on the ablebodiedness, marginalises 'physical, mental, neuronal, cognitive or behavioural' differences as deviant (Wolbring, 2012: 78) and describes the disabled or chronically ill body 'as a diminished state of being human' (Campbell, 2001: 44, 2009). This is where the narratives and the lived experiences of disabled, chronically ill and/or neurodivergent staff in academia play a vital role in resisting the discourses of marginalisation.

Experiences of ableism in academia

Although ableism and internalised ableism are endemic in academia (see Brown and Leigh, 2020), little is known about the actual lived experiences of disabled, chronically ill and/or neurodivergent academics. The authors here are experienced writers and scholars in their own respective fields, although not necessarily in the field of disability studies. As such, this book is not situated within a specific disciplinary tradition such as disability studies, sociology, education and the like. Instead, the contributions are focused on the personal experiences of individuals to provide an insight into what it feels like to live and work in academia as someone who is neurodivergent and/or has a disability or chronic illness.

With this book we all aim to provide an insight into the lives and works of non-stereotypical academics, and to offer practical ideas and strategies for implementation in order to improve working conditions and learning environments for staff and students within academia.

Chapter overviews

In the opening chapter Laura Ellingson specifically uses emotional attachment through irony to illuminate her experiences of ableism in academia. Her account of being physically disabled draws on irony and feminist readings to theorise and exemplify autoethnography as a way of producing knowledge that provokes and evokes and is therefore a valid, robust and important framework for disability and ableism studies.

Angharad Butler-Rees (Chapter 2) draws on her experiences as a visually impaired academic to explore the circumstances of higher education in the 21st century that lead to the distinct rejection of emotions. Angharad demonstrates how academia demands a way of working that is devoid of emotions, thereby showing how this results in an emotional toll on the individual.

Chapter 3 by Jennifer Leigh argues that embodiment incorporates a conscious self-awareness of information, sensations and emotions that arise from the body and the mind, which, in turn, impacts on the generation of knowledge and research that gives us an insight into embodied experience. Jennifer shows that a research that centralises embodiment and authenticity is another robust framework to illuminate ableism and the experience of disability, chronic illness and/or neurodivergence.

In her chapter (Chapter 4), Sharon Smith discusses the use of language and its impact on how experiences of disability, chronic illness and/or neurodivergence are viewed. Sharon argues that the current terminology in use tends to focus on a deficit model rather than on the inclusive approach needed to develop truly inclusive practices in higher education, and she concludes with a call for allowing individuality.

Following a brief intermezzo, Oliver Daddow opens the second part of the book (Chapter 5) and presents his experiences of colour blindness and how the invisible impairment has not only shaped his educational formation, but also impacts the way he undertakes research. Despite its light-hearted narrative, Oliver's story helps us realise the kinds of assumption we make on an everyday basis, thereby unintentionally excluding individuals, yet excluding them nonetheless.

The subsequent chapter by Robert H. Mann and Bryan C. Clift provides insight into the life of a scholar who has a stammer (Chapter 6). The two scenes presented make evident the discrepancy between the academic's internal monologue and external conversations, the emotions and feelings of frustration and the embarrassment and failure associated with not being able to hold the conversation as would have been wanted or planned.

Feelings of frustration and failure are also a key component in Jeanne Barczewska's Chapter 7, in which she presents her experiences of losing her voice due to vocal cord nodules, an ulcer on her larynx and laryngopharyngeal reflux. However, she not only speaks to the lost vocal cords, she also uses her chapter to explore the theme of having metaphorically lost her voice in her academic role due to uncomfortable leave and return to work arrangements.

Nicole Brown then considers the experience of hearing loss and deafness in contemporary academia (Chapter 8). Drawing on her own experiences of ever-increasing hearing loss, she highlights how difficult it may be for an individual to come to terms with the inevitable, while at the same time demonstrating that there are no neat categories, only messiness when it comes to embodied experiences.

In her contribution (Chapter 9), Rosalind Janssen explores the messiness of experiences that are at intersections; in her case, at the intersection of chronic illness, age and gender. She openly discusses collagenous colitis, an inflammatory disease affecting the large bowel, and the impact this has when, for example, you need to leave a seminar room mid-lecture. As such, she not only explores gendered ageism alongside chronic illness, she also covers the taboo of bodily functions in a refreshingly honest way. Chapter 10 by Chris Mounsey and Stan Booth begins with a light-hearted account of Chris's successful relationship with his Access to Work partner Stan. The chapter highlights Chris's experience in relation to disability schemes currently commonly propagated in the UK, the Disability Confident Scheme and the Access to Work provisions. The chapter concludes with a specific afterword by Stan, who reflects, in turn, on his experience as an Access to Work partner for Chris.

Emma Sheppard's Chapter 11 is the first in a group that considers the academic in the context of working with and for students. Emma chooses not to name her diagnosis, as ultimately this should not be and indeed is not relevant. For her, the importance is to focus on making invisible needs visible for others in order to create empathy and understanding.

In Chapter 12, Chloe Farahar and Annette Foster also present the theme of invisible needs in their treatise on Autistic people in academia. Using their personal experiences, Chloe and Annette highlight that for some being Autistic[1] is a clear identity, which needs to be respected accordingly, that being Autistic is not a dichotomy, and that our stereotypical views of autism are an example for our very limited understanding of the multitude of experiences that are possible.

The subsequent chapter by Jo Sullivan (Chapter 13) focuses specifically on the experience of autism within nurse education. Jo's contribution needs to be seen as an example for the interaction between neurodivergence and work-based learning courses and professional routes into academia.

The composer Ben Lunn provides an entirely different approach to exploring differences, disabilities and neurodivergences, when he explores ableism in music academicism in Chapter 14. In his critically reflective opinion piece, he focuses on the endemic problems that disabled people come up against, and which need to be rectified.

In their chapter about dyslexia (Chapter 15), Jennifer Hiscock and Jennifer Leigh present an insight into the experiences of an academic with dyslexia and an academic supporting others with dyslexia. They specifically critique commonly available coping strategies and support tools in order to present a more realistic picture of dyslexia in the academy.

Chapter 16 by Mikael Vejdemo-Johansson and Ian P. Gent focuses on the difficult topics of mental health issues and suicide in academia. Referring to their experience of setting up the group blog Depressed Academics and using the blog as evidence, Mikael and Ian present the brutal reality for many academics who experience depression.

In a similar vein, Nicola Martin deals with difficult emotions resulting from bereavement alongside personal experiences of cancer. In her contribution (Chapter 17), Nicola highlights the messiness of life which means that, sometimes, experiences strongly interconnect and intersect, although in Nicola's personal timeline narrative, there is the before and the after.

Clare Lewis also refers to the before and after when she openly discusses how, in the aftermaths of major traumatic injury, she had to learn to come terms with what had happened to her (Chapter 18). Clare's chapter in a way epitomises and summarises all previous chapters and experiences, when she discusses the difficulty of making sense of our identity, and of deciding which elements of our identity we are able and willing to share with others.

In her conclusion, Nicole Brown reflects on the connecting threads through all the chapters and provides an outlook at what the future might bring for academics with disabilities, chronic illnesses and/or neurodivergences. Yet, this is not an attempt to provide a quick-fix for 'reasonable adjustments' or support. Instead, every single one of us contributing to this book tells a personal story that readers may relate to, that may provoke emotive reactions, that may result in real actions leading to the attitudinal change so needed in higher education.

Note
[1]   This book uses capitalised and non-capitalised terms such as autism and Autism, deaf and Deaf, to mark when a specific identity is intended.

References

Advance HE. (2019a). *Equality in Higher Education: Students Statistical Report 2019.* Retrieved from: www.advance-he.ac.uk/knowledge-hub/equality-higher-education-statistical-report-2019 [Last accessed: March 2020].

Advance HE. (2019b). *Equality in Higher Education: Staff Statistical Report 2019.* Retrieved from: www.advance-he.ac.uk/knowledge-hub/equality-higher-education-statistical-report-2019 [Last accessed: March 2020].

Advance HE. (2019c). *Equality in Higher Education: Statistical Report 2019 – Staff Infographics PDF version.* Retrieved from: www.advance-he.ac.uk/knowledge-hub/equality-higher-education-statistical-report-2019 [Last accessed: March 2020].

Barnartt, S.N. (2010). Disability as a fluid state: Introduction. In: Barnartt, S.N. (ed). *Disability as a Fluid State: Research in Social Science and Disability,* Vol 5. Bingley: Emerald Group Publishing, 1–22.

Blackmore, P. (2015). *Prestige in Academic Life: Excellence and Exclusion.* London: Routledge.

Brown, N. (2020a). Disclosure in academia: A sensitive issue. In: Brown, N., & Leigh, J.S. (eds) *Ableism in Academia: Theorising Experiences of Disabilities and Chronic Illnesses in Higher Education.* London: UCL Press.

Brown, N. (2020b). Introduction: Theorising ableism in academia. In: Brown, N., & Leigh, J.S. (eds) *Ableism in Academia: Theorising Experiences of Disabilities and Chronic Illnesses in Higher Education.* London: UCL Press.

Brown, N. & Leigh, J.S. (2018). Ableism in academia: Where are the disabled and ill academics? *Disability and Society,* 33(6), 985–989.

Brown, N. & Leigh, J.S. (eds) (2020). *Ableism in Academia: Theorising Experiences of Disabilities and Chronic Illnesses in Higher Education.* London: UCL Press.

Brown, R., & Carasso, H. (2013). *Everything for Sale? The Marketisation of UK Higher Education.* London: Routledge.

Campbell, F.K. (2001). Inciting legal fictions: Disability's date with ontology and the ableist body of the law. *Griffith Law Review,* 10, 42–62.

Campbell, F.K. (2009). *Contours of Ableism: The Production of Disability and Abledness.* New York: Springer.

Chouinard, V. (1997). Making space for disabling difference: Challenging ableist geographies. *Environment and Planning D: Society and Space*, 15, 379–387.

Darabi, M., Macaskill, A. & Reidy, L. (2017). Stress among UK academics: Identifying who copes best. *Journal of Further and Higher Education*, 41(3), 393–412.

Deegan, M.J. (2010). 'Feeling normal' and 'feeling disabled'. In: Barnartt, S.N. (ed). *Disability as a Fluid State: Research in Social Science and Disability*, Vol 5. Bingley: Emerald Group Publishing, 25–48.

del Cerro Santamaría, G. (2020). Challenges and drawbacks in the marketisation of higher education within neoliberalism. *Review of European Studies*, 12(1), 1–22.

Faulkner, S.L. (2018). Poetic inquiry. In: Leavy, P. (ed). *Handbook of Arts-Based Research*, New York: Guildford Press. 208–230.

Gornall, L., & Salisbury, J. (2012). Compulsive working, 'hyperprofessionality' and the unseen pleasures of academic work. *Higher Education Quarterly*, 66(2), 135–154.

HESA. (2020). *Higher Education Student Statistics: UK, 2018/19 – Student Numbers and Characteristics.* Retrieved from: www.hesa.ac.uk/news/16-01-2020/sb255-higher-education-student-statistics/numbers [Last accessed: March 2020].

Kelan, E. (2011). Moving bodies and minds: The quest for embodiment in teaching and learning. *Higher Education Research Network Journal*, 3, 39–46.

Leder, D. (1990). *The Absent Body.* Chicago, IL: University of Chicago Press.

Molesworth, M., Scullion, R., & Nixon, E. (eds). (2010). *The Marketisation of Higher Education and the Student as Consumer.* New York: Routledge.

Oliver, M. (1983). *Social Work with Disabled People.* Basingstoke: Macmillan.

Oliver, M. (2013). The social model of disability: Thirty years on. *Disability and Society*, 28(7), 1024–1026.

Opstrup, N., & Pihl-Thingvad, S. (2016). Stressing academia? Stress-as-offence-to-self at Danish universities. *Journal of Higher Education Policy and Management*, 38(1), 39–52.

Richardson, L. (2000). Writing: A method of inquiry. In: Denzin, N., & Lincoln, Y. (eds). *The Sage Handbook of Qualitative Research* (2nd edn). Thousand Oaks, CA: Sage. 923–943.

Richardson, L. (2003). Writing: A method of inquiry. In: Lincoln, Y., & Denzin, N. (eds). *Turning Points in Qualitative Research: Tying Knots in a Handkerchief.* Walnut Creek, CA: Altamira. 379–396.

Taris, T.W., Schreurs, J., & Van Iersel-Van Silfhout, I.J. (2001). Job stress, job strain, and psychological withdrawal among Dutch university staff: Towards a dual process model for the effects of occupational stress. *Work and Stress*, 15(4), 283–296.

Taylor, Y., & Lahad, K. (eds). (2018). *Feeling Academic in the Neoliberal University: Feminist Flights, Fights and Failures.* New York: Springer.

Watermeyer, R. (2015). Lost in the 'third space': The impact of public engagement in higher education on academic identity, research practice and career progression. *European Journal of Higher Education*, 5(3), 331–347.

Wolbring, G. (2012). Expanding ableism: Taking down the ghettoization of impact of disability studies scholars. *Societies*, 2(3), 75–83.

PART I

Ways of knowing

Expectations within academia result in specific ways of working and knowledge production being favoured. These tend to be linked to post-positivist frameworks and paradigms, even within the qualitative realm. This tendency is further compounded by government strategies and initiatives that emphasise the role and relevance of the hard sciences as compared to the contributions the soft sciences or creative industries may have to offer. These trends towards an absolute, rational knowledge are at odds with individuals' personal experiences of illness and disabilities and their needs to make sense of what happens in their everyday lives.

Part I of this book therefore considers ways of working and knowledge production to generate data and provide context of experiences. The contributions in this part present a range of frameworks to exploring the lived experiences of disability and illnesses within academia. The autoethnographic, autobiographical and embodied perspectives presented in this section provide structured and insightful lenses through which disability experiences can be explored critically, analytically and rigorously.

By the second decade of the 21st century, interpretative methods and approaches within qualitative research are no longer unique, innovative or outlandish. Yet, the process of undertaking autoethnography, self-narrative or embodied inquiry is not without risks. As will be shown in the subsequent chapters, this form of inquiry is incredibly personal (Bochner and Ellis, 2002), which may be considered self-indulgent or narcissistic (Salzman, 2002; Sparkes, 2002). However, through the consistent application of self-examination and self-reflection, self-inquiry helps in making sense of one's own experiences, which in turn leads to better understanding of others (Chang, 2016). Finally, by sharing the self-inquiry the researcher-authors are able to affect their readers and initiate transformation (Berry, 2006).

The ambitious aim in this part of the book lies in demonstrating the value of autoethnographic, autobiographical and embodied perspectives in making sense of and presenting lived experiences.

References

Berry, K. (2006). Implicated audience member seeks understanding: Reexamining the 'gift' of autoethnography. *International Journal of Qualitative Methods*, 5(3), 94–108.

Bochner, A.P., & Ellis, C. (eds). (2002). *Ethnographically Speaking: Autoethnography, Literature, and Aesthetics*, Vol. 9. Lanham, MD: Rowman Altamira.

Chang, H. (2016). *Autoethnography as Method*, Vol. 1. New York: Routledge.

Salzman, P.C. (2002). On reflexivity. *American Anthropologist*, 104(3), 805–811.

Sparkes, A.C. (2002). Autoethnography: Self-indulgence or something more. In: Bochner, A.P., & Ellis, C. (eds). *Ethnographically Speaking: Autoethnography, Literature, and Aesthetics*, Vol. 9. Lanham, MD: Rowman Altamira, 209–232.

1

A leg to stand on: irony, autoethnography and ableism in the academy

Laura L. Ellingson

Introduction

Harsh fluorescent lights glare down on me as I enter the tiny, beige room that houses my department's photocopier. The sharp scent of hot toner wafts from the machine as it spits out page after page of what appears to be an exam. Resigned, I place my biannual, state-issued disabled parking certificate on the copier and press several buttons to scan it into an electronic image.

"Hey! How are you?" asks my colleague Ben, as he enters the room and reaches for the pile of copies on the lower tray.

I roll my eyes. "I'm okay, just scanning proof that my leg is still amputated – for next year's parking pass."

Ben looks back at me incredulously. "Seriously?"

"Yup," I nod. Sneering, I continue, "My leg *still* hasn't grown back – *shocking!*"

"So your permanent disability is actually *permanent?*" he asks with mock surprise.

"Indeed. If only I came from a family of starfish, maybe there would be hope for regenerating a leg," I quip.

Ben shakes his head. "That's ridiculous. What a waste of your time and theirs."

Grateful for his understanding, I say goodbye to Ben and return to my office to dutifully email the scanned certificate to the university parking office.

The demand that I repeatedly provide current documentation of my status as a disabled motorist to my university is, of course, a minor institutional barrier. The parking office's stated goal of 'accurate and up-to-date record keeping' requires wasting my time and theirs with bureaucratic nonsense born of an endless well of suspicion. I sarcastically refer to this policy as 'proving that my leg still has not grown back', following amputation above the knee due to complications of bone cancer, after almost 20 years of limb-salvaging surgeries. A widespread belief has been articulated to me over the years by various students, faculty, staff and administrators that some (manipulative, even deceitful) disabled faculty unfairly take advantage of university policies such as the small discount in parking rates or priority scheduling of courses, necessitating administrative vigilance. When I do secure a disability accommodation, the cost is an implicit requirement that I be demonstrably appreciative of my university's generosity, performing a relentless, cheerful gratitude and remaining polite, patient and nonconfrontational in the face of ableist policies, practices and microaggressions on my campus.

In this 'layered account' (Rambo Ronai, 1995), I review research on disabled university faculty staff and narrate some of my own lived experiences as a disabled professor at a private liberal arts university in the US. In so doing, I theorise the potential of autoethnography as an intervention into intractable, inequitable higher education systems encountered by disabled faculty. Specifically, I employ evocative autoethnographic narrative moments (Ellis, 2004) to illustrate my use of irony, in the form of humour and sarcasm, as a subversive tool against institutionalised and interpersonal ableism; by playing the fool, I hope to highlight just how foolish the rationales constructed to deny or justify inequities and illuminate how disabled faculty cope with microaggressions.

Before I go any further, I want to acknowledge that in many ways, I am one of the privileged disabled faculty. Despite its ableist culture, my institution has been supportive of me in a number of ways, such as providing my full salary while I was on medical leave (rather than only the considerably smaller disability insurance payments) shortly into my second year on tenure track. More significantly, at no time did anyone insinuate (at least within my hearing) that my medical leave would jeopardise the likelihood of my earning tenure, nor that my second, longer medical leave during my seventh year would delay my promotion to full professor. Having reached both of those milestones has granted me the freedom to write this chapter frankly and honestly without concern for negative consequences to my career. I am further insulated by White and heteronormative privileges that many disabled faculty do not enjoy; these both increased the likelihood that I would earn tenure and will decrease the risks I face in speaking as a disabled professor (Campbell, 2008). Autoethnography provides a generative method for documenting and reflecting on the embodied complexities of navigating an ableist culture among the well-meaning and the somewhat less well-meaning members of academia.

I'm sitting through a faculty affairs committee meeting in the Provost's conference room, shifting uncomfortably in my chair over and over again as I struggle to get the angle of my prosthetic socket just right so that it is parallel to the floor. When I sit with it at an angle the edge of the socket pushes up into the right side of my bottom, irritating the skin and muscle there. Shifting again, I try to re-enter the conversation in progress, figuring out where we are in the process of revising a proposed change to a governance procedure.

In the background of the quiet conversation, the air pump on my prosthetic socket (the part that keeps the prosthesis attached to what's left of my leg) begins to vibrate audibly as it sucks air out, reestablishing the optimal level of vacuum pressure. I start to cringe but instead straighten my spine, refusing to apologise or explain the noise that is part of my daily routine. Two people begin to look around, wondering where the buzzing noise is coming from.

A faculty colleague who has become a friend over our years of working together on various campus initiatives, whom I will call Nicholas (not his real name), is sitting next to me. When the buzzing noise continues unabated after a few seconds, he looks at me impatiently and reaches over to grab my smartphone where it rests on the wooden table, assuming it is responsible for the noise. Holding my phone out to me, he pushes the button on the side that should silence the buzzing of an incoming call or text.

I watch his face as the buzzing continues unabated. Annoyance turns to confusion, dismay, and then embarrassment as he gradually realises that his attempt to silently but very visibly admonish me for failure to follow proper smartphone etiquette has instead drawn further attention to my still-vibrating prosthetic pump. Everyone is looking at me now, and I flush but keep my chin up, refusing to apologise for my body. After a pause, the chair of the committee resumes the meeting.

I look over at Nicholas, giving him a sardonic, exaggerated version of the look he had given me as he reached for my phone, clearly conveying that I did not appreciate his behaviour.
"Sorry," he mumbles, red faced and contrite.
I offer him a small smile and nod, letting it go.

What is autoethnography?

Autoethnography is research, writing, story and method that connect the autobiographical and personal to the cultural, social and political; it is both a process and a product (Ellingson and Ellis, 2008; Ellis, 2004; Ellis and Bochner, 2000). The author incorporates the 'I' into research and writing, yet analyses self as if studying 'others' in a culture of which the researcher is a part. Evocative autoethnographic accounts portray meaning through dialogue, scenes, characterization and plot, claiming the conventions of literary storytelling and through poetic language (Faulkner, 2017). Toward the other end of an art–science methodological continuum, analytic forms of autoethnography highlight more systematic approaches to documenting and analysing researchers' past experiences (Chang, 2016). Layered autoethnography features alternating segments of academic writing with story, poetry, or other artistic representations (Rambo Ronai, 1995). A strength of this form is the mirroring of complex relationships, organisations and cultural tropes by the construction of research, reflection, and story (or other art) into an account that flows back and forth between ways of sensemaking (Ellingson, 2009).

Faculty and graduate students embarking on academic careers have used autoethnography to explore experiences of being teachers and researchers (Bochner, 1997; Pillay et al, 2016). Disabled and chronically ill faculty and graduate students have embraced autoethnography to illuminate their unique struggles (and joys) in academia (Birk, 2013; Castrodale and Zingaro, 2015; Esposito, 2014; Morant Williams and Morant, 2018; Scott, 2013; Sobchack, 2010), including those living with mental illness and psychiatric disability (Campbell, 2018; Jago, 2002; Johnston and Sanscartier, 2019). Faculty also document discrimination and exclusion based on embodied experiences of pregnancy (Kannen, 2013; Zhang, 2017), which is treated as a 'short-term disability' under US employment law.

Disabled faculty autoethnographies fit within a larger context of marginalised academics at all stages of their careers who turn to autoethnography to voice experiences of bias, exclusion and microaggressions, including racism (Alexander, 1999; Johnson, 2013), sexism (Dahl, 2015; Edwards, 2017), heteronormativity and homophobia (Check and Ballard, 2014; Jones and Adams, 2016), classism (McIlveen et al, 2010; Romo, 2005), intersections of marginalised identities (Boylorn, 2013; Griffin, 2012; Robinson and Clardy, 2010) and colonisation (LeFrançois, 2013) – all of which intersect with disability, of course. Far fewer academics have reflected on their Whiteness and other privileges (Myers, 2008; Potter, 2015; Warren, 2011).

My colleague Mike lounges in the comfortable stuffed chair in one corner of my office as I prattle on about the latest campus controversy. "What did you say at the open forum?" he asks, sipping from his insulated coffee mug.

Waving my Diet Coke can with a flourish, I launch into a passionate tirade against an unfair policy imposed by our administration. Mike smiles, amused by the intensity of my response. Lightening my tone a bit, I continue, "I'm putting my *one* remaining foot down on this issue!" I mirror my words with an exaggerated stomp of my left foot and snicker. "Yeah, that'll work," laughs Mike.

Irony as a lens

I identify as an intersectional feminist scholar, that is, one who supports the social, political and economic equality of the sexes (which I acknowledge are nonbinary and multiple, though viewed as binary within dominant Western cultures), and who understands those identities as intersecting with other meaningful categories such as race, sexuality, class and, of course, disability. Further, I am an irreverent feminist who embraces irony in the form of humorous sarcasm – from the most gentle and playful to the most biting and acerbic – as a tool of subversion, education, role modelling and resistance. Irony is a source of laughter and playfulness, something needed by feminists and others dedicated to promoting social justice within (and beyond) universities (Chess, 2010; Ellingson, 2013). Some evidence even suggests that sarcasm boosts creativity for both those who use it to express themselves and the recipients (Huang et al, 2015).

> [F]eminist irony draws on a poststructuralist commitment to the discursive struggle over meaning. Irony is best known as a humorous juxtaposition of literal and intended meanings or an exaggerated disjuncture between what is expected and what actually unfolds. Ferguson [1993] argues that from a poststructuralist feminist perspective, ironies challenge the claims about experience and subjectivity in dominant ideologies by highlighting inconsistencies and contradictions and by positioning those who laugh (or grin wryly) as complicit in such textual subversions. (Sotirin et al, 2007: 251)

As with other forms of activism to counter racism, sexism, anti-immigrant sentiment and so on, disabled activism within and beyond the academy challenges dominant ideologies by revealing the absurdly exclusionary logics in the cultural norms and practices taken for granted as equitable or just. Rohrer (2005) builds on Ferguson's (1993) and Haraway's (1991) work on feminist irony by linking it explicitly to disability (see also Bartsch et al, 2001). She argues that:

> [t]he disabled subject position produces irony through the inescapable friction between living in a disqualified body and *living* at all … For years, disability activists and artists have been using irony to "keep themselves in a situation that resists resolution" to act discursively and materially to unsettle ableism. They use ironic language to call attention to imposed (mis)representations and new self-definitions while at the same time acknowledging the contingency and fluidity of their identity claims. (Rohrer, 2005: 44)

Feminist irony is embodied in the figure of the trickster, which can serve as a generative trope for disability activism. Lugones (1987) explains:

> When I travel from one "world" to another, I have this image, this memory of myself as playful in this other "world." I can then be in a particular "world" and have a double image of myself as, for example, playful and as not playful... and to the extent that I can materialize or animate both images at the same time I become an ambiguous being. This is very much a part of trickery and foolery. It is worth remembering that the trickster and the fool are significant characters in many non-dominant or outsider cultures. One then sees any particular "world" with these double edges and sees absurdity in them and so inhabits oneself differently. (Lugones, 1987: 13)

With a nod to both the Lugones (1987) feminist trickster and the crip of critical disability theorising (Kafer, 2013; McRuer, 2006), I propose an ironic, sarcastic, humorous *cripster*. Through cripster autoethnography, I play on and with expectations of my embodied disabled self in the university and give voice to (some of) the many painful, embarrassing, messy, frustrating and occasionally funny experiences of leaking, falling, breaking, blushing and limping through the hallowed halls of my ivory tower. As disability activist Nancy Mairs pointed out, 'Speaking out loud is an antidote to shame' (Mairs, 1997: 102), and I prefer to speak out loud with delicious, subversive, ironic wit whenever possible.

Anxiously, I scroll through the file of notes I keep ready for when I have to compile my faculty activity report. I have internalised the metrics of the neoliberal university despite my ideological rejection of them. This is the first time I have used the new online system for documenting my productivity. I feel confident that I have done enough to be evaluated well, but I struggle to place my publications, awards, pedagogical development and service tasks in the correct sections and subcategories.

Slurping my ever-present Diet Coke to keep caffeine flowing into my blood stream, I succumb to 'the isolating, embodied effects of neoliberal temporal regimes' of academia that keep me tied to my laptop at 9pm (Mountz et al, 2015: 1238). My eyes leave the screen in search of a fleeting distraction. Grabbing my phone, I text a friend in another department at my university who lives with a debilitating chronic illness.

> Me: In what box on [system] do we put all the hours wasted in useless meetings?
> Her: The box after the one for all the time we waste filling out these online forms.
> Me: LOL. How do we document the hours reading hundreds of emails?
> Her: Ha. Or the time spent recovering from our departmental 'retreats'?!
> Me: Still searching for the box to document what it takes to make it look like everything is fine when I'm in terrible pain.
> Her: Let me know if you find it. [crying-laughing emoji]

Neoliberalist logics

Garland-Thomson (2011) articulated the notion of disabled people as 'misfits', that is, people whose needs and abilities do not fit with current expectations, built environments and normative standards that are both rigidly enforced and never specifically articulated. It is the *misfitting* or lack of fit that engenders ableism, placing blame, lack and stigma on disabled people rather than on exclusionary cultures and places. The 'notion of a normative optimal academic ... [is] one who is not disabled and who is responsible for managing any problems that they may encounter in the university' (Waterfield et al, 2018: 333). Ableism obscures the very idea that it is in and through material bodies that faculty produce all of the desirable academic achievements so valued by neoliberal governments and universities (Ellingson, 2017). Disabled faculty often are nervous about getting tenure, about whether they have enough of those individualised metrics. As autonomous neoliberal subjects, 'academics are exhorted to demonstrate their value through such indicators as grant funding, patents, training of "highly qualified personnel", social media "likes", journal impact factors and standardized indices for productivity such as the h-index and the i10-index measuring citations' (Waterfield et al, 2018: 331). In this context, 'overwork is normalised' (Brown and Leigh, 2018: 986). For disabled faculty staff with mental illness another layer of irony exists: 'our ability to find success in writing and publishing is borne of the same forces that cause us our "craziness"' (Johnston and Sanscartier, 2019: 134). Like other faculty with disabilities I face implicit bias and feel pressure to over perform so that I do not risk poor performance evaluations. Ironically, my relatively high level of achievement is offered up as evidence by some that I do not need accommodations. Worse, my accomplishments are mobilised to shame other disabled faculty judged to be insufficiently productive, reflecting an academic version of 'crip nationalism' (Markotić and McRuer, 2012) 'the hailing of some disabilities as socially productive for national economies and ideologies to further marginalize other disabilities' (Puar, 2015: 49–50). Ironically for many faculty staff with psychiatric or mad disorders, some mental illnesses actually promote intense periods of concentration and productivity, which the university rewards while being intolerant of the negative aspects of those same conditions. Further, it is ironic that doing academic jobs well can lead to disabilities such as repetitive stress injury, back pain, stress induced conditions such as sleep difficulties, migraines, or exacerbation of autoimmune disorders and so on (see, for example, Guelke, 2003).

Returning from an academic conference, I caught a connecting flight in Minneapolis, an airport with an efficient system of electric carts to transport people with disabilities from gate to gate. Aboard one such vehicle with a friendly African American woman as our driver, I sat next to a woman with crutches whose right leg was immobilised in a large, Velcro-strapped brace. We made slow progress through a crowded terminal. People either did not know or did not care that our cart was trying to pass them. Both exhausted and exhilarated by the conference, I winced as intermittent shocks of phantom pain seared my missing limb, a problem exacerbated by insufficient sleep. Meanwhile the skin beneath my prosthetic socket burned and itched, sore from so much walking as I wandered through hotel conference rooms and endless hallways for four days.

Pausing yet again because the mass of people swarming through the terminal did not respond to her repeated calls of "Excuse me!" the cart driver shook her head in frustration. I checked the time yet again, anxious about missing my flight. As we stalled, a tall, White man with curly brown hair walked toward us. He spread his arms wide and leaned over in front of me, violating my personal space.
"Hey, hey, how do I get in on this?" he asked with a disingenuous smile, waving his hand to indicate the electric cart.
Rolling my eyes, I retorted, "Cut off your leg. That's what I did."
The driver broke through the crowd, and I lost sight of the man just after his face registered surprise and indignation.

Visibly disabled faculty are highly stigmatised; our existence on campuses continually surprises university community members and visitors. This reflects the assumption that '[d]isabled people are expected to be recipients of professional attention, not professionals themselves' (Waterfield et al, 2018: 332). Many faculty who can pass for non-disabled struggle in continuing doing so rather than disclosing their disability. They 'fear that they [will be] suddenly no longer seen as academics or persons, but as their disability or health condition. In this sense, academics themselves are the physical manifestation of internalised ableism within academia' (Brown and Leigh, 2018: 988). Faculty must disclose disabilities in order to access needed accommodations, leaving them vulnerable to 'underlying notions of disability as a weakness or hindrance to professional and competent job performance' (Waterfield et al. 2018: 332; see also Stone et al, 2013). Even worse, disabled faculty can disclose conditions only to be disbelieved when '[i]nvisible, less known or contested conditions are dismissed as a fabrication, malingering and an act of a fundamentally lazy or overwhelmed worker seeking validation. Considering such strong views, the act of disclosing automatically links the personal and private to the public' (Brown & Leigh, 2018: 987). Social stigma and being subjected to disrespect and disbelief is further intensified for disabled faculty who are also faculty of color, immigrants, gender-nonconforming or outside heteronormative norms, members of religious minorities or other marginalised identities.

The better we become at hiding our disabilities completely, or in over-functioning to provide industrious cover to our visible disabilities, the more we reinforce the ableist assumption that disabled scholars do not belong in the academy until or unless we can function without needing accommodations. This strengthens the idea that we also do not really need accommodations, given that at times we have managed to succeed despite their absence. Our resilience, creativity and exhaustion are taken as proof that there is nothing wrong with the status quo instead of evidence of the extraordinary lengths that we go to succeed and prove we can contribute positively to our universities. The stigma is intensified for disabled faculty who are also people of colour, immigrants, gender-nonconforming or outside heteronormative norms, members of religious minorities, or of other marginalised identities.

Sweating profusely, I reach for my insulated water bottle and drink deeply. I continue pedalling my indoor exercise bike smoothly, speeding up again when I catch myself going slower than I intended. Bright sun floods the den/exercise room at the back of my house. Five more minutes until I reach my goal of 40 minutes, so I keep puffing away.

My bright blue cotton t-shirt clings to my sides, breasts and belly, a clammy, smelly testament to my efforts to manage my ongoing stress with moderate, comfortable exercise. I look down at the front of my shirt and smirk. The shirt is the precise shade of a US disabled parking placard, and the standard insignia of a stick figure using a wheelchair is emblazoned across my chest. Beneath the figure it reads: 'I'm just in it for the parking'. With a snort I think of other great t-shirts I have that offer playful, sarcastic portrayals of disability. One features jagged claw marks and quips, 'The bear was faster', while another riffs on a classic Monty Python comedy sketch about a wounded-yet-persistent knight in battle by proclaiming, 'It's only a flesh wound!' I declined to purchase one that cracked, 'Keep staring and maybe I'll do a trick', fearing it was a bit too biting in its sarcasm for most audiences, but I appreciate the sentiment nonetheless.

Autoethnography as intervention

Through this autoethnographic account, I have offered readers a glimpse into the radical specificity (Sotirin, 2010) of one disabled faculty member's experiences and my use of ironic humour and sarcasm to resist ableist policies and practices. In this way, I frame my 'narratives not as universal but ubiquitous' (Mountz et al, 2015: 1239). Autoethnographic narratives invite readers to *think with* a story of disability rather than break it apart for analysis (Frank, 1995). Through the invocation of cripster autoethnography, I invite readers to snicker and smirk with my stories, empathising with my snarky resistance, while also illustrating some of the ways in which coping with irony and humour makes little progress in dismantling ableist structures.

Disabled faculty staff are accustomed to being the object of sarcastic comments about how we are "gaming the system", don't *look* sick, exaggerate our pain or incapacities, or demand special considerations that drain limited resources while benefiting only a few people, after all. Through autoethnography that incorporates sarcasm and humour, we may become the instigator of sarcastic humour rather than its object. This is a generative way of denying the false dichotomy that typically (albeit not exclusively) frames activism as sombre rather than powerful in and through playfulness (Chess, 2010). Cripster autoethnography functions as an imperfect but meaningful intervention into the academy when disabled faculty members (and staff and students) become the ones offering sarcastic observations about our campus climates, poking fun at ridiculous regulations, laughing and taking pleasure in our clever quips and critiques rather than only grimly surviving bureaucratic barriers to our inclusion and flourishing.

I prepared to ride my Ninebot (a two-wheeled, self-balancing, electric transportation device) over to a meeting across campus at the wellness centre. Pressing the button on the key fob, I turned it on and it responded with a series of beeps. When I left my office, I noticed that it had only three (of eight) bars showing on the battery power indicator, but I figured that it would be sufficient to get me there and back.

Two bars remained when I hopped aboard to return following the meeting. About a quarter of the way back to my office on the other side of campus, the display went from two bars to none in only a few seconds. The Ninebot started beeping wildly at me and then shut itself off while I was still riding it. Never having had this problem before, I didn't know that the machine would not remain upright for much longer. As it powered down, I lost my balance and went flying through the air, landing flat on my back. I was mortified and fought back against the tears that burned in my eyes.

Thankfully, my pride was hurt worse than my back. As I lay there, a kind (and very surprised) young woman stopped. "Do you need some help?" she asked kindly.

"Yes, um, thanks. Thank you. I, ah, I'm not sure what happened," I said. I clasped her offered hand and prayed that her slight frame would provide sufficient to raise my much larger body from the ground, a process further complicated by my inability to bend my prosthetic leg as I rose from my prone position. "Thanks again," I said, not meeting her eyes. I tried desperately to think of something funny or light-hearted to say but I came up blank.

"Sure," she said softly and continued on her way.

Placing a call to the Communication Department office, I tried to make light of my plight. "Once again my optimism was clearly unfounded!" I joked through my tears. Our wonderful administrative assistant sent a student worker running over with the charger cord from my office. I dragged my Ninebot into the nearby student centre and plugged it in.

The metaphorical and material realities of the depleted battery mocked me silently as I waited, trapped, until I accumulated enough power to carry on.

References

Alexander, B.K. (1999). Performing culture in the classroom: An instructional (auto) ethnography. *Text and Performance Quarterly*, 19(4), 307–331.

Bartsch, I., DiPalma, C., & Sells, L. (2001). Witnessing the postmodern jeremiad: (Mis)understanding Donna Haraway's method of inquiry. *Configurations*, 9(1), 127–164.

Birk, L.B. (2013). Erasure of the credible subject: An autoethnographic account of chronic pain. *Cultural Studies? Critical Methodologies*, 13(5), 390–399.

Bochner, A.P. (1997). It's about time: Narrative and the divided self. *Qualitative Inquiry*, 3(4), 418–438.

Boylorn, R.M. (2013). Blackgirl blogs, auto/ethnography, and crunk feminism. *Liminalities: A Journal of Performance Studies*, 9(2), 73–82.

Brown, N., & Leigh, J. (2018). Ableism in academia: Where are the disabled and ill academics? *Disability & Society*, 33(6), 985–989.

Campbell, E. (2018). Reconstructing my identity: An autoethnographic exploration of depression and anxiety in academia. *Journal of Organizational Ethnography*, 7(3), 235–246.

Castrodale, M.A., & Zingaro, D. (2015). "You're such a good friend": A woven autoethnographic narrative discussion of disability and friendship in higher education. *Disability Studies Quarterly*, 35(1). Retrieved from: https://dsq-sds.org/article/view/3762/3827

Chang, H. (2016). *Autoethnography as Method*. New York: Routledge.

Check, E., & Ballard, K. (2014). Navigating emotional, intellectual, and physical violence directed toward LGBTQ students and educators. *Art Education*, 67(3), 6–11.

Chess, S. (2010). How to play a feminist. *Thirdspace: A Journal of Feminist Theory & Culture*, 9(1). Retrieved from: http://journals.sfu.ca/thirdspace/index.php/journal/article/view/273

Collins, J.C. (2017). Leveraging three lessons learned from teaching an HRD undergraduate diversity and inclusion course: An autoethnography of one professor's perceptions. *Advances in Developing Human Resources*, 19(2), 157–175.

Dahl, U. (2015). Sexism: A femme-inist perspective. *New Formations*, 86, 54–73.

Edwards, J. (2017). Narrating experiences of sexism in higher education: A critical feminist autoethnography to make meaning of the past, challenge the status quo and consider the future. *International Journal of Qualitative Studies in Education*, 30(7), 621–634.

Ellingson, L.L. (2009). *Engaging Crystallization in Qualitative Research: An Introduction*. Thousand Oaks, CA: Sage.

Ellingson, L.L. (2013). Are you serious? Playing, performing, and producing an academic self. In: M. Giardina & N. Denzin (eds). *Qualitative Inquiry as Global Endeavor* (pp. 195–209). Walnut Creek, CA: Left Coast.

Ellingson, L.L. (2017). *Embodiment in Qualitative Research*. New York: Routledge.

Ellingson, L.L., & Ellis, C. (2008). Autoethnography as constructionist project. In: J.A. Holstein, & J.F. Gubrium (eds), *Handbook of Constructionist Research* (pp. 445–465). New York: Guilford.

Ellis, C. (2004). *The Ethnographic I: A Methodological Novel about Autoethnography*. Walnut Creek, CA: AltaMira Press.

Ellis, C., & Bochner, A.P. (2000). Autoethnography, personal narrative, reflexivity: Researcher as subject. In: N.K. Denzin & Y.S. Lincoln (eds), *Handbook of Qualitative Research* (2nd edn, pp. 733–768). Thousand Oaks, CA: Sage.

Esposito, J. (2014). Pain is a social construction until it hurts: Living theory on my body. *Qualitative Inquiry*, 20(10), 1179–1190.

Faulkner, S.L. (2017). Poetry is politics: An autoethnographic poetry manifesto. *International Review of Qualitative Research*, 10(1), 89–96.

Ferguson, K.E. (1993). *The Man Question: Visions of Subjectivity in Feminist Theory*. Berkeley, CA: University of California Press.

Frank, A.W. (1995). *The Wounded Storyteller: Body, Illness, and Ethics*. Chicago, IL: University of Chicago Press.

Garland-Thomson, R. (2011). Misfits: A feminist materialist disability concept. *Hypatia*, 26(3), 591–609.

Griffin, R.A. (2012). I AM an angry Black woman: Black feminist autoethnography, voice, and resistance. *Women's Studies in Communication*, 35(2), 138–157.

Guelke, J.K. (2003). Road-kill on the information highway: Repetitive strain injury in the academy. *Canadian Geographer/Le Géographe canadien*, 47(4), 386–399.

Haraway, D.J. (1991) *Simians, Cyborgs and Women: The Reinvention of Nature*. London: Free Association Books.

Hernandez, K.A.C., Ngunjiri, F.W., & Chang, H. (2015). Exploiting the margins in higher education: A collaborative autoethnography of three foreign-born female faculty of color. *International Journal of Qualitative Studies in Education*, 28(5), 533–551.

Huang, L., Gino, F., & Galinsky, A.D. (2015). The highest form of intelligence: Sarcasm increases creativity for both expressers and recipients. *Organizational Behavior and Human Decision Processes*, 131, 162–177.

Jago, B.J. (2002). Chronicling an academic depression. *Journal of Contemporary Ethnography*, 31(6), 729–757.

Johnson, R.M. (2013). Black and male on campus: An autoethnographic account. *Journal of African American Males in Education*, 4(2).

Johnston, M.S., & Sanscartier, M.D. (2019). Our madness is invisible: Notes on being privileged (non) disabled researchers. *Canadian Journal of Disability Studies*, 8(5), 120–140.

Jones, S.H., & Adams, T.E. (2016). Autoethnography is a queer method. In: C.J. Nash (ed), *Queer Methods and Methodologies* (pp. 195–214). New York: Routledge.

Kafer, A. (2013). *Feminist, Queer, Crip*. Bloomington, IN: Indiana University Press.

Kannen, V. (2013). Pregnant, privileged and PhDing: Exploring embodiments in qualitative research. *Journal of Gender Studies*, 22(2), 178–191.

Khalifa, M.A., & Briscoe, F. (2015). A counternarrative autoethnography exploring school districts' role in reproducing racism: Willful blindness to racial inequities. *Teachers College Record*, 117, 080305.

Klinker, J.F., & Todd, R.H. (2007). Two autoethnographies: A search for understanding of gender and age. *The Qualitative Report*, 12(2), 166–183.

LeFrançois, B.A. (2013). The psychiatrization of our children, or, an autoethnographic narrative of perpetuating First Nations genocide through 'benevolent' institutions. *Decolonization: Indigeneity, Education & Society*, 2(1), 108–123.

Lugones, M. (1987). Playfulness, 'world'-travelling, and loving perception. *Hypatia*, 2(2), 3–19.

Mairs, N. (1997). Carnal acts. In: K. Conboy, N. Medina, & S. Stanbury (eds), *Writing on the Body: Female Embodiment and Feminist Theory* (pp. 296–305). New York: Columbia University Press.

Markotić, N., & McRuer, R. (2012). Leading with your head: On the borders of disability, sexuality, and the nation. In: N. Markotić & A. Mollow (eds), *Sex and Disability* (pp. 165–182). Durham, NC: Duke University Press.

McIlveen, P., Beccaria, G., du Preez, J., & Patton, W. (2010). Autoethnography in vocational psychology: Wearing your class on your sleeve. *Journal of Career Development*, 37(3), 599–615.

McRuer, R. (2006). *Crip Theory: Cultural Signs of Queerness and Disability*, Vol. 9. New York: New York University Press.

Morant Williams, K., & Morant, F.S. (eds) (2018). *Reifying Women's Experiences with Invisible Illness: Illusions, Delusions, Reality?* Lanham, MD: Lexington.

Mountz, A., Bonds, A., Mansfield, B., Loyd, J., Hyndman, J., Walton-Roberts, M., Basu, R., Whitson, R., Hawkins, R., Hamilton, T., & Curran, W. (2015). For slow scholarship: A feminist politics of resistance through collective action in the neoliberal university. *ACME: An International E-journal for Critical Geographies*, 14(4), 1235–1259.

Myers, W.B. (2008). Straight and white: Talking with my mouth full. *Qualitative Inquiry*, 14(1), 160–171.

Pillay, D., Naicker, I., & Pithouse-Morgan, K. (eds). (2016). *Academic Autoethnographies: Inside Teaching in Higher Education*. New York: Springer.

Potter, J.E. (2015). The whiteness of silence: A critical autoethnographic tale of a strategic rhetoric. *The Qualitative Report*, 20(9), 1434–1447.

Puar, J.K. (2015). Bodies with new organs: Becoming trans, becoming disabled. *Social Text*, 33(3 (124)), 45–73.

Rambo Ronai, C. (1995). Multiple reflections of child sex abuse: An argument for a layered account. *Journal of Contemporary Ethnography*, 23(4), 395–426.

Robinson, C.C., & Clardy, P. (eds). (2010). *Tedious Journeys: Autoethnography by Women of Color in Academe*. Oxford: Peter Lang.

Rohrer, J. (2005). Toward a full-inclusion feminism: A feminist deployment of disability analysis. *Feminist Studies*, 31(1), 34–63.

Romo, J. (2005). Border pedagogy from the inside out: An autoethnographic study. *Journal of Latinos and Education*, 4(3), 193–210.

Scott, J.A. (2013). Problematizing a researcher's performance of 'insider status': An autoethnography of 'designer disabled' identity. *Qualitative Inquiry*, 19(2), 101–115.

Snyder, S., & Mitchell, D. (2010). Ablenationalism and the geo-politics of disability. *Journal of Literary & Cultural Disability Studies*, 4(2), 113–125.

Sobchack, V. (2010). Living a 'phantom limb': On the phenomenology of bodily integrity. *Body & Society*, 16(3), 51–67.

Sotirin, P. (2010). Autoethnographic mother-writing: Advocating radical specificity. *Journal of Research Practice*, 6(1). Article M9. Retrieved from: http://jrp.icaap.org/index.php/jrp/article/view/220/220

Sotirin, P., Buzzanell, P.M., & Turner, L.H. (2007). Colonizing family: A feminist critique of family management texts. *Journal of Family Communication*, 7(4), 245–263.

Stone, S.D., Crooks, V.A. and Owen, M. (2013). Going through the back door: Chronically ill academics' experiences as 'unexpected workers'. *Social Theory and Health*, 11(2), 151–174.

Warren, J.T. (2011). Reflexive teaching: Toward critical autoethnographic practices of/in/on pedagogy. *Cultural Studies ↔ Critical Methodologies*, 11(2), 139–144.

Waterfield, B., Beagan, B.B., & Weinberg, M. (2018). Disabled academics: A case study in Canadian universities. *Disability & Society*, 33(3), 327–348.

Zhang, K. (2017). Being pregnant as an international PhD student: A poetic autoethnography. In: Cahnmann-Taylor, M., & Siegesmund, R. (eds), *Arts-Based Research in Education* (pp. 67–81). New York: Routledge.

2

"There's no place for emotions in academia": experiences of the neoliberal academy as a disabled scholar

Angharad Butler-Rees

Introduction

Through this chapter I intend to draw attention to some of the silences and secrets of academic life. Over the past few decades, we have observed the gradual neoliberalisation of the academy, with profound changes to the structures of higher education that have included growing corporatisation and privatisation (Graham, 2002; Evans, 2005; Marginson and Considine, 2000; Taylor and Lahad, 2018; Washburn, 2003). Such neoliberalisation has been accompanied by increasing pressures and workloads placed upon academics, with scholars expected to both work harder and faster (Archer, 2008; Clegg, 2010; Harris, 2005; Henderson, 2018; Morrissey, 2013; Read and Bradley, 2018). Academics as a result frequently experience anxiety, stress and shame about their failure to keep up and/or about receiving rejection (Harrowell et al, 2018); this is framed predominantly in an individualistic discourse.

In this chapter, I will draw upon my own experiences as a visually impaired PhD student, highlighting the challenges I face in keeping up with the increasing demands and speed of academic life, along with how such intolerable demands may impede both my personal progress as a disabled scholar and my future career. This may be made even harder by the lack of space created within academia to talk through the emotions, such as feelings of anxiety, stress and personal failure. There are a number of potential reasons why academics may not discuss such feelings, including the potential for it to be professionally embarrassing; it may also leave the researcher feeling exposed or vulnerable (Harrowell et al, 2018). This chapter will be formulated as a political call for change; advocating for (i) recognition of the ways in which exclusions may be brought about through the intensification, 'extensification' (Jarvis and Pratt, 2006) and speeding up of academic life, and (ii) the need to create a safe 'shared emotional space' (Lacey, 2005: 289) in which academics may explore and work 'vulnerably' through the emotions brought about through their daily work.

The neoliberal academy

Over recent decades, neoliberalisation has come to both infiltrate and reshape most aspects of our society through the expansion of free-market logic (Mirowski, 2013). Brown (2015: 176) highlights the extent to which neoliberal logic has impacted upon our society in stating: 'Neoliberalisam does not merely privatise – turn over to the market for individual production and consumption – what was formerly publicly supported and valued. Rather, it formulates everything, everywhere, in terms of capital investment and appreciation, including and especially humans themselves.'

Neoliberal logic has increasingly come to permeate higher education. There has been growing critique of the neoliberalisation and structural transformations in higher education, focusing on how higher education has become marketised and transformed into a commodity (see, for example: Bok, 2003; Evans, 2005; Graham, 2002; Naidoo and Jamieson, 2005; Shumar, 1997, 2004; Washburn, 2003). Such transformations have been accompanied by significant reductions in financial resources, wages and deteriorating working conditions, including the intensification of workloads and growing casualisation of employment (Murray, 2018). These changes have made both staying and progressing in academia an increasingly volatile venture. Perhaps surprisingly there has been relatively limited organised resistance until recently, from trade unions and other bodies, against such changes (Gill, 2009). However, 2018 saw a surge in visible resistance with a number of strikes and pickets organised by the University and College Union (UCU) around changes to staff pensions and the emergence of numerous online campaigns including 'Anti-Precarity Cymru' and #zinesagainstprecarity.

There appear to be very few articles on the neoliberal academy that explore the emotional impacts of rising pressure and expectations placed upon academics (Gill, 2009; Henderson, 2018). Recent decades have seen both the intensification and extensification of work (Jarvis and Pratt, 2006), along with an inflation of what is expected of academics (Gill, 2009). Academics appear to be expected to work ever harder and faster (keeping to restricted timescales), and to deal with increasing workloads, driven predominantly by the chronic underfunding of universities and the audit culture, which has become internalised (Henderson, 2018; Lynch, 2006; Morley, 2003; Shipley, 2018). Both success and failure have increasingly become monitored and analysed through impact evaluation assessments such as the Research Excellence Framework (REF) and the Teaching Excellence Framework (TEF) (Taylor, 2018). Gill (2009) suggests that we might draw upon Nigel Thrift's (2000) concept of 'fast management', which builds upon the idea of 'fast-capitalism', to describe how academics are required to be increasingly fast and nimble – responding to new calls for papers, new sources of funding and the ever-changing demands of funders and stakeholders. In addition to the intensification of academics' workloads, academic work has also, as noted by Jarvis and Pratt (2006), 'extensified' over time and space. As Gill (2009) notes, work in today's universities may be regarded as 'academia without walls', this has been enabled through technological advances, which make it possible for academics to be 'always on' (Gregg, 2009); able to continue their work, regardless of location or time of day (Shipley, 2018). Gornall and Salisbury (2012: 151) similarly note how, 'there are not many professional jobs you can do in your dressing gown', albeit this has radically changed with the onset of the COVID-19 pandemic. This image unsettles the conventional spatial and temporal boundaries of home and work. The increasing use of shared offices, along with noise, interruptions (predominantly in the form of emails) and student demands, has meant that many academics feel unable to work while at work. As such, many academics now work evenings and weekends in order to keep up with their overloaded workloads (Gill, 2009).

While universities have sought to 'help' their employees to deal with the intensification of academic labour, this has largely been done through numerous training courses. These courses cover various topics that relate to stress and time management, and demand that academics improve themselves in order to keep up with increasing workloads and demands (Gill, 2009). Such approaches have served to silence complaints and resistance, with individuals seeing their inability to keep up as a personal failure, which may be overcome through self-discipline and self-governance. Academics present themselves as model neoliberal subjects through their engagement in practices of self-management and monitoring, often internalising new mechanisms of auditing (Henderson, 2018; Lovin, 2018; Shipley, 2018). Neoliberal forms of governmentality such as that produced through auditing have therefore been incredibly successful in bringing about surplus labour and value, with a much greater amount of time now being spent working than ever before (Gill, 2009; Gregg, 2009; Lovin, 2018; Schuurman, 2009).

Academics as a result frequently experience anxiety, stress and shame about their failure to keep up with such demands; this is framed predominantly in an individualistic discourse. These anxieties are privatised and deemed to reflect an individual's self-worth (Gill, 2009). As a result, individuals are unlikely to share such experiences with fellow co-workers, if they are seen to be unsympathetic or competitive as opposed to being supportive and solidaristic. It is thought that the neoliberal university structures have been largely responsible for the reverberation, diffusion and internalisation of both competition and audit, creating somewhat of an uneasy and competitive environment in which scholars are often directly pitted against one another (Lovin, 2018; Shipley, 2018), and thus potentially dismantling any previous sense of collective belonging. There are a number of reasons why individuals may not wish to discuss their sense of failure, these may include: the potential for it to be professionally embarrassing and uncomfortable; it might also present itself as a risk for scholars pursuing an increasingly precarious career in academia, leaving the researcher feeling exposed or vulnerable (Harrowell et al, 2018).

The limited resistance to the neoliberalisation of higher education and its increasing expectations of academics is therefore in part a consequence of these individualising processes and that individuals are too drained to resist. Moreover, academics, as Gill (2009) argues, are often unaware of what to resist or how they might do so. While there is a temptation to sanitise the realities of our work and to overlook our feelings of self-failure, this chapter would instead like to suggest that there is great value in both writing and speaking openly about our experiences. I would like to encourage scholars to 'write vulnerably' (Behar, 2014: 16) in their reflective scholarship, so as to build a more solidaristic and supportive community, in which individuals may feel more able to openly share their experiences and anxieties. In doing so, feelings of shame, self-blame and isolation could be reduced.

The emotional toll of being a disabled academic

As a disabled scholar, I have found the framing of an individual's inability to keep up with the intolerable workload of academia as an individualised form of personal failure that may be overcome through self-discipline and self-governance (Breeze, 2018), rather than as a structural feature of the contemporary university, to be particularly troubling. This discourse places itself in complete opposition to the social model of disability, upon which the Disabled People's Movement has traditionally been based. The social model of disability places responsibility for disablement with the structures and attitudes of society rather than with the individual, their body and their impairment (Brisenden, 1986 and Oliver, 1990). As such, a clear differentiation was made between 'impairment' as the functional limitation of an individual and 'disability' as the limitation to take part in society on an equal footing with others, due to ableist oppression and exclusionary practices (Disability Awareness in Action, 2009), for example, attitudes, poor employment opportunities, inaccessible transport and design. This has been explained clearly by Rob Kitchin (2003: 8) who states, 'at the core of the "social model of disability" is the notion that it is not impairment that disables people, it is society'.

In complete contrast to this, the prevailing individualistic, neoliberal discourses circulating academic institutions place the problem and the accompanying blame with the individual rather than on the operating structures of universities, which make unsustainable and intolerable demands of academics. If an academic is unable to keep up with their increasing workloads, it is thus deemed as being a direct result of a personal deficit or characteristic held by the individual, such as their assumed disorganisation, laziness or carelessness.

While the increased intensification and extensification of work (Jarvis and Pratt, 2006) will indeed have impacted upon all academics, I would argue here that such changes are particularly problematic for disabled scholars. This prevailing individualistic discourse suggests that one may simply overcome the barriers or challenges they face (that is, growing expectations and increasingly short deadlines/turnarounds) by simply working harder and – implicit within this – faster. Harris (2005), for example, draws upon the concept of 'speed-up time', while Read and Bradley (2018) notion towards 'time squeezing' (Southerton 2003), whereby academics seek to condense time through trying to complete as many tasks as possible within an increasingly constrained time period. Both of the above notion towards how time has sped up in the neoliberal university and academics must consequently seek to keep pace (do Mar Pereira, 2015). The individual is therefore conceptualised as the only person who has the means of alleviating their own situation.

I find this particularly concerning as a disabled academic, as I am not always necessarily able to work 'harder', that is for longer hours, due to migraines, exhaustion and reduced vision brought about as a direct result of eye strain from intensive reading and writing. Similarly, regardless of how hard I work, I will never be able to work at the same pace as my fully sighted colleagues, because it simply takes me longer to access and process visual information. As such, it is likely that putting such pressures upon myself will lead to a deterioration in both my physical and mental health. There are also likely to be other disabled scholars who are, for example, unable to work for extended hours due to their restricted access to support such as personal assistants, whose hours are being increasingly cut back. The increasing workload and expectations of academics may therefore further exclude and marginalise disabled scholars, who are likely to find it near impossible to keep up with such demands. The concept of time can be experienced and negotiated differently in line with varying formations of identity and privilege and has for long been a significant disabling factor for people with impairments, spanning back to the Industrial Revolution, where many disabled people were excluded due to their inability to keep up with the increasing time pressures and intensification of labour. Not only am I forced to place myself at risk (through seeking to keep up with such demands), further I am not allowed to express any emotion about this, without being seen as moaning or incompetent.

Neoliberal discourses of individualised responsibility may also make disabled scholars such as myself even more acutely aware of our own impairments and to foster a negativity towards our impairments, causing disabled scholars to either feel inadequate or simply not good enough. Such internalised feelings of shame, failure and inadequacy are also intensified by the lack of place to talk about such feelings and emotions in academia. It can be incredibly difficult to externalise and gain emotional solidarity in an environment which is somewhat hostile to the expression of emotion, potentially leading to an increased sense of isolation among academics (Lovin, 2018). Academia and academic scholarship have long sought to distance themselves from both the emotional and the subjective, in an attempt to assert both their own objectivity and rationality (Jayaratne and Stewart, 1991; Oakley, 1981; Smith, 1974).

Despite feminist scholars emphasising the importance of emotions and the emotional in motivating and sustaining our research, there still remains limited open and frank discussion around the everyday emotions and emotional labour involved in our everyday work (Bellas, 1999; Berg et al, 2016; Harrowell et al, 2018; Hochschild, 1985). Academics are frequently called upon to engage in emotional labour such as care-giving towards students and/or fellow colleagues; this may include demonstrations of empathy and sympathy, development of personal relationships, counselling and lifting of spirits. Meeting the pastoral needs of students may further involve extending office hours, being continuously contactable via email for emergencies, counselling those experiencing grief and radiating sincerity and approachability (Lawless, 2018). Studies show that women disproportionally take on emotional labour within academia; they are predominantly the ones listening to students' personal struggles and trepidations, reassuring fellow colleagues of their capabilities and highlighting issues of equality, diversity and inclusion within their departments. This burden also appears to be disproportionately placed upon academics from minority backgrounds, who are often institutionally encouraged to stand out, disclose and make difference known (Taylor, 2018). Responsibility is often placed upon them to stand for diversity, widening participation or internationalisation (Taylor, 2018). Like Lawless (2018), I am not arguing here that we should not be undertaking this sort of work, but instead I would like to call upon individuals to both identify and make explicit the forms of work they are undertaking. Through identifying emotional labour as work, we may then start to reconsider discursive markers of professionalism, productivity and success (Lawless, 2018).

Both scientists and social scientists have traditionally been educated and trained to suppress and censor their emotions (Bellas, 1999). Such practices, as Bellas (1999) argues, are particularly visible within older textbooks such as *The Practice of Social Research* by Earle Babbie (1995). Babbie (1995) notes how, during interviews with respondents, interviewers should be a '*neutral* medium through which questions and answers are transmitted' (264, italics in original). Impression management has therefore traditionally been regarded as essential within interviewing techniques. There has, however, been growing recognition of the way in which an interviewer's subjectivity may inadvertently impact upon the interview and the wider research process, preventing them from serving as a 'neutral medium' (Hill, 2002). Furthermore, such practices are perhaps neither feasible nor desirable within much social science research where there is a need to build rapport, empathy and understanding between the researcher and their informants. Despite the insistence on objectivity and emotional detachment, it is not uncommon for researchers to become emotionally entangled and/or invested in the lives of participants. This is particularly the case when there is continued contact between researcher and participant, beyond that of solely an individual interview (Bellas, 1999). Additionally, neutrality can be particularly challenging when the research topic relates to the personal lived experiences of the researcher and thus has the potential to cut very close to the bone (Bellas, 1999). To be open and honest about the everyday mental and emotional labour involved in academia can therefore be particularly challenging in such an environment.

The expression of emotion has been seen as synonymous with femininity and vulnerability, and as such, sharing one's everyday mental and emotional struggles is seen to risk presenting oneself as vulnerable, incapable or simply out of one's depth (Hacker, 2018; Harrowell et al, 2018). Consequently, many academics feel prevented from speaking openly about their personal experiences, instead confining such emotions and emotional anxieties to the private space of their homes or offices. Individuals must engage in emotional management while at work, continually restraining their emotions, seeking to appear as content or as what Murray (2018) describes as the 'happy worker' – the ideal neoliberal subject. Performing happiness, holding back anger and/or despair can be incredibly exhausting. Similarly, crying, as Hacker (2018) argues, has little place on campus with academics made to perform according to masculine standards of emotional detachment, objectivity and self-control (Bellas, 1999; Petersen, 2007). This silencing or policing of the emotions is evident across the vast majority of male-dominated academic institutions and is a practice which is very rarely challenged or resisted. It operates through the standardised professional expectations placed upon scholars and the traditional distancing of the academy from the emotional and the emotive. Here, I would like to draw attention to the risks of such forms of emotional silencing and to suggest how we might resist such practices by creating a space which is more supportive and nurturing of the emotions.

What the future holds

As academics it is important that we become more aware of our own practices in excluding emotions, because not doing so jeopardises our emotional wellbeing and our ability to sustain an academic career. This may be achieved through, for example, creating a safe 'shared emotional space' (Lacey, 2005: 289) in which academics may explore the emotional nature of their work, perhaps through the form of online discussion forums, coffee breaks or informal meetings. Such spaces could encourage a form of shared vulnerability, in which disabled and non-disabled scholars alike could openly express the ways in which they may be struggling with the increasing and insurmountable demands of academic life. Such an approach would hopefully help to reduce feelings of isolation and self-blame, particularly among disabled colleagues, enabling individuals to see how they are not alone in facing such difficulties. Such practices may also have the potential to foster increased empathy, solidarity and a greater 'ethic of care' among the academic community (Tronto, 1998). Dickson-Swift and colleagues (2009) have similarly noted the importance of institutional and individual support in order to enable such practice.

Without the support of an empathetic academic community, it is likely that scholars will continue to individually internalise feelings of shame, self-blame and failure brought about as a direct result of their increasing workloads and pressures, rather than coming together to both recognise and resist the ways in which the very structures of academia are leading to increased hardship, deteriorating working conditions, poor mental health among academics and a less diverse workforce. Academia has ever since its inception been a highly gendered, class-based and racialised space that puts particular bodies at a distinct advantage. The conditions of the neoliberal higher education sector have, however, served to both further capitalise upon and deepen existing inequalities.

I would encourage more academics to speak openly and 'vulnerably' about the daily challenges of neoliberal academia. It should, however, be recognised that there may be times in which individuals may choose not to challenge or 'speak out', in order to sustain oneself and one's career. It may as such be easier for more permanent staff to 'speak out'. Similarly, there is an imperative for more senior academics to listen, consider and speak up for their colleagues in more precarious employment.

There appears to be very little understanding among the wider academic community of how structural transformations in higher education and changes in working conditions, such as the intensification of workload and increasing precarity of academic careers, have (disproportionately) affected disabled people. I would encourage members of the academic community to take greater time to listen to the experiences and trepidations of disabled academics. It is hoped that, in doing this, individuals will become more aware of how they may best support fellow disabled colleagues in their daily work and resistance.

It can be easy to feel isolated and alone as a disabled scholar. I would encourage disabled academics to become members of national networks such as the National Association of Disabled Staff Networks and online support groups like Chronically Academic, and Disabled Women Academic Professionals #DWAP, in order to overcome feelings of isolation and support one another in attaining their rights. Alongside this, I would also encourage disabled academics to form peer support groups within their institutions, creating spaces in which disabled academics may more comfortably share their experiences, gain mutual support through building supportive relationships and learn from one another.

It has at times been difficult to gain support, solidarity and understanding from fellow non-disabled academics, who understandably have been very much focused on maintaining their own academic careers and getting by in an increasingly precarious and overworked sector (Murray, 2018). I would therefore advocate for the building of alliances between groups who have been disproportionately affected by recent structural changes in higher education, for example female academics, scholars from overseas and parents/carers (Murray, 2018), in order to both draw attention to their increasing exclusion from the academy and to build a greater resistance.

Very little to date has been written about disabled academics experiences of working in the neoliberal academy. I would therefore encourage more disabled academics to study themselves and write about their own experiences, in order to both increase public understanding and inform policy and practice.

References

Archer, L. (2008). The new neoliberal subjects? Young/er academics' constructions of professional identity. *Journal of Education Policy*, 23(3), 265–285.

Babbie, E. (1995). *The Practice of Social Research*. Belmont, CA: Wadsworth.

Behar, R. (2014). *The Vulnerable Observer: Anthropology that Breaks Your Heart*. Boston, MA: Beacon Press.

Bellas, M.L. (1999) Emotional labour in academia: The case of professors, *The Annals of the American Academy of Political and Social Science*, 561(1): 96–110.

Berg, L.D., Huijbens, E.H. & Larsen, H.G. (2016). Producing anxiety in the neoliberal university. *The Canadian Geographer/ Le Geographe Canadien*, 60, 168–180.

Bok, D. (2003). *Universities in the Marketplace: The Commercialization of Higher Education*. Princeton, NJ: Princeton University Press.

Breeze, M. (2018). Imposter syndrome as a public feeling. In: Taylor, Y., & Lahad, K. (eds). *Feeling Academic in the Neoliberal University*. New York: Springer Nature, 191–220.

Brisenden, S. (1986). Independent living and the medical model of disability. *Disability, Handicap & Society*, 1(2), 173–178.

Brown, W. (2015). *Undoing the Demos: Neoliberalism's Stealth Revolution*. Brooklyn, NY: Zone Books.

Clegg, S. (2010). Time future: The dominant discourse of higher education. *Time & Society*, 19(3), 345–364.

Dickson-Swift, V., James, E.L., & Kippen, S. (2009). Researching sensitive topics: Qualitative research as emotion work. *Qualitative Research*, 9(1): 61–79.

Disability Awareness in Action (2009). *Newsletter*. Available from: www.daa.org.uk/?page=newsletter/ [Accessed 5 November 2018].

do Mar Pereira, M. (2016). Struggling within and beyond the Performative University: Articulating activism and work in an 'academia without walls'. *Women's Studies International Forum*, 54, 100–10.

Evans, M. (2005). *Killing Thinking: The Death of the University*. London: Continuum.

Gill, R. (2009). Breaking the silence: The hidden injuries of neo-liberal academia. In: Flood, R., & Gill, R. (eds). *Secrecy and Silence in the Research Process: Feminist Reflections*. London: Routledge, 228–44.

Gornall, L., & Salisbury, J. (2012). Compulsive working, 'hyperprofessionality' and the unseen pleasures of academic work. *Higher Education Quarterly*, 66(2), 135–154.

Graham, G. (2002). *Universities: The Recovery of an Idea*. Exeter: Imprint Academic.

Gregg, M. (2009). Function creep: Communication technologies and anticipatory labour in the information workplace. *New Media and Society*.

Hacker, D. (2018). Crying on campus. In: Taylor, Y., & Lahad, K. (eds). *Feeling Academic in the Neoliberal University*. New York: Springer Nature, 281–300.

Harris, S. (2005). Rethinking academic identities in neo-liberal times. *Teaching in Higher Education*, 10(4), 421–433.

Harrowell, E., Davies, T., & Disney, T. (2018). Making space for failure in geographic research, *The Professional Geographer*, 70(2), 230–238.

Henderson, E.F. (2018). Feminist conference time: Aiming (not) to have been there. In: Taylor, Y., & Lahad, K. (eds). *Feeling Academic in the Neoliberal University*. New York: Springer Nature, 33–60.

Hill, M.E. (2002). Race of the interviewer and perception of skin color: Evidence from the multi-city study of urban inequality. *American Sociological Review*, 67(1): 99–108.

Hochschild, A.R. (1985). *The Managed Heart: Commercialization of Human Feeling*. Berkeley, CA: University of California Press.

Jarvis, H., & Pratt, A. (2006). Bringing it all back home: The extensification and 'overflowing' of work: the case of San Francisco's new media households. *Geoforum*, 37, 331–9.

Jayaratne, T.E., & Stewart, A.T. (1991). Quantitative and qualitative methods in the social sciences: Current feminist issues and practical strategies. In: Fonow, M.M., & Cook, J.A. (eds). *Beyond Methodology: Feminist Scholarship as Lived Research*. Bloomington, IN: Indiana University Press.

Kitchin, R. (2003). Architects disable: A challenge to transform. *Building Material*, 10, 8–13.

Lacey, A. (2005). Networked communities: Social centers and activist spaces in contemporary Britain. *Space and Culture*, 8(3), 286–301.

Lawless, B. (2018). Documenting a labor of love: Emotional labor as academic labor. *Review of Communication*, 18(2), 85–97.

Lovin, C.L. (2018). Feelings of change: Alternative feminist professional trajectories. In: Taylor, Y., & Lahad, K. (eds). *Feeling Academic in the Neoliberal University*. New York: Springer Nature, 137–162.

Lynch, K. (2006). Neo-liberalism and marketisation: The implications for higher education. *European Educational Research Journal*, 5(1), 1–17.

Marginson, S., & Considine, M. (2000). *The Enterprise University: Power, Governance and Reinvention in Australia*. Cambridge: Cambridge University Press.

Mirowski, P. (2013). *Never Let a Serious Crisis Go to Waste: How Neoliberalism Survived the Financial Meltdown*. New York: Verso.

Morley, L. (2003). *Quality and Power in Higher Education*. Maidenhead: SRHE and Open University Press.

Morrissey, J. (2013). Regimes of performance: Practices of the normalised self in the neoliberal university. *British Journal of Sociology of Education*, 36(4), 614–34.

Murray, O.M. (2018). Feel the fear and killjoy anyway: Being a challenging feminist presence in precarious academia. In: Taylor, Y., & Lahad, K. (eds). *Feeling Academic in the Neoliberal University*. New York: Springer Nature, 163–190.

Naidoo, R., & Jamieson, I.M. (2005). Knowledge in the marketplace: The global commodification of teaching and learning in higher education. In: Ninnes, P., & Hellsten, M. (eds). *Internationalizing Higher Education: Critical Explorations of Pedagogy and Policy*. New York: Springer, 33.

Oakley, A. (1981). Interviewing women: A contradiction in terms? In: Roberts, H. (ed). *Doing Feminist Research*. London: Routledge and Kegan Paul, 30–61.

Oliver, M. (1990). *The Politics of Disablement*. Basingstoke: Macmillan.

Petersen, E.B. (2007). Negotiating academicity: Postgraduate research supervision as category boundary work. *Studies in Higher Education*, 32(4), 475–487.

Read, B., & Bradley, L. (2018). Gender, time and 'waiting' in everyday academic life. In: Taylor, Y., & Lahad, K. (eds). *Feeling Academic in the Neoliberal University*. New York: Springer Nature, 221–242.

Schuurman, N. (2009). Work, life, and creativity amongst academic geographers. *Progress in Human Geography*, 33(3), 307–312.

Shipley, H. (2018). Failure to launch? Feminist endeavors as a partial academic. In: Taylor, Y., & Lahad, K. (eds). *Feeling Academic in the Neoliberal University*. New York: Springer Nature, 17–32.

Shumar, W. (1997). *College for Sale: A Critique of the Commodification of Higher Education*. London: Falmer Press.

Shumar, W. (2004). Global pressures, local reactions: Higher education and neo-liberal economic policies. *International Journal of Qualitative Studies in Education*, 17(6), 823–839.

Smith, D.E. (1974). Women's perspective as a radical critique of sociology. *Sociological Inquiry*, 44(1), 7–13.

Southerton, D. (2003). Squeezing time: Allocating practices, co-ordinating networks and scheduling society. *Time and Society*, 12(1), 12–25.

Taylor, Y. (2018). Navigating the emotional landscapes of academia: Queer encounters. In: Taylor, Y., & Lahad, K. (eds). *Feeling Academic in the Neoliberal University*. Springer Nature, 61–86.

Taylor, Y., & Lahad, K. (2018). Introduction: Feeling academic in the neoliberal university: feminist flights, fights, and failures'. In: Taylor, Y. and Lahad, K. (eds). *Feeling Academic in the Neoliberal University*. Cham: Palgrave Macmillan, 1–16.

Thrift, N. (2000). Performing cultures in the new economy. *Annals of the Association of American Geographers*, 90, 674–692.

Tronto, J.C. (1998). An ethic of care. *Generations: Journal of the American Society on Aging*, 22(3), 15–20.

Washburn, J. (2003). *University, Inc.: The Corporate Corruption of Higher Education*. New York: Basic Books.

3

Embodiment and authenticity: how embodied research might shed light on experiences of disability and chronic illness

Jennifer Leigh

Introduction

Embodiment as a term is becoming widely used in mainstream society, and is generally associated with the physical body in some way. However, the definition of embodiment is more esoteric. It is defined by lexicographers as 'a tangible or visible form of an idea, quality, or feeling' (Oxford Dictionary, 2019). As such it has no immediate connection with the physical, lived and experienced body. There are a number of theoretical positions on embodiment, and this has implications for the ways in which it is used to conceptualise lived experience. My position is that embodiment incorporates a conscious self-awareness of the information, sensations, proprioception, images, feelings and emotions that arise from the body and the mind. In this chapter I briefly explore differences of understanding and conceptualisations of embodiment, reflect on how I understand and use the concept of embodiment and embodied and how this in turn impacts on the generation of knowledge and research that gives us an insight into embodied experience. I show how this is particularly relevant for those interested in researching the experiences of those with embodied differences, such as those with disability, chronic illness or neurodivergence.

Embodiment

The term embodiment is contested (Sheets-Johnstone, 2015), and part of the battle of using the word is the need to continuously define and determine what we mean by it. For some sociologists the idea of embodiment relates to how we perform our identity, the clothes we wear, whether we choose to have tattoos, piercings, or the way that we display to others how we choose to identify ourselves within society (Evans et al, 2004). When it comes to performing our identity through our bodies, this can mean how we use ideas of discipline (Foucault, 1977) to train our bodies to be a certain way – through weight lifting, ballet training (Green, 1999) or couch-potatoing, for example. Forms such as yoga (Iyengar, 2010), dance (Green, 2003; Claid, 2016) and martial arts (Ralston and Ralston, 2006) train and discipline our bodies in different ways, and can be used to bring awareness to how we use them in space, as well as increase physical qualities such as strength and flexibility. There is even an industry around embodied practitioners, who work with others to train, to mend, to facilitate our bodies in different ways, exemplified in the virtual embodiment conference held each year since 2018 (Walsh, 2018) when over 15,000 people joined in virtual discussions and lectures.

We use our bodies to show others who we want to be, and we judge others on who they appear to be from their bodies. This can be very superficial – who has not seen a magazine which comments on who has lost weight, gained weight, who is wearing the right or wrong clothes – or a means for us to try and portray a sense of belonging to a particular 'group'.[1]

I experienced this myself when I worked as a yoga teacher. If I wore clothes in a particular style, my students would adopt the same to express and be seen as one of the group. The idea of using our bodies in a certain way denoting a sense of belonging is particularly interesting. When it comes to physicality and forms of movement and exercise, it is possible to 'see' the types of practice that an individual regularly uses. A yoga body is and moves differently from a gym body, a ballet body, Alexander technique body, martial arts body or a weight lifting body. It is even possible to differentiate to a finer level, and distinguish between the different types of yoga and how they perform themselves on how we move through the world. This can be likened to Bourdieu's *hexis*, the way that we unconsciously use our bodies, that forms part of his more familiar *habitus* (Bourdieu, 1977). It is more than conforming to a stereotype, although there is an element of typicality in this kind of bodily compliance. This is one version of bodywork, though bodywork can also be seen as how we use our body in the world (Brown, 2019), or to denote hands-on body therapies such as Rolfing, Alexander technique, Feldenkrais and the like (Juhan, 1987), which can be used in a similar way to movement and exercise forms to bring awareness to and around our physical body.

Sociologists (Shilling, 2012; Evans et al, 2004; Dyck and Archetti, 2003) emphasise that we are all embodied, and everything we do is by necessity embodied, because we have these meaty, fleshy, breathing bodies that carry us through the world. It is not possible to separate ourselves from our embodied experience. This understanding is a movement on from Descartes' idea that the mind and body are totally separated (Descartes, 1641/1993), and yet can be used in a way that almost implies we are just brains in boxes of bodies. Anthropological theories of embodiment (Csordas, 2002; Pink, 2009) take a more reflexive approach to research and awareness of the sensory to shape their understandings of the world and the people who live within it.

Philosophers such as Drew Leder and Maurice Merleau-Ponty extol the importance of our embodied experience, while at the same time distancing themselves from it (Carman, 1999). Leder (1990), for example, argues that our bodies only become visible when they are not working – when they are ill or injured or disabled – and the rest of the time they are invisible, they dis-appear. If we apply this to the idea of disability, this would imply that the disabled body is always visible. My issue with these philosophers is that when I read their work, while I agree fundamentally with the idea that we need to take account of our embodied experiences, I get the sense that they write, and sit, and yet are not aware of their bodies, of moving and using them in a consciously aware way. They think, rather than do.

My understanding of embodiment is that it is both a state of being and a process (Leigh, 2012). Embodiment in this way is a conscious self-awareness of the thoughts, feelings, emotions and sensations that arise from and within the body as we move through the world. In this sense, embodied practices are any practices we do that enable us to increase this conscious self-awareness (Leigh and Bailey, 2013). This understanding of embodiment starts from the premise that there is no Cartesian split between body and mind (Descartes, 1641/1993), where our body is seen as a continual source of trouble (Plato, 2009), inferior to the intellect. Instead, intelligence is seeded in the flesh (Lakoff and Johnson, 1999; Johnson, 1995). In this way, movement bridges the 'gap' between body and mind, allowing us to become conscious and feel (Juhan, 1987). This conceptualisation is inclusive. Movement does not mean we need to be elite athletes or yogis to be aware of our bodies as Leder suggests (1990). We are all moving all the time. We move as we breathe, as we blink, our hearts beating and blood and lymph rushing through our bodies. Our very cells move within us respiring and motilating. In knowledge of this, Maxine Sheets-Johnstone, a dancer philosopher, contests the use of the word embodied (Sheets-Johnstone, 2015). For Sheets-Johnstone, it is not embodiment but a kinaesthetic sense of proprioception, how and where we move our body through space (Sheets-Johnstone, 2010; 2015). While this is true, I generally use the term embodied. Though it is contested, it has some meaning for many, and so does not come across as jargon. Embodied incorporates the idea that it is not just the body, but thoughts, feelings, emotions and senses that arise from, within and around the body. This self-awareness allows us to reflect and to be reflexive, alert to ourselves and how we experience the world around us.

But this is all words, and embodiment is something we do, something we are, not something we read about. I invite you to pause for a moment after this paragraph. Pause, and notice your breathing. Notice whether it is fast or slow. The pattern that it makes in your body. Is it the same? Does it change? Do not judge yourself, just notice it. Notice where in your body you are breathing. Is it in your chest? Your belly? Your back? Notice your body. Become aware of how you are sitting, standing or lying. Notice the places of contact between your body and where it touches the ground, itself, or the furniture beneath you. Notice whether you are comfortable and adjust yourself if you choose. Notice the thoughts in your head. Are they active? Quiet? Note any that are important to you, and then let them all go. Notice the sounds around you. Notice the warmth of your clothes on your skin, the temperature of the air. Notice the air in your nose as you breath in and out and the feeling of air as it does so. Notice how you are feeling. Is it a combination of emotions and feelings? Again, allow yourself to let go of any that are not useful to you as you breathe out. Bring your attention to your breath again, noticing if the pattern has changed. Allow your eyes to close and pause.

Embodiment and knowledge production

So how did I come to this understanding of embodiment? Where does it fit within academia? And where does it have relevance for researching into lived experiences of disability? Research in and around embodiment is happening in many different disciplinary areas, including visual anthropology (Csordas, 2002; Pink, 2009), geography (Back, 2007), martial arts (Bowman, 2015), drama and dance (Claid, 2016; Chaiklin, 2009), education (Bailey, 2003; Barrow, 2008) and sport (Bain, 1987; Wright, 2000; Lu et al, 2009). It is often allied with the use of creative or multi-modal approaches (Harvey et al, 2019; Bradley et al, 2018) and these have applications to the study of disability and the experience of living with a disability and chronic illness. A thread that runs through all of these examples is the demonstration of reflexivity, and a high level of self-awareness on the part of the researcher (Leigh and Bailey, 2013).

There are two main definitions for and of disability (Leonardi et al, 2006) which are often considered in relation to each other (see, for example Oliver, 2013; Shakespeare, 2006). The medical model, still commonly subscribed to in continental Europe, is the idea that disability is a medical impairment. That is, our bodies or minds are dis-abled in some way that stops us being able to 'do' or feel things in the same way as 'normal' or 'neurotypical' or 'healthy' people. The medical model is a model of impairment and pathology. In contrast, the social model of disability, utilised by many critical disability theorists in the UK, states that it is society that disables us by not allowing us to access things with the same ease as those without a disability. While the medical model cannot be dismissed completely, the social model would suggest that being blind is not the disability, the fact that not all PDF files are screen-readable disables us. Similarly, it is not the fact that we need a wheelchair that means we have a disability, but the fact that not all buildings have ramps and lifts that enable us to have access. For those with a chronic illness or invisible condition, these models, and the tension between them, can feel confusing (Asch, 1984; Leicester and Lovell, 1997; Toombs, 1995). It may feel that our conditions do disable us, particularly if we remember how we were in our bodies or minds before we became ill. Disability, and claiming that identity of having a disability, is not straightforward (Brown and Leigh, 2020). It often results from a personal journey of acceptance and acknowledgement (Charmaz, 1991). It follows, then, that one aspect of research into and on disability is to be aware of and attentive to embodied experiences. What might embodied research look like?[2] Here I want to highlight different ways embodied research generates knowledge, and how these processes might be useful to those researching disability.

Reflectivity and autoethnography can be used to highlight individual responses, and draw them out to wider sociological issues to evoke responses and raise questions for the reader (Bochner and Ellis, 2016). While reflexivity, and its importance within the research process is becoming more widespread, the influence of the researcher's own body is not always a consideration. Some research approaches, such as narrative work (Moen, 2006) and phenomenology (Pollio et al, 1997) may foreground reflexivity, however we should not feel we have to limit ourselves to these in order to embed an embodied approach to research. Embodiment can acknowledge the physical presence of bodies in research. For example, Ian Wellard (2015; 2019) uses embodied research in sport by utilising a reflective and autoethnographic approach in his work on the moving, physical body in the context of sport and activity. He writes from his own experiences, and uses reflections and memory to evoke responses.

During a research project where his body was the site of research, Wellard recounts a fall during a CrossFit session, in the context of likening his body to that of a performance artist: 'My bleeding legs also make me think about the social context of blood and the places in which it is acceptable' (Wellard, 2019: 144). The social acceptableness of blood and other bodily fluids is particularly relevant to research around disability and chronic illness. Blood, vomit, bile, sweat, tears and snot are visceral materials with associated smells that evoke memories and reactions from those who witness them. The embodied experience of living with a disability or chronic illness is not restricted to the 'superhuman' aspects that we see portrayed in adverts for the Paralympics (Campaign Live, 2016). Autoethnography requires an awareness of positionality, where the researcher is situated in and on the research to be explicit. As such, it can be a way to contend with criticisms of autoethnographical research (Allen-Collinson and Hockey, 2005) being too personal. These objections are often aimed at Black, Indigenous and People of Colour (BIPOC) academics by Kalwant Bhopal (2015). She argues that research on White people carried out by White people is not seen in the same way as research on BIPOC people carried out by BIPOC academics, which is labelled 'personal' and less rigorous. Similarly, the same criticisms can be applied to feminist research and critical disability studies if they rely on reflexive autoethnographic methods and subjective voices.

The idea of embodied knowing and resonance with others' experiences underlies Kimber Andrews's work (2019). She used a framework based on Polanyi's (1966) two-part process of acquiring embodied knowledge from dance and choreography to first observe, sense in her own body, copy and then reinterpret to probe and explore two very different teaching styles. Andrews approached this task, and the inherent embodied nature of teaching (an idea echoed in Brown, 2019), from the perspective of both a researcher and dancer, and the tensions make her observations meaningful and interesting:

> After a few weeks of writing detailed descriptions, I began to question what a detailed analysis would provide a reader in regards to better understandings

how teachers *use* movement in the classroom, fearing that these analyses were too detailed to provide a better understanding of what the movement looked like. These descriptions were not only tedious to read but also to write … I worked to translate my experiences and observations into language that would capture the *connotation* of what was communicated through movement. (Andrews, 2019: 129–30)

Practice as research as a method is accepted in performance and creative disciplines such as drama, dance and creative writing (Trimingham, 2002), however it is less recognised within the wider academy. In the social sciences and sciences, the idea of practice 'counting' as research is still innovative and barely accepted. Ben Spatz (Spatz, 2020; Pin Ang et al, 2019; Spatz, Forthcoming) advocates using the body as a research tool, and has utilised a 'laboratory' where they[3] 'experiment' and explore it. Spatz draws on scientific terminology in order to create a practice that emulates the scientific laboratory, creating a controlled, contained environment in which to practise and to generate new knowledge. Embodied practice can bring challenges. Spatz is from the discipline of drama, and their work focuses around performance and dissemination using technology and audio-visual recording in order to capture the experimental work.

Being seen, or how we are portrayed is tangential to Paul Bowman's work in culture, media and around martial arts. He uses his own embodied, private, personal practice in mixed martial arts to contextualise and to shape his work on film and martial arts within the media (Bowman, 2019). As a younger academic he was intrigued by the representation of embodied martial arts in films with actors such as Bruce Lee, in ethnographic texts such as Loïc Wacquant's *Body and Soul: Ethnographic Notebooks of an Apprentice-boxer* (2004) and how these related to theorists such as Michel Foucault and Jacques Derrida. Bowman describes the disconnect between his textual analysis of films, books and media compared to his own embodied practice of mixed martial arts and the challenge that he saw in trying (to use Wacquant's words') 'to go from the guts to the intellect, from the comprehension of the flesh to the knowledge of the text' (Wacquant, 2009: 122).

Culture impacts on embodied experience. The popularisation of Bruce Lee's work created a rise in participation in martial arts classes and as a result impacted on people's lived experience. Similarly, media portrayals of disability and chronic illness impact on the lived experience and feelings of those with chronic illness and disability. If those with disabilities are portrayed as superhuman, how do we feel if we struggle to shower, to hold down a job, to meet that ideal? If those with disabilities are portrayed as scroungers, lazy and unclean, then how do we integrate and incorporate that into our own self-image?

Academic research often, if not always, requires a recognised output. Depending on the discipline this generally needs to be a peer-reviewed, high quality research output that can be rated and recognised in order to fit within one of the many metrics used to grade and rank university work, such as the Research Excellence Framework (REF) in the UK. If embodied research asks embodied research questions and uses embodied methods (Leigh and Brown, Forthcoming), how can we best do this in an embodied manner? Audio-visual and creative methodological approaches can be incredibly valuable (see, for example, Brown and Leigh, 2019; Kara, 2015; Leigh and Brown, Forthcoming). Regardless of the methods we use, we must be mindful of the additional ethical and moral considerations that are placed on us as researchers, particularly when we are working with groups who may be considered to be vulnerable (Kara, 2018). Embodied research often asks a lot of its researchers and researched (Leigh and Brown, Forthcoming). If we are consciously aware of our own embodied experiences, and bring them in by way of the questions we ask, the methods we employ, the ways we disseminate and the words we write, we are asking for a lot of honesty, openness and vulnerability in order to be authentic. This creates a further emotional burden than if we were to make more 'objective' or less embodied choices.

Embodied autoethnography

I am in favour of being authentic and honest, and in the process revealing of my own vulnerability and position on the work and research I undertake. The kind of academic writing I admire is the kind where scholars are human, allow me to hear their voice and see from their eyes. My understanding of embodiment is not unique, and it can be justified from a variety of disciplinary perspectives including dance, drama, anthropology and sociology.

My own perspective is somewhat more eclectic. I am a star-child born of hippies. I grew up a vegetarian, my parents were both osteopaths and naturopaths, and as such the innate healing power of our bodies and the importance of healthy, strong bodies were grounded in me from early childhood. We practised some yoga at home, as children and then a bit more as a teenager. My first degree was in chemistry with analytical science, and I became pregnant aged 19 part-way during this. I returned to yoga, first ante-natal, and then Iyengar yoga (Iyengar, 1966). After my degree I started a PhD in computational chemistry and at the same time trained as a yoga teacher over three years (BWoY, 2010). I had another child, took specialist courses in peri-natal yoga and yoga for babies and children with special needs. I trained as a somatic movement therapist and educator (ISMETA, n.d.). My doctoral studies explored how children reflected, experienced and perceived their sense of embodiment through movement (Leigh, 2012). I undertook two post-doctoral positions in psychology before accepting a lectureship in higher education and academic practice. My role now combines educational development with higher education research (Leigh, 2019d).

After returning from maternity leave with my youngest child, I was invited by my then director of research to think carefully about where I wanted my research to go. Up until then my focus had been one of necessity. In the current culture of overwork (Acker and Armenti, 2004) and precariousness (Gill, 2010), my work had been focused on maintaining a job. I had changed fields several times, on each occasion learning a new terminology, a new disciplinary language. This was an opportunity to be authentic to my background, to bring more of my embodied self into my work. And yet I was aware of the tensions between my embodied practice, with its ideas of acceptance and presence, and the academic culture of criticality, competition and judgement (Leigh, 2019a). I started to have conversations with scholars about how they had negotiated these tensions. These conversations snowballed, and eventually became an edited book (Leigh, 2019b) in which I purposefully brought together scholars from across the disciplines in order to share, and to enter into conversation about their ideas and understandings of embodiment. My own work took on a particular interest in reflective practice and reflexivity (Leigh and Bailey, 2013; Leigh, 2016), how creative research methods can facilitate reflection and research (Leigh, 2017; Leigh, 2020; Brown and Leigh, 2019) and ideas of embodied academic identity (Leigh, 2019c).

My embodied experiences colour and affect the work I undertake and how I go about it. I rely on my practice of yoga to centre myself and orientate myself within the world. Missing practice impacts on my physical and mental health. I struggle during periods of illness, feeling disconnected not only from my body, but also from my awareness of who I am, what I have to say and how I can creatively weave together words into an authentic story. I find that embodied experiences give weight and authenticity to what I write and experience. It is only when I am honest about my own position on a subject that I am able to write in a way that is evocative and poignant for others to read.

As an embodied researcher I want my work to do the same: to evoke and trigger in those who have experienced similar stories, and to resonate with the imagination of those who have not. Whether I am writing about ableism, academic identity, or other aspects of higher education, I want to be authentic to my own embodied experience, and by doing this, I hope and intend to touch others.

Conclusion

In this chapter I have shown how academics can apply embodied research and how this might in turn be utilised to explore experiences of disability, chronic illness, neurodivergence and ableism. I particularly wanted to draw on theories beyond the field of critical disability studies to widen the perspective on how embodied research and embodied approaches might be used to generate new knowledge.

What embodiment is, and what it means to each of us, is subjective and personal. In a live performance I saw Spatz and their co-investigators model their research process, where they worked as a trio, each taking a role. One 'experimenting' with movement, voice, sound around the topic they were investigating (in this case Jewish songs and stories), another acted as director, directing, encouraging and shaping the experimental work. The third held a camera, videoing the session, moving in and around the other two as they wanted. I am always struck by the performance aspect in this type of work. I work under the assumption that drama (and often dance) are intrinsically created and explored in order to perform them to an audience, adding an extra layer. In yoga and somatic therapy there is no audience. Embodied experiences are personal, often emotional, and their intrinsic purpose is for the individual and not for others. We could explicitly use the performativity of research, disseminating to an audience through an article, chapter or film, to showcase what we want to be seen, or conversely, we must acknowledge that disseminating our more internal perspectives can be construed as self-indulgent navel-gazing.

When we choose to use embodied research approaches on ourselves or others, we need to be conscious of the impact of shining a light onto these internal and personal processes whether we are collecting data from others, performing for an audience or sharing our innermost reflections. This process is necessary for me in order to be authentic to my background, my upbringing and my experiences. However, I acknowledge that working and researching in this way can be considered riskier, particularly for those who are less established or working in environments which are more constrained or precarious. When it comes to researching embodied difference, by choosing an embodied research perspective we are choosing to honour the rich, varied and 'thick' qualitative experiences that embodied difference results in. Simultaneously we risk exposing ourselves, our vulnerabilities and those of our participants in a judgemental and critical academic environment. We risk putting our heads above the parapet in a highly critical and competitive academic environment if we present work that differs from the norm, that does not conform to expected dimensions for outputs. We risk pitting ourselves against the expectations of academics and what constitutes academic research and academic work. We are making the invisible emotional and physical labour of the chronically ill or disabled academic highly visible. By acknowledging the pain, the differences and the difficulties in embodied experiences and embodied research, we open ourselves up to the richness and deepness of them.

When I disseminate my work, when I sit down to write a chapter such as this, or show a film that has been born out of a research project, I have to figuratively and literally take a deep breath, release my shoulders from up by my ears, feel my feet ground into the floor, accepting the pain and tension in my right foot and ankle from old injuries and adjusting the balance of weight as I balance myself against an anticipated onslaught. And yet, I feel that it is worth the pain and the preparation because it is a way to be authentic and to share that authenticity with my audience. When we are working within a contested field, authenticity, and embodied authenticity, allows us to follow a path that helps avoid assumptions and preconceptions, honour the experiences of our participants and ourselves, and evoke a meaningful response in return.

As I finish writing I wanted to return to my authentic here and now, and be present, pause and acknowledge where I am in this chapter. This morning I intended to practise, so I could approach the 'end-game' with a clear head, and be physically comfortable as I sit, laptop on knees, cushion behind my back. I started, but all too aware of pain shooting down my right calf, snot and pressure building in my head, weight in my bones from all-encompassing fatigue and a drag of 'wasting time' in my heart, I 'only' completed the sun salutes that form the first part of my full practice before going downstairs and making breakfast. My youngest is on half-term, and I am aware that my thinking and writing is likely to be interrupted through the day to attend to her needs. I try not to feel guilt, and instead honour that this is where my body is today. This is all I have. Forcing myself through my practice as I 'have' to, to teach effectively, is not authentically honouring my voice in this writing.

So, I invite you to pause with me now. Pause, and notice. Notice your breath, the pattern it makes in your body as you breathe in and breathe out. Notice whether it is the same or different from earlier. Do not judge yourself, just notice. Notice any tension you carry, acknowledge it and let it go. Let go of all that does not serve you.

Breathe in. Breathe out.

In a small, embodied act of rebellion against the neoliberal, overcritical and depersonalised academy:

Allow your eyes to close and pause.

Notes

[1] The word tribe is often used in this context, but it is problematic https://hownottotravellikeabasicbitch.com/is-using-the-word-tribe-or-spirit-animal-offensive-to-native-americans/. It is, however, consistently used within sociological and educational contexts to denote group identities (Becher and Trowler, 1989).

[2] For a more comprehensive discussion of Embodied Inquiry as a research method along with practical discussions of research design, analysis, ethics and dissemination, please see Leigh and Brown (2021).

[3] Ben Spatz identifies as non-binary and uses they/them pronouns.

References

Acker, S., & Armenti, C. (2004). Sleepless in academia. *Gender and Education*, 16(1): 3–24.

Allen-Collinson, J., & Hockey, J. (2005). Autoethnography: Self indulgence or rigorous methodology? In: M. McNamee (ed). *Philosophy and the sciences of xercise, health and sport: Critical perspectives on research methods*. London: Routledge, pp. 187–202.

Andrews, K. (2019). Finding the dance in the everyday: A flesh and bones approach to studying embodiment. In: *Conversations on embodiment across higher education: Teaching, practice and resarch*. Abingdon: Routledge, pp. 122–135.

Asch, A. (1984). The experience of disability: A challenge for psychology. *American Psychologist*, 39(5): 529.

Back, L. (2007). *The art of listening*. London: Bloomsbury.

Bailey, R. (2003). Learning to be human: Teaching, culture and human cognitive evolution. *London Review of Education*, 1(3): 177–190.

Bain, L. (1987). Modern sports and the Eastern tradition of physical culture: Emphasizing Nishida's theory of the body. *Joural of the Philosophy of Sport*, 14: 44–47.

Barrow, R. (2008). Education and the body: Prolegomena. *British Journal of Educational Studies*, 56(3): 272–285.

Becher, T. & Trowler, P. (1989). *Academic tribes and territories*. 2nd edn. Buckingham: Open University Press.

Bhopal, K. (2015). *A comparative study of the unequal academy*. Abingdon: Routledge.

Bochner, A., & Ellis, C. (2016). *Evocative autoethnography: Writing lives and telling stories*. London: Routledge.

Bourdieu, P. (1977). *Outline of a theory of practice*. Cambridge: Cambridge University Press.

Bowman, P. (2015). Asking the question: Is martial arts studies an academic field? *Martial Arts Studies*, 1: 3–19.

Bowman, P. (2019). Embodiment as embodiment of. In: J. Leigh (ed). *Conversations on embodiment across higher education: Teaching, practice and research*. Abingdon: Routledge, pp. 11–24.

Bradley, J., Moore, E., Simpson, J., & Atkinson, L. (2018). Translanguaging space and creative activity: Theorising collaborative arts-based learning. *Language and Intercultural Communication*, 18(1): 54–73.

Brown, N. (2019). The embodied academic: Body work in teacher education. In: J. Leigh (ed). *Conversations on embodiment across higher education: Teaching, practice and research*. Abingdon: Routledge, pp. 86–96.

Brown, N. & Leigh, J. (2018). Ableism in academia: Where are all the disabled and ill academics? *Disability and Society*, 33(6): 985–989.

Brown, N. & Leigh, J. (2019). Creativity and playfulness in higher education research. In: M. Tight & J. Huisman (eds). *Theory and method in higher education research*, Vol. 4. Bingley: Emerald, pp. 49–66.

Brown, N. & Leigh, J. (eds) (2020). *Ableism in academia: Theorising experiences of disabilities and chronic illness in higher education*. London: UCL Press.

BWoY (2010). *The British wheel of yoga*. Available at: www.bwy. org.uk/ [Accessed 19 July 2010].

Campaign Live, 2016. *Channel 4 We are superhumans*. Available at: www.campaignlive.co.uk/article/campaign-year-2016-channel-4-were-superhumans/1418721 [Accessed 21 September 2019].

Carman, T. (1999). The body in Husserl and Merleau-Ponty. *Philosophical Topics*, 27(2): 205–226.

Chaiklin, S. (2009). We dance from the moment our feet touch the earth. In: S. Chaiklin & H. Wengrower (eds). *The art and science of dance/movement therapy*. Hove: Routledge, pp. 3–11.

Charmaz, K. (1991). *Good days, bad days: The self in chronic illness and time*. Chicago, IL: Rutgers University Press.

Claid, E. (2016). I am because you are. *Journal of Dance and Somatic Practices*, 8(2):115–128.

Csordas, T. (2002). *Body/meaning/healing*. Basingstoke: Palgrave Macmillan.

Descartes, R. (1641/1993). *Meditations on first philosophy*. Indianapolis, IN: Hacket Publishing Company.

Dyck, N., & Archetti, E. (eds). (2003). *Sport, dance and embodied identities*. Oxford: Berg.

Evans, J., Davies, B., & Wright, J. (eds). (2004). *Body knowledge and control: Studies in the sociology of physical education and health*. Abingdon: Routledge.

Foucault, M. (1977). *Discipline and punish: The birth of prison*. New York: Random House.

Gill, R. (2010). Breaking the silence: The hidden injuries of the neoliberal university. In: R. Ryan-Flood & R. Gill (eds). *Secrecy and silence in the research process: Feminist reflections*. Abingdon: Routledge, pp. 288–344.

Green, J. (1999). Somatic authority and the myth of the ideal body in education. *Dance Research Journal*, 31(2): 80–100.

Green, J. (2003). Foucault and the training of docile bodies in dance education. *Arts and Learning Research Journal*, 19(1): 99–125.

Harvey, L., McCormick, B., & Vanden, K. (2019). Becoming at the boundaries of language: Dramatic enquiry for intercultural learning in UK higher education. *Language and Intercultural Communication*, 19(6): 451–470.

ISMETA, n.d. *ISMETA*. Available at: www.ismeta.org/ [Accessed 18 July 2010].

Iyengar, B.K.S. (1966). *Light on yoga*. London: HarperCollins.

Iyengar, B.K.S. (2010). *Iyengar yoga*. Available at: www.bksiyengar.com [Accessed 20 July 2010].

Johnson, D.H. (1995). *Bone, breath and gesture*. Berkeley, CA: North Atlantic Books.

Journal of Embodied Research (2019). Available at: https://jer.openlibhums.org/ [Accessed 21 September 2019].

Juhan, D. (1987). *Job's body*. Barrytown, NY: Station Hill Press.

Kara, H. (2015). *Creative research methods in the social sciences: A practical guide*. Bristol: Policy Press.

Kara, H. (2018). *Research ethics in the real world: Euro-Western and indigenous perspectives*. Bristol: Policy Press.

Lakoff, G. & Johnson, M. (1999). *Philosophy in the flesh: The embodied mind and its challenge to Western thought*. New York: Basic Books.

Leavy, P. (2015). *Method meets art: Arts-based research practice*. New York: Guildford Press.

Leder, D. (1990). *The absent body*. Chicago, IL: University of Chicago Press.

Lefebvre, H. (2004). *Rhythmanalysis: Space, time and everyday life*. London: Continuum.

Leicester, M. & Lovell, T. (1997). Disability voice: Educational experience and disability. *Disability & Society*, 12(1): 111–8.

Leigh, J. (2019d). *Somatic movement and education: A phenomenological study of young children's perceptions, expressions and reflections of embodiment through movement*. PhD thesis, University of Birmingham.

Leigh, J. (2016). An embodied perspective on judgements of written reflective practice for professional development in Higher Education. *Reflective Practice: International and Multidisciplinary Perspectives*, 17(1).

Leigh, J. (2017). Experiencing emotion: Children's perceptions, reflections and self-regulation. *Body, Movement and Dance in Psychotherapy*, 12(2): 128–144.

Leigh, J. (2019a). Embodied practice and academic embodied identity. In: *Conversations on embodiment: Teaching, practice, and research*. Abingdon: Routledge.

Leigh, J. (ed). (2019b). *Conversations on embodiment across higher education: Teaching, research and practice*. Abingdon: Routledge.

Leigh, J. (2019c). An embodied approach in a cognitive discipline. In: *Educational futures and fractures*. London: Palgrave.

Leigh, J. (2019d). Exploring multiple identities: An embodied perspective on academic development and higher education research. *Journal of Somatic and Dance Practices*, 11(1): 99–114.

Leigh, J. (2020). Using creative methods and movement to encourage reflection in children. *Journal of Early Childhood Research*, 18(2): 130–142.

Leigh, J. & Bailey, R. (2013). Reflection, reflective practice and embodied reflective practice. *Body, Movement and Dance in Psychotherapy*, 8(3): 160–171.

Leigh, J. & Blackburn, C. (2018). *Exploring embodied academic identity through creative research methods*. Canterbury.

Leigh, J. & Brown, N. (2020) *Embodied inquiry: Research methods*. London: Bloomsbury

Leigh, J. & Brown, N. (Forthcoming). Exploring interdisciplinary research.

Leigh, J., Brown, N., & Blackburn, C. (2018). *something*. Canterbury.

Leonardi, M. et al (2006). The definition of disability: What is in a name? *The Lancet*, 368(9543): 1219–1221.

Lu, C., Tito, J.M., & Kentel, J.A. (2009). Eastern Movement Disciplines (EMDs) and mindfulness: A new path to subjective knowledge in Western physical education. *Quest*, pp. 353–370.

Moen, T. (2006). Reflections on the narrative research approach. *International Journal of Qualitative Methods*, 5(4), pp. 56–69.

Oliver, M. (2013). The social model of disability: Thirty years on. *Disability & Society*, 28(7):1024–26.

Oxford Dictionary (2019). *Lexicographers at Oxford Dictionary's definition of embodiment*. Available at: www.lexico.com/en/definition/embodiment [Accessed 21 September 2019].

Pin Ang, G. et al (2019). What is a song? *Performance Research*, 24(1):80–93.

Pink, S. (2009). *Doing sensory ethnography*. London: Sage.

Plato (2009). *Phaedo*. Oxford: Oxford Paperbacks.

Polanyi, M., 1966. *The tacit dimension*. Garden City, NY: Doubleday.

Pollio, H., Henley, T., & Thompson, C. (1997). *The phenomenology of everday life*. Cambridge: Cambridge University Press.

Ralston, P. & Ralston, L. (2006). *Zen body-being*. Berkeley, CA: Frog.

Shakespeare, T. (2006). The social model of disability. *The Disability Studies Reader*, 2: 197–204.

Sheets-Johnstone, M. (2010). Kinesthetic experience: understanding movement inside and out. *Body, Movement and Dance in Psychotherapy*, 5(2): 111–127.

Sheets-Johnstone, M. (2015). Embodiment on trial: A phenomnenological investigation. *Continental Philosophy Review*, 48:23–39.

Shilling, C. (2012). *The body and social theory*. 3rd edn. London: Sage.

Single White Female [film] (1992). Directed by Barbet Schroeder. United States: Barbet Schroeder.

Spatz, B. (2015). *What a body can do: Technique as knowledge, practice as research*. Abingdon: Routledge.

Spatz, B. (2020). *Blue sky body: Thresholds for embodied research*. Abingdon: Routledge.

Spatz, B. (Forthcoming). *Making a laboratory: Dynamic configurations with transversal video*. Brooklyn, NY: Punctum Books.

Toombs, S. (1995). The lived experience of disability. *Human Studies*, 18(1): 9–23.

Trimingham, M. (2002). A methodology for practice as research. *Studies in Theatre Performance*, 22(1): 54–60.

Wacquant, L. (2004). *Body and soul: Ethnographic notebooks of an apprentice-boxer*. New York: Oxford University Press.

Wacquant, L. (2009). The body, the ghetto, and the penal state. *Qualitative Sociology*, 32: 01–129.

Walsh, M. (2018). *The embodiment conference*. Available at: https://embodiedfacilitator.com/embodiment-conference-2018/ [Accessed 21 September 2019].

Wellard, I. (2015). *Researching embodied sport: Exploring movement cultures*. London: Routledge.

Wellard, I. (2019). Researching embodied sport and movement cultures: Theoretical and methodological considerations. In: J. Leigh (ed). *Conversations on embodiment across higher education: Teaching, practice and research*. Abingdon: Routledge, pp. 139–150.

Wright, J. (2000). Bodies, meanings and movement: A comparison of the language of a physical education lesson and a Feldenkrais movement class. *Sport, Education and Society*, 5(1): 35–49.

4

What's in a word? Rephrasing and reframing disability

Sharon Smith

Introduction

Academia is directed by policy and government legislation when managing students and, as such, the requirements of the Equality Act 2010 to meet the accessibility needs of disabled students are fulfilled. We can see, however, that even within society the inequalities and needs of individuals are not always met (Smith, 2017). Alongside this sits the discussion about the terminology we use and how that impacts on the social construct of disability.

By exploring some of the historical perspectives and definitions that have emerged, and in considering society's construct of disability through the influences of media and language, I argue that we need to develop a more inclusive approach that exceeds the policy requirements and develops a 'value' approach to meeting individual needs.

A personal perspective

I encountered a period of life-threatening illness in 2003, my approach to which was a positive one. The 'big C' word was a negative term in 2003, and my cancer treatment was invasive and followed by chemotherapy. At that time cancer was not classed as a disability; it became defined as such under the Equality Act

2010. Cancer can be defined as a 'hidden disability' as, although the signs are often evident during chemotherapy, the lasting effect of chemo continues unseen for many years afterwards with many side effects, such as neuropathy (The National Cancer Institute, 2010) and immune deficiencies. During recovery I was supported well; however, trying to return to work during the last cycle of chemotherapy was a challenge. I felt very strongly that returning to work would enable a more positive mental wellbeing. I acknowledge that the well-meaning gestures from colleagues and friends were for my own care but, on reflection, I remember the level of their knowledge and understanding was limited and misjudged. In identifying this response, it becomes apparent that many disabilities are misunderstood and the lack of understanding and awareness results in discrimination. Brown and Leigh recognise that there is a distance between policy and practice. They state that many academics with disabilities are not taken seriously, and that their professional status is seen 'through the lens of their disability status' and that this can result in the 'fear that they are suddenly no longer seen as academics or persons, but as their disability or health condition' (Brown and Leigh, 2018: 987).

In developing approaches which support ableism there are several points to consider, such as the historical construct of disability, the definitions of medical and social models and the legal requirements of managing disability. Around the debate lie several other considerations, such as values and beliefs defined by culture and language.

Societal and historical perspectives

If we consider how cultural perspectives impact on our language, we can identify how we then make sense of the world we live in, which in turn creates our responses to different aspects of living within a society. The Oxford English Dictionary (2007: 556) defines disability as first a 'lack' and notably as 'incapacity' in the eyes of the law. This definition, as Mallet and Runswick-Cole (2014) highlight, focuses on what the individual cannot do rather than what they can do. In defining disabilities in this way, we focus more on the medical model than the social model of disabilities. Mallet and Runswick-Cole (2014: 4) argue that the 'medical model emphasises individual pathology, individual (personal) deficit and individual medical treatment'. In reviewing this definition, the Equality Act 2010 provides a legal expectation for individuals where 'he or she has a "physical or mental impairment"' and 'the impairment has a substantial and long-term adverse effect on [his or her] ability to carry out normal day-to-day activities'.

In considering the debate around inclusion and the approach to enabling students' access to learning and teaching, my own personal perspective of managing an 'impairment' provides a case study about how academics face the challenges of dealing with their individual needs. In supporting students, we are required to meet their needs; this is often part of an induction process and the appropriate services manage the students' access to their support. However, we expect students to disclose their needs and very often this is not the case, especially with regard to mental health needs. Society must make 'reasonable adjustments', as deemed originally under the Disability Discrimination Act (DDA, 1995), to promote a social model approach. The DDA highlighted that, wherever possible, adaptations should be made in the workplace and to the access to opportunities, for example equal access to a building or classroom. Using the terms 'adjustment' and 'adaptations' enabled the individual to access environments and opportunities on an equal basis, and where this condition could not be met then reasonable adjustment would be made (Smith, 2017).

Brown (2019: 93) debates the concept of embodiment and what this means and, discussing how the way we see ourselves can impact on our own viewpoint and how we adjust our conceptual thinking, she argues: 'instead of seeing disability as deviance from normality, instead of viewing the world from the perspective of able and normal; instead of undertaking the kind of body we do to cover up deficiencies to fit into normal society, we are called to refine normality and disability'. In turn, our perceptions are determined by our mind's conceptions; Brown's (2019: 94) analogy is likening the mind and body to two sides of a coin. The impact of any disability can be seen in the approach highlighted within this chapter, in examining the impact of chemotherapy on the body. Do we allow the mind to control the body or enable the body by adjusting the belief that disability is a disadvantage? I return here to my discussion on recognising diff/abilities and celebrating the different approaches we all have to daily life.

I recognise that we need to make some adaptations to our thinking first, to ensure an equal starting point. Let's consider the analogy of being short-sighted: without glasses individuals may struggle to see but with adjustment by wearing glasses individuals can access the world around them. While this may be regarded as an over-simplification, it argues that with adaptation we can enable mobility, accessibility and provide greater equality. I find the terminology used within recognising individual needs rather dis-abling as a concept and argue we should refer to disabilities as differ-abilities. I argue that we start from a deficit point when constructing a definition of disability, and I strongly believe that the terminology we use should be enabling rather than disabling. Swain and French (2000: 573) support an affirmation model where it is the 'assumption that disabled people want to be normal'. But indeed what is 'normal'? I would consider this is referring to the mass of individuals rather than a person's own identity. In reviewing Alison Lapper's case later in the chapter, we can see that Alison refers to herself as neither 'normal' nor 'disabled'.

I advocate that our language determines our thinking and, within my teaching, I stress that we should also place the person first and then the needs afterwards, and that language should reflect this. An example would be 'a learner with disability' rather than 'a disabled learner'. Mallet and Runswick-Cole (2014: 4) concur with this viewpoint, recognising that we should consider a 'person with a disability' rather than 'disabled person' and that it is: 'through "language" that our ideas and assumptions are shaped, and these, in turn, directly affect the ways people are treated and language has a material impact upon the lives we all lead'.

In considering terminology and language, the term impairment sits well with many societies, although within the deaf community there are some who would prefer to be called deaf rather than hearing impaired. As Goodley (2001) argues, there are two definitions to consider, one using the term impairment, which is seen as a function of limitations, or one using the term disability, which highlights the loss or limitations of opportunities. Mallet and Runswick-Cole (2014: 9, Diagram 1) cite the Manchester City Council (no date) definitions that highlight what are acceptable terms, those that the council felt were appropriate to use when referring to disabled people. The terminology (exemplified in their diagram) is negative, such as 'afflicted, suffering from, victim', and these words provide us with a tragic discourse of disability. We have moved away from terminology which presents a historical label, such as 'crippled' and 'handicapped', and these were redefined within the Disability Discrimination Act (DDA, 1995) and *Diagnostic and Statistical Manual of Mental Disorders* (DSM V5) (World Health Organization, 2001). These definitions and redefinitions highlight how language can be detrimental to individuals, as in the example presented by Mallet and Runswick-Cole: 'Able-bodied – The preferred term is non-disabled. Able-bodied suggests that all abilities are physical and ignores unseen disability'. I agree with Mallet and Runswick-Cole. In the English language we use negative prefixes such as that found in 'dis'-ability or 'invalid' to detrimental effect. Using the example 'invalid', an experience can be seen as literally 'non' valid.

Exploring historical perspectives, we can see that we have begun to move away from a medical model of disability (Mallet and Runswick-Cole, 2014), enabling a social model of disability to become more prominent. Notably, images from historical documents and media show disability in a negative form, such as the image of Tiny Tim, in Charles Dickens' *A Christmas Carol*, and the film *The Elephant Man* (1980), an example of a man with a physical disability who became exploited as a freak show, after having been institutionalised for deformities caused by Proteus syndrome. Historically we can see that disability has emerged from the institutionalised approach to become a more inclusive social approach. Recognising this inclusive approach highlights a change in attitude and approaches in facilitating individual requirements. The medical model has defined both the approach required by law to support the individual and the DSM V5 (World Health Organization, 2001). The structure of the DSM V5, and the language used within it, reflects the medical definitions; using such a document to assess or define an individual's needs does not take into account the social model and the impact that environment and approaches might have on an individual's access to the world around them.

Historically, the approach to disability was a negative one and many disabled people were hidden or institutionalised. Haegele and Hodge (2016) argue that the definition has changed as it has been altered through 'society's' dialogue, highlighting that disability was originally framed in religious discourse. Haegele and Hodge also concur that language defines how we view disability and, in using the two terms 'medical and social model', they argue for further discussion of the two models. In doing so they consider a definition of disability in regard to the two models, the medical model highlighting the deficit model and the social model recognising that an individual can be different from the 'norm' (Table 4.1).

Considering the following vignette presented in Smith (2017: 1), an individual can be 'disabled' by the environment when adaptations are not successful. This highlights that requirements under the Equality Act 2010 are exercised but they are not always suitable in terms of an inclusive approach to a social inclusion:

> We all face barriers in our lives but problems accessing basic activities can develop into huge barriers for those living with particular needs and requirements. This became a reality for me when I recently planned a well-earned short break away at a luxury hotel with my husband, who has a mobility difficulty. Having made them aware that we would require a room with an accessible shower, preferably close to all the hotel facilities, they assured me that they would book us into one of their disabled suites.
>
> On arrival, we discovered that our room was on the second floor and that the service lift (not the guest lift) was the only access to it, through the Spa. The entrance to the Spa building was at the top of the hotel drive. Suitcases in tow, with no help offered by

Table 4.1: Comparisons between the medical and social model of disability discourse

Topic	Medical model	Social model
What is disability?	An individual or medical phenomenon that results from impairments in body functions; a deficiency in body functions or structures; a deficiency or abnormality	A social construct that is imposed on top of impairments by society; a difference
Access to treatment or services	Referral by diagnosis	Self-referral, experience driven
Target of intervention	'Fixing' the disability to the greatest extent possible	Social or political change in an effort to decrease environmental barriers and increase levels of understanding
Outcomes of interventions	Normalizing functions; functioning member of existing society	Self-advocacy, changes in environment and understanding, social inclusion
The agent of remedy	The professional	Can be the individual, an advocate, or anyone who positively affects the arrangements between individual and society
Effects on individuals who are typically functioning	Society remains the same	Society evolves to be more inclusive
Perceptions towards individuals with disabilities	The individual is faulty	The individual is unique
Cognitive authority	Society and doctors	Academics and advocates with disabilities
Perception of disability	Being disabled is negative	Being disabled in itself, is neither positive or negative

Source: Haegele and Hodge, 2016: 194

the hotel staff, the next obstacle was to pass through five fire doors. We entered into our room to see the only access to the balcony was over a step. (Smith, 2017: 1)

Alison Lapper (2006) illustrates clearly how an individual's approach to their disability can determine how society might define a particular individual. Alison's needs were as a result of a congenital malformation called phocomelia. Her case study highlights that she viewed her needs as different and not as a disability (Smith, 2017: 97). Alison highlights that she 'was considered to be severely disabled and hates that phrase with a passion' (Lapper, 2006: 18). We have certainly developed a more open dialogue with individuals since Alison's childhood, and individuals are more involved with assessment and negotiating their needs. Alison's case highlights how she was automatically given prosthetics to make her 'normal' but she found this difficult and disabling and preferred to function without them. I believe the message is quite clear: the individual must be the central point in any decisions about meeting their needs. Alison states 'the results would have been more impressive' (Lapper, 2006: 37) if she had been consulted, rather than others deciding for her what her needs were.

I argue that if all resources are aimed at the needs of a range of individuals then there is no need to be 'disabled'. If we provide appropriate environments, model appropriate language and develop cultures that value the individual, we should then consider whether the person is in fact disabled. Swain and French (2000: 569–578) consider that many people who are not defined as disabled do indeed have impairments, and that we all have some elements of oppression, whether through disability or 'through poverty, racism, sexism and sexual preference as indeed do many disabled people'. This argues for the ethos of inclusion for all. The view of disability being a tragic model is explored by Swain and French; they present an argument for an affirmation model that presents an acceptance of the individual and which highlights a positive social identity. Indeed, they argue that it is only non-disabled people who view individuals with disabilities through the tragic model, and not disabled people. They conclude that the affirmation model is generated by disabled individuals rejecting the tragic model of disability, and that individuals with disabilities 'assert a positive identity'. Irrespective of societal perception of disabilities, it remains that inclusion values all individuals as different; this applies therefore not only to disabilities to but other aspects of society's differences, such as gender or ethnicity.

Hochwald (1957, cited in Holler, 2019) presents a dialogue discussing the 'tragedy discourse'. Hochwald views the deficiency model as a means for individuals to present a personal tragedy, and further argues that disabled individuals view themselves as 'a victim of destiny'. Holler (2019) conversely presents the argument that personality and coping strategies are key to defining and constructing attitudes to disability. This can be seen in the earlier vignette; the argument is that the individual presents and regards themselves as 'less able' rather than 'able with adaptation': the 'normal' access to the hotel via the main entrance was not available, so adjustments had been made; however, these only created a dis/abled access.

Family attitudes to disability also play a part in how we construct our understanding of disability, and how in turn we develop our values and beliefs of how disabilities should be managed. In some cases, family expectations that there is a 'cure' creates barriers to accepting the difference presented in the way an individual is and how they deal with life events (Larson 1998). Larson's (1998) research focuses on how six families of Mexican origin manage with what is labelled as 'high burden' children with disability, between 5–11 years of age. Larson highlighted the maternal desire demonstrated within the study for the child with the disability to be 'normal'. Larson argues that maternal expectations are for a normal child that would enable a more normal life for the family; as Larson highlights it 'they are clinging to a desire for change'. The research concludes that maternal relationships needed to be 'reformed and recast' and the relationship and the dialogue with professionals needs to be more open and address some of the emotional issues. I recall during my own illness that attitudes from individuals varied from the 'tragedy' mode to 'thank goodness it's not me, how would I cope?'. This highlights that attitudes to disability are often derived from an individual's perception of the disability/ need and the fear of how they would cope with it. As Larson highlights, the individual person's approach to their disability determines their ability to manage the circumstances.

Many physical and mental disabilities are not visible and therefore not recognised by society (Larson, 1998). We might consider that this is due to the individuals' choice to remain unlabelled or it could be that they feel their disability might be judged. I am aware from my own experience that individual perceptions of disability are often misunderstood, resulting in inappropriate responses, such as misguided adaptations. In most cases, individuals manage their needs rather than opening the situation up to discussions of large discrepancies in supplying adaptations. I found, for example, that in my workplace access to the lift was perceived as reserved for people with disabilities; in an effort to manage my wellbeing and energy levels I made use of the lift, but this could result in negative attitudes as to why I was doing so.

The construction of media influences

Cultural and social perspectives of disability are constructed through language, visual representation, historical representation such as in stories and novels, and social events such as 'freak shows' at circuses: these have all impacted on social definitions and understanding. 'The way media views disability and transmits this to society can determine a societal outlook and portray either a positive or negative viewpoint' (Smith, 2017: 93). Ellis (2016: 12) argues that the media often 'perpetuates stereotyping' rather than allowing the representation of disability to be defined by the individual's lived experiences, such as in the case of Alison Lapper. Jackson et al (2015) identify some main themes when considering how we construct perceptions of disability: first, they consider that empowerment is central, they go on to recognise that within this there is the need to recognise voice, and then look at how we construct the language we use in defining individuals with disability and represent their voices. How we represent the voice of individuals is an important key to how society constructs its understanding and perceptions of disability.

The language we use

In using the term 'disability' we are perpetuating a negative view of individual differences; however, it is difficult to rephrase language we have become familiar with, as this not only takes a change in attitude but also a reconditioning of how we convey our viewpoints. As Alison Lapper's perspective illustrates, we can resituate our thinking through the language we use. This can also be seen in Stephen Hawking's opening speech at the London Paralympics (2012):

> We are all different: the Paralympic Games is also about transforming our perception of the world. We are all different. There is no such thing as a standard or run-of-the-mill human being, but we share the same human spirit. What is important is that we have the ability to create. This creativity can take many forms, from physical achievement to theoretical physics. However difficult life may seem, there is always something you can do and succeed at. (Hawking, 2012)

In recognising that society's language and attitudes can affect the opportunities available for individuals, the debate around terminology is relevant. This can also be seen in managing attitudes to gender and transgender. Rosen (2018) considers how both the terminology we have used in describing gender and individuals' self-identity construct how society makes meaning of those preferences. It can be argued that language determines our thoughts and beliefs and in turn the actions we then take. Rosen (2018) highlights that the term 'transvestite' was an acceptable term in the 1900s and debates with Dr Laura Wright the use of terms and outlines that language considers the individual's preferences in describing them. The example highlighted was how we describe individuals as 'he' or 'she', where a gender-neutral stance would consider the term 'they'. Using this in our language would begin to remove the bias we see. An everyday example of this can be seen in the growing use of the term 'accessibility toilets' rather than having 'male or female'; the term accessibility then fits a number of individual concerns, other than just gender.

Boroditsky (2018) states that language can shape the way we think and argues that 'Language guides our reasoning and events'. It could be argued that events affect the language we use; examples of this can be seen in how some languages use 'masculine and feminine' verbs. Boroditsky gives an example of this in her TED Talk, examining the idea that the way in which different languages are constructed can alter the perceptions and ideas. For example, Aboriginal communities use directional language and they do not use left or right. Instead the language is situational: it revolves around you, for example, in saying which way you are going you would say 'North-northeast in the far distance'. The use of directional language is employed to situate the person in terms of their position and is understood as doing so by others.

Language can also determine how events are perceived. Boroditsky (2018) provides an example of this in stating that language can indicate blame: for example, when we say 'I broke my arm', does this mean you actually broke it yourself or did it happen as a result of something happening to you? Another example, 'I broke the vase' implies blame, and this could be rephrased to say 'the vase broke'. How we construct our reaction to issues can highlight how we react to each other and our social actions and notions. From this viewpoint, the term disability is a negative one, using a negative prefix (Smith, 2017) and a more fluid term would be 'differ/ability'.

My involvement in an Erasmus project highlighted how language can affect understanding. The GUIDE project (2013) provides a good example of how understanding and concepts can be misinterpreted. The partners within the project were defining their terminology for the project from DSM V4 (World Health Organization, 1992) which still used negative terms. The progression from terms such as 'mental retardation' (DSM V4) to terms such as 'impairment' in DSM V5 (World Health Organization, 2001) made a considerable difference to the context and outcomes of the project (Smith, 2017). This opportunity enabled us to construct both a more updated concept of what inclusion meant and a more inclusive approach in designing resources to support teachers in schools.

Reflecting on practice and understanding needs

With the move towards widening participation in higher education, the impact of the Equality Act 2010 and changes in Disabled Students' Allowance (2019), lecturers are required to provide a broader inclusive offer. This may be through the design of resources and the access to the teaching environment. This has prompted an inclusive approach whereby the curriculum is designed taking the needs of a range of learners into account. We could define this as inclusive or universal design, both of which adapt and enable those with individual needs to access the curriculum. In considering the importance of Universal Design for Learning, Bracken (2019: 364) highlights that: 'Over the past fifty years or so, national and transnational educational systems have shifted more toward valuing human diversity and, as a result, there is much greater scope within HEIs for students from more diverse backgrounds.'

Bracken considers that the use of Universal Design for Learning allows for a more 'student-centred' approach and argues for a whole university approach to inclusive learning. I consider this will not only impact on the students' learning but also allow for a broader teaching tool for lecturers, enabling those with individual needs themselves to be facilitated. This focus on Universal Design for Learning requires not only a culture shift but also resourcing, with changes in the environments and in the technical support provided. It can be seen from the discussion in Bracken et al (2019) that shifts in stakeholders' beliefs and institutional policy are required for the success of Universal Design for Learning.

I recognise that within my own practice I miss opportunities to enable students, not from a lack of understanding but from being misinformed or from lack of adapting my style of teaching. While I consider my approach to be inclusive, minor elements of my teaching become difficult for students. An example of this was during a formative task in which the students were asked to complete an audit of their skills to date. The audit was presented in reverse form (see Table 4.2). This seemingly obvious audit became a very difficult task for a student who was dyslexic. In the case of this student they were also a staff member and I had

Table 4.2: Diagram audit

Learning Outcomes: Colleagues will be able to ...	A	B	C	D	E
1 Design appropriate teaching programmes in your subject discipline and critically evaluate their effectiveness					
2 Evaluate and apply appropriately a wide range of learning and teaching methods, to work with a range of group sizes					
3 Use and value appropriate learning technologies to develop effective learning materials, learning environments and learning support systems					
4 Use an innovative range of assessment techniques to support effective learning and enable students to monitor their own progress					
5 Deploy appropriate methods of evaluating your own teaching and learning practices					
6 Undertake personal development planning to audit, critically reflect upon, plan and record your development					

Key
The table is labelled A–E but the key is labelled E–A

E I have not really considered how to do this nor do I have any direct experience to reflect on. I can thus produce no evidence of achieving this outcome/value.

D I have started to think about this but I have only limited experience to draw upon. I can produce little or no evidence to demonstrate I have achieved this.

C I have thought about this and I have experience of doing it. However I can produce little or no evidence to demonstrate that I have achieved this outcome/value.

B I have thought carefully about this and have had experience of doing it. I can produce some examples that demonstrate I have achieved this.

A I have thought carefully about this and have various experiences of doing it. I can produce a range of examples that demonstrates I have achieved this outcome/value.

made assumptions of their 'abilities'. The discussion with the student/staff member highlighted how we can miss opportunities to support staff in their daily work life. In this case, I adapted the approach to the task by reversing the audit key (Table 4.2), shading the table and changing the font; these adaptations made the task more enabling. This example highlighted that we often do not meet the needs of staff/students with difficulties. Some psychical disabilities are managed through adaptation to the workplace, where environment and design are not always suitable for individual needs. It opens up the debate about how organisations support staff in managing their role, and whether 'human resources' departments are fully prepared and able to support staff or even if they are fully aware of how to support staff. This is not a deed of negligence but one of misinformed approaches or lack of awareness. In most cases, staff with individual needs are dealt with in a reactive and not a proactive manner, based on the construction of attitudes (as demonstrated in my case study earlier within the chapter); understanding individual needs and recognising our perception of needs can impact on both how individuals feel and how they are placed within society.

Conclusion

How we define ourselves within our workplace is an individual preference and in identifying differences we need to consider why should these should define who an individual is and possibly what sets them apart. It is important to consider how we meet a balanced approach of supporting those with particular needs without attaching a label to individuals. I believe the answer is in an acceptance that we are all different and have individual needs and that these present as 'differ/ability': they should not be defined by a particular need, *typical societal* resource or requirement.

How we construct communities of disabilities is highlighted in the affirmation model (Swain and French, 2000: 540–578); this highlights that communities can 'affirm their disability as seen in the Disability Arts Movement and in doing so disabled people are actively repudiating the dominant value of normality'. Jackson (2019) argues that individuals can find it hard to share their needs, but ableism in academia requires an openness to doing so. Brown and Leigh (2018) emphasise that disclosing your individual needs can present some personal difficulties.

Understandably, many students find that, in declaring their needs on entry to university, they face personal acceptance; for staff, however, such a declaration also means that professional status can be affected. In supporting 'Ableism in Academia', there are costs to institutions in providing and planning for the individual: the attitudes of organisations and institutions need to shift for more staff to be comfortable with their own disabilities. The problem of ingrained attitudes to disabilities as creating barriers still exists. Alternatively, we have to be accessible for all, and this requires an openness to understand that the world is a complex place and that we may not be able to meet everyone's needs.

Inclusion is therefore a choice by the individual to be included through using their preferred and learned approaches, which also enhance their view of the everyday world and enable them to participate more effectively within it. Some disabilities, such as mental health and neuropathy, are hidden. These disabilities may not be apparent because the individual prefers to hide their needs as they feel they will be judged. This raises the question as to whether we openly accept the needs of others or whether the attitudes around disabilities still impair access. Alongside my argument of differ/ability sits the empowerment of individuals to speak out; many academics hide their individual needs as they are worried such visibility will impact on their professional standing. This can be seen within Brown's (2019) discussion, which asks the question as to whether we speak out and how others will view the information. Gates (2019) highlights the empowerment of women; she presents an example of empowering women to speak out and how this then impacts on the community they live in. If we use language to convey and develop culture beliefs, then actions and empowerment can also present opportunities for change.

This chapter has highlighted Alison Lapper's desire to be seen for her ability and individuality. However, in a recent report about her son's death in August 2019 she was referred to as 'disabled Alison Lapper'; after twenty years of empowering herself and campaigning for change she still is identified by her disability rather than by her ability and achievements. Brown and Leigh (2018: 987) consider that a 'societal shift in relation to our understanding of disabilities is needed'.

References

Boroditsky, L. (2018). How language shapes the way we think. *TED Talks*. Retrieved from: https://binged.it/2Gb9Uv9

Bracken, S., & Novak, K. (2019). *Transforming Higher Education through Universal Design for Learning: An International Perspective.* London: Routledge.

Brown, N. (2019) The embodied academic: Body work in teacher education. In: Leigh, J.S. (ed). *Conversations on Embodiment across Higher Education: Teaching, Practice and Research.* London: Routledge, 86–95.

Brown, N., & Leigh, J. (2018). Ableism in academia: Where are the disabled and ill academics? *Disability & Society*, 33(6), 33:6.

Disability Discrimination Act (DDA, 1995). London: HMSO. Retrieved from: www.legislation.gov.uk/ukpga/1995/50/contents

Elephant Man, The [film] (1980). Directed by David Lynch.

Ellis, L. (2016). Reframing disability: Media, (dis)empowerment and voice in the 2012 Paralympic Games, *Disability & Society*, 31(2), 291–293.

Equality Act. (2010) Retrieved from: www.legislation.gov.uk/ukpga/2010/15/contents

Gates, M. (2019). *The Moment of Lift: Empowering Women Changing the World.* London: Bluebird.

Goodley, D. (2001). Learning difficulties, the social model of disability and impairment: Challenging epistemologies. *Disability & Society*, 16, 207–231.

GUIDE. (2013). *Guidelines for Teachers Working with Students with Medium-light Cognitive Impairment.* Retrieved from: www.project-guide.eu/

Haegele, J., & Hodge, S. (2016). *Disability Discourse: Overview and Critiques of the Medical and Social Models.* Quest, 68(2), 193–206.

Hawking, S. (2012). Opening speech at Paralympics, 14 March. London. Retrieved from: http://olympics.nbcsports.com/2018/03/14/stephen-hawking-paralympics-speech-video-opening-ceremony-london-2012/

Help if you're a student with a learning difficulty, health problem or disability. (2019). Retrieved from: www.gov.uk/disabled-students-allowances-dsas

Holler, R. (2019). 'Rebuilding a shattered life and a broken body': Social work and disability discourses in Israel's first decades, *The British Journal of Social Work*, 49(2), 448–465.

Jackson, D., Hodges, C., Molesworth, M., & Scullion, R. (2015). *Reframing Disability? Media, (Dis)Empowerment, and Voice in the 2012 Paralympics*. Oxford: Routledge.

Jackson, R. (2019). *Promoting Universal Accessibility in Higher Education*, presented at University of Worcester. Unpublished.

Lapper, A. (2006). *My Life in My Hands*. London: Pocket.

Larson, E. (1998). Reframing the meaning of disabilities to families: The embrace of paradox. *Social Science and Meaning*, 47 (7), 865–975.

Mallet, R., & Runswick-Cole, K. (2014). *Approaching Disability*. London: Routledge.

Rosen, M. (2018). Michael Rosen talks language and gender identity with C.N. Lester. *Word of Mouth* (radio programme). Retrieved from: www.bbc.co.uk/programmes/b09r4k4l

Smith, S. (2017). Dis/ability. In: Woolley, R. (ed). *Understanding Inclusion Core Concepts, Policy and Practice*. London: Taylor and Francis.

Swain, J., & French, S. (2000). Towards an affirmation model of disability. *Disability & Society*, 15(4), 569–582.

The National Cancer Institute. (2010). Retrieved from: www.cancer.gov/about-cancer/treatment/side-effects/nerve-problems

World Health Organization (1992). *The ICD-10 Classification of Mental and Behavioural Disorders: Clinical Descriptions and Diagnostic Guidelines*. Geneva: World Health Organization.

World Health Organization (2001). *International Classification of Functioning, Disability and Health (ICIDH-2)*. Geneva: World Health Organization.

Intermezzo

Ellingson, Butler-Rees, Leigh and Smith have all taken their very own approach to understanding autoethnography, self-narrative and embodied inquiry. Yet, at the core of all four contributions lies the focus on the self and reflexivity. Indeed, self-narratives and autoethnographic work emphasise the need to gain deep understanding of the self (*auto*) in order to be able to analytically engage (*graphy*) with wider socio-cultural issues (*ethno*) (Ellis and Bochner, 2000).

The general critique and criticism of self-narratives lies in the potential lack of rigour of the analytical engagement with culture. However, as the four chapters have demonstrated the emphasis on the self, the lived experience and the body-as-lived enables an understanding that impacts the reader viscerally.

At the same time, these four contributions are in themselves critiques of the kinds of knowledges that are favoured in academia. Ellingson, Butler-Rees, Leigh and Smith highlight that their knowing and experiencing are highly relational and contextual. Life experiences do not occur in a vacuum, but shape and are shaped by the interactions and connections with other human beings in the specific contexts in which they occur (Leigh and Brown, 2021). This relational and contextual nature of experiences in turn requires a strong look inside oneself, thus a focus on the self and reflexivity to make sense of and analyse the meanings of experiences. In other words, the authors' inward-look enables them to reflect, to look outwards, to make connections and to develop their theorisations of their own experiences. Instead of questioning the rigour of this kind of analysis or knowledge, we as readers should be taking this outward-look another step further to make our own connections, to reflect on our roles within these or similar experiences, to develop theories on what can be done and to take action, thus to be transformed (Berry, 2006; Chang, 2016).

The academics' personal, professional experiences and scholarly engagement provide an impetus for change within academia, but also provide practical examples for initiatives and strategies to be implemented for the benefit of disabled, chronically ill and/ or neurodivergent academics and students. And therein lies the strength of this second part of the book.

References

Berry, K. (2006). Implicated audience member seeks understanding: Reexamining the 'gift' of autoethnography. *International Journal of Qualitative Methods*, 5(3), 94–108.

Chang, H. (2016). *Autoethnography as Method.* (Vol. 1). Routledge.

Ellis, C., & Bochner, A. (2000). Autoethnography, personal narrative, reflexivity: Researcher as subject. In: Denzin, N., & Lincoln, Y. (eds). *Handbook of Qualitative Research.* (2nd edn). London: Sage, 733–68.

Leigh, J., & Brown, N. (2021). *Embodied Inquiry: Research Methods.* London: Bloomsbury.

PART II

Lived experiences

Although ableism in academia is endemic (Brown and Leigh, 2018, 2020), there have been few publications specifically exploring the experiences of disabled, chronically ill and/or neurodivergent members of staff in academia. Over the past three years the conversations around ableism and issues of equality, diversity and inclusion have certainly intensified. And still, there are too many members of staff in academia who do not feel that they can disclose their conditions and/or needs (see Brown, 2020). It is therefore only the more humbling and refreshing to be able to present so many chapters in Part II of this book to provide insights into the lived experiences of disabled, chronically ill and/or neurodivergent individuals.

The contributors tell their stories through emotional and scholarly engagement with disability, from an embodied perspective or using an autobiographical, autoethnographic, self-narrative approach. Even if methodological choices are perhaps not always transparent all contributors were required to think with stories (Frank, 2013) and to use writing as a method of inquiry (Richardson, 2000, 2003). The result is a representation of very personal experiences embedded in relevant, scholarly literature, 'not to evoke a sense of empathy, cultural insight or deep significance, but to confront us with the *radical specificity* of living a life … in the sense that life is lived in the flows, multiplicities, and provisionality of each moment, event, emotion' (Sotirin, 2010, n.p., section 6, original emphasis).

The chapters in Part II, therefore, are not representations of all experiences of disabilities, chronic illnesses and/or neurodivergences, but the radical specificity of each individual's experience, thus the usually subjugated and marginalised (Ellingson, 2017). As a collective, the contributors do not wish to reinforce a hierarchy of marginalisation or to ignore their potential privileges, such as race, gender or positions in academia, which are more secure for some than others. Instead, irrespective of their personal circumstances, the contributors emphasise the exemplariness of their lived experiences. Despite the many differences across the chapters, experiences are nonetheless comparable in relation to the disability experience as a societal barrier and challenge for individuals. Each chapter finishes with reflection questions and practical recommendations and strategies for more inclusive practices in higher education to stimulate further thoughts and actions across the sector.

References

Brown, N. (2020). Disclosure in academia: A sensitive issue. In: Brown, N., & Leigh, J.S. (eds). *Ableism in Academia: Theorising Experiences of Disabilities and Chronic Illnesses in Higher Education*. London: UCL Press.

Brown, N., & Leigh, J.S. (2018). Ableism in academia: Where are the disabled and ill academics? *Disability and Society*, 33(6), 985–989.

Brown, N., & Leigh, J.S. (eds) (2020). *Ableism in Academia: Theorising Experiences of Disabilities and Chronic Illnesses in Higher Education*. London: UCL Press.

Ellingson, L.L. (2017). *Embodiment in Qualitative Research*. Routledge.

Frank, A.W. (2013). *The Wounded Storyteller: Body, Illness, and Ethics*. (2nd edn). Chicago, IL: University of Chicago Press.

Richardson, L. (2000). Writing: A method of inquiry. In: Denzin, N., & Lincoln, Y. (eds). *The Sage Handbook of Qualitative Research*. (2nd edn). Thousand Oaks, CA: Sage. 923–943.

Richardson, L. (2003). Writing: A method of inquiry. In: Lincoln, Y. & Denzin, N. (eds). *Turning Points in Qualitative Research: Tying Knots in a Handkerchief*. Walnut Creek, CA: Altamira. 379–396.

Sotirin, P. (2010). Autoethnographic mother-writing: Advocating radical specificity. *Journal of Research Practice*, 6(1), M9.

5

Colour blindness in academia: the challenges of an invisible impairment

Oliver Daddow

Introduction

The majority of people share a common sensory experience in terms of perceiving, naming, discussing and using the colours they see. A sizeable minority of people, however, experience the world differently because they have a more limited perception of colour. Statistics show that 1 in 12 males and 1 in 200 females with Northern European ancestry live with what is colloquially, but inaccurately, known as colour blindness[1] – approximately 4.5 per cent of the population. This means that, globally, hundreds of millions of people are not as aware, if they are aware at all, of differences between colours or hues that the majority of us take for granted: 'Worldwide, there are approximately 300 million people with colour blindness, almost the same number of people as the entire population of the USA' (Colour Blind Awareness, 2018a). In the UK, approximately 450,000 children, or one child in every co-educational classroom, are unable to identify many different colours (Scope, 2018) because they have defects in the three kinds of retinal cones that respond to red, blue and green light (National Eye Institute, 2015).

Colour blindness can be brought on by conditions such as diabetes or multiple sclerosis and it can also accompany the natural ageing process in humans (Colour Blind Awareness,

2018a). That said, it is most commonly an inherited condition, one for which there is no known cure. Regarding inherited colour blindness, as the statistics above indicate, males are more likely to be affected than females because the gene responsible is carried in the X chromosome and, unlike females, males do not have a second X chromosome that usually overrides the faulty one. The most common form of colour blindness is red-green confusion; the second most common is blue-yellow confusion; the rarest type is monochromacy, where one sees in shades of grey from black to white (Colour Blind Awareness 2018b).

The purpose of this chapter is to explore the everyday challenges in academia from my perspective as someone who has inherited deuteranomaly (green-deficient cone sensitivity). The first part of the chapter briefly explains the daily lived effects of the condition and how they have impacted negatively on my educational experiences and work as an academic. It includes a ten-point scale of offensive responses when colour blind challenges are raised. The second part is more specifically on research, exploring how living with colour blindness has moulded my preference for text analysis as my main research method.

The primary argument pursued in what follows is that the treatment of colour blindness in education seems to be at one with forms of 'discrimination and oppression that many disabled people experience in society' (Hehir, 2002: 3). Living in a world of colour is incredibly tiring physically and mentally, but reasonable adjustments for it are in short supply because there is such limited awareness of colour blindness and its consequences. In our schools and universities colour vision deficiency is an invisible 'site of inequality' on an 'ableist landscape' in education (Penketh, 2017: 113). The very nature of education itself requires re-imagining to improve the experiences of all in society. The pre-requisite to this is improved understanding. Simply being listened to, not talked at, would be a useful step. The secondary argument moves from the general to the specific, and is that my preference for text analysis as academic research method is reflective of my desire to exert a form of 'control' over colour that I do not experience elsewhere in academia or life in general.

Living with colour blindness

I was diagnosed with colour blindness in primary school when I was around 6 years of age. As, remarkably, is still the case today, colour blindness screening in UK schools the early 1980s was patchy to non-existent. My impairment was picked up by luck as much as anything else. I was keen on art at home and at school but I painted the sky purple, tree trunks green and grass brown or dark red. My repeated 'mistakes' formed a pattern that drew the attention of a combination of my parents and teacher, who I believe had some knowledge of the condition from prior classroom experience. One day, I was kept back after school to look through a book of circles filled with coloured dots, some of which showed numbers and lines, some of which did not. This was the Ishihara 38 Plate Colour Vision Deficiency Test (Colblindor, 2018), which confirmed my colour blindness.

Out of interest, I just retook the full test online and the diagnosis, it confirms, is that I have a 'moderate' form of red-green colour blindness. This is the second strongest categorisation after 'severe' on a four-point scale. I was not aware of their shock or fears at the time, but my mother later revealed that my parents, and father in particular, were devastated by the diagnosis. They initially planned to spend whatever money it took to 'make me right', but were swiftly advised there was no cure. My mother spent hours patiently labelling coloured pencils and felt tip pens, so I could get by at school. I do not remember being bullied or picked out for being 'different', although I might have blocked it out, or my mind could be playing tricks. Undoubtedly my mum's labelling helped limit my exposure to ridicule by helping me select the 'right' colours in art and so on.

So at school I do not recall any of my peers knowing they had colour blindness, or discussing it if they did. My teachers were informed but there was no policy on it. I was not 'statemented' as requiring a special educational need or extra support. Teachers (mostly) listened empathetically to my difficulties and made allowances, such as not using dark chalk on the blackboard. The move to whiteboards is an improvement, but they are not perfect. I was put off the natural sciences because of the use of colour in experiments and assessments. For example, in chemistry I could not read the colours on litmus paper. In physics I could not rewire a plug or grasp light diffraction.

Mathematics was just as much a nightmare because of the graphs and presentation of statistical data (see later in this chapter). Geography was also off-putting because of the use of colour coding to designate rainfall patterns in weather systems, different countries in an atlas and the percentages of the population living in poverty in global human rights indicators. I always dreaded these subjects' assessments for reasons which seemed irrational at the time because I enjoyed studying and worked hard. Now I know that it was because I was not able to process the requisite information and was consequently less engaged than peers were with the learning materials. Before assessments began I knew I would not perform to my best, even though I was a diligent student.

Colour blindness impacts on my life in many ways, some minor, some major and all impactful. Simply opening my eyes and looking around reminds me that I am 'different', having a genetic condition that means I might be missing out on nature and colours in all their glory. I will give just a few examples of the daily grind of being colour blind before homing in on the academic impact through school education and beyond.

Imagine being in the toilets of a busy train station. All the doors look closed. You are trying to ascertain the unlocked ones. A small red circle the size of a UK 5p piece above the handle indicates the cubicle is engaged, while a green one tells you it is free. Now imagine not being able to distinguish red from green and you will appreciate the difficulty and potential embarrassment colour blindness can cause. You either have to go down the row pushing at each and every door to find an unlocked one, or you have to ask someone to help you identify the green one. I have had some very awkward moments in train station toilets; my coping strategy is to avoid them wherever possible. Meanwhile, although I did learn to drive I found it abnormally exhausting and stressful and never passed my driving test. Looking back, this was a blessing for my safety and others'. With colour blindness you learn to not trust your eyes even though you are certain to be seeing the 'correct' colour. I was always pausing just that little bit too long at traffic lights – long enough to annoy other drivers and frustrate me.

Other daily challenges include not being able to: read red-green LED indicators for charging batteries; read food packaging labels, which can be dangerous if one also has a deadly health issue such as a peanut allergy; tell apart unripe fruit and vegetables from their ripe counterparts; book seats at the theatre when the seat map is colour coded; and know which till is free at the supermarket if the store uses a colour coded check-out system.

One of my passions is watching and playing sport, but rarely can I distinguish between the two teams, not to mention that red, green or brown kits against grass that make the players invisible. I cannot easily pick up red or pink cricket balls; I struggle with on-screen golf scorecards; I cannot keep up with tennis balls against the clay court at Roland Garros; nor can I work out what is going on in a football (soccer) penalty shoot-out when the graphic uses red/green circles for miss/score respectively. I long ago gave up watching international rugby encounters between Wales and Ireland because when they wear their home kits (red versus green) all the players look the same colour. Growing up, my brothers, who are not colour blind, had to get used to playing with one team always in white on our beloved computer football games so I could tell them apart. Software designers are belatedly catching on to the colour blindness issue in game design, some now coming with optional colour blind modes (Johnson, 2010).

In academia, the sorry picture of how colour blindness is understood and catered for (or not) is no different. As I have experienced it in 20 years as a scholar who has worked in several universities, colour blind issues are not acknowledged in any meaningful way in academic training or professional development courses. Gender, diversity and equality are, rightly, hot topics, but colour blindness is not part of the discussion. Awareness that the condition even exists is patently lacking and catering for it is, therefore, just about non-existent, reflecting the finding that 'people are often unaware of the constraining impact of disability'. For that reason, suggests Margaret McLean (2011: 13) 'they are likely to assume that the circumstances of their able-bodied world are universal.' In other words, ableist assumptions are institutionalised in universities, creating 'barriers to equitable social participation for many disabled people'.

To give some examples, the results of my university's National Student Survey were processed into tables colour coded using the dreaded traffic light system, including black numbers on a red background, which makes them invisible; the same goes for yellow against white. University Virtual Learning Environments (VLEs) routinely use pastel shades and faded texts, especially when editing, which is tiring on my eyes. I often sit in lectures, conferences and workshops confused by PowerPoint slides I cannot read and handouts I cannot fathom because they are not colour blind friendly. Confronted with such visuals I tend to switch off, choosing not to participate in my own discrimination. On the plus side, I integrate discussion of colour blindness into my lectures and presentation guides, meaning that I can reach hundreds of students per year who otherwise might remain oblivious to colour blind matters.

Higher education's obliviousness to colour blindness parallels that in wider society. Crucially, it reflects the appalling state of print and broadcast media coverage of colour blindness, which is beyond the scope of this chapter only on the grounds of space. This includes publicly funded broadcasters such as the BBC which 'failed colour blind viewers' during its 2015 general election coverage (Harding, 2016), but which still has not learned its lesson. Suffice to say it is an exacerbating factor in everything discussed here, notably journalists' depiction of colour blind people as stupid, being abused by famous journalists and broadcasters for mentioning it on social media and the production of inaccessible visuals on television, including on game shows, making them impossible to follow.

The range of challenges one faces as a colour blind person is, ironically, matched only by the range of ways in which people try to tell you it is not a problem and that one should remain silent about them. Ableist assumptions clearly structure the kinds of responses one receives to raising colour blind challenges, inside and outside academia. They can be mapped on a 10-point scale of increasing offence:

1. Silence (the most common).
2. 'Use an app' (the technological solution).

3. 'I can send you a programme to fix it' (the even more time consuming and cumbersome technological solution).
4. 'Ask someone to help you' (infantilising discourse).
5. 'This is how it's always been done' (path dependency).
6. 'The majority can see it, pipe down' (lack of empathy).
7. 'If you can see red and green you're not colour blind: concentrate harder' (denial by misunderstanding).
8. 'Do not impose your lifestyle choice on society' (denial informed by misunderstanding and prejudice).
9. 'Women cannot be colour blind' (gendered denial).
10. 'You should be put up against a wall and shot for having a genetic deficiency' (internet trolling by toxic White supremacists).

Responses up and down this scale will no doubt be familiar to anyone raising concerns in public about how their particular impairment or disability is catered for by society. Just as worryingly, and even in a world of 'political correctness', colour blindness seems to be one of the few physical impairments about which it is still 'fair game' to make jokes – and their quality has not improved since the 1970s. This approach to 'dealing' with colour blindness in academia was summed up by a former boss who always made a joke when he saw me, in public or otherwise, about my 'yellow' tie (it was blue or purple). I laughed of course, as we tend to do, but inside I felt rather different. This experience is rare but is the tip of the iceberg when the rest of the responses come into the equation. Having described some of the ways in which being colour blind impinges negatively on my life and job, the next part will highlight the practical effects of the condition on my academic research choices.

Colour blindness in academic research

The background to the ensuing reflection on the way in which my relationship to colour affects my research lies in the world of social media. I am of the view that the association between my colour blindness and my academic pursuits only crystallised properly after I, rather reluctantly, signed up to Twitter for professional reasons in February 2017. Twitter is a veritable riot of colour, a constant flow of pictures, memes, gifs, cartoons, tables, graphs and charts. I try not to follow too many people to limit my exposure as far as possible, but the intensity of the colour experience is palpable nonetheless.

For the majority of people myriad colours on social media are no issue. They can process the information, 'like' it or otherwise and scroll on. However, I noticed that I was having to linger on many of the images and even then could not interpret them. I began to take a second and then a third look at the graphs, images, figures and tables that are a staple of timelines and retweets for the politically interested. Polls of voting intentions, leader approval ratings, PowerPoint slides, heat maps, country comparison indexes, pie charts of attitudes towards immigration, Brexit negotiation flow charts: on social media they get the full colour treatment.

Using colour is a staple of communication and education and very few people would, understandably, question its use. I can imagine these images look aesthetically pleasing and informative if one can see the full colour spectrum. However, after being on Twitter for 24 months, at the time of writing, I estimate that I can process 'normally' around half the images I see on the platform. I can spend time deciphering what is going on in a few of the remainder if I concentrate hard. The rest remain an impenetrable morass of shapes and numbers, the content of which is meaningless if not invisible. Even if I can distinguish colours in, say, a line graph, it is usually impossible to translate from legend to graph. My eyes do not 'hold' the strength of a colour for long. So, I do not know which line represents what trend, as in the example in Figure 5.1, from Public Health England, a government body. If one were to print this out in black and white, or lived with monochromacy, the image would be no more revealing. Like all of its ilk, this graph's fundamental design flaw is that it relies on the use of colour alone to convey the key information.

The problems are of equal magnitude whether the images are viewed on mobile phone or large screen PC:[2] for me, at least, the size of the image is less important than the choice of colour. Thus, I would not feel confident using such material in

Figure 5.1: Example of an inaccessible graph for those with colour blindness

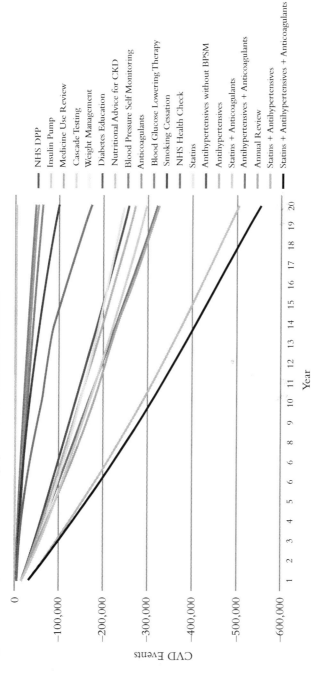

Note: A colour version of this image can be found at https://policy.bristoluniversitypress.co.uk/lived-experiences-of-ableism-in-academia/fig-5-1-col.
Source: Public Health England, 2018

research without getting it wrong and thereby being accused of fabricating evidence. Nor would I feel confident producing such images in the first place, because while I might be able to read them I am well aware others may not.

And this is the crux. Following on from what was said in the first part about my self-exclusion from subjects at school requiring or promoting the coloured presentation of data, I have ended up researching in the social sciences where I can stick to simple text and not be overwhelmed by, or have to present my research in, data visualisation formats with which I am uncomfortable. In particular, I have homed in on discourse analysis, the systematic study of language in context used to get at the mental life worlds and belief systems of the people responsible (for instance Daddow, 2011; Daddow, 2015). I could not imagine even sitting in quantitative panels at a political science conference because I know I would not be able to process around half the key data. It would be a futile exercise for me and my colleagues.

I answer my research questions about the management of British European policy by political elites by immersing myself in the words and phrases that help us understand the worldviews of British prime ministers and foreign secretaries as seen in the recurring tropes, metaphors, frames and keywords they deploy to describe and legitimise their policies in speeches (see Daddow, 2011), statements, parliamentary debates and policy documents. I have applied this method to British foreign policy more widely and have also branched out to explore how the media constructs political scandals, such as that befalling Oxfam in 2018.

I used to put my choice of method down to an innate geekiness and a keen eye for the detail of what politicians say and how they say it. But it transpires that my awkward relationship to colour itself explains my choice of method and has sharpened this aspect of my learning and encounters with the primary material. I first of all ruled myself out of certain subjects (see previous section) in which the use of colour was routine. Then, within my chosen field, I narrowed down to a method that would enable me to work from black and white, which I fill with my own 'colour', literally and metaphorically. Onto the print outs of the relevant texts I code the key words and phrases I need using bright, contrasting colours I can distinguish, usually yellow, blue and pink. I then draw the connections from the colour coded data, with the written report of the findings being at the heart of my publications. In other words, my work in the field text analysis has both benefits from, and is structured by, my experiences of living and managing colour blindness in my daily life.

As for how others have reacted to this approach, I have never properly discussed it with anyone so I assume I am tolerated on social media as something of a 'quirk' but it is not something anyone has ever felt comfortable raising with me directly. The discourse approach is controversial enough in some quarters of the discipline (is it 'science' they ask?). To explain it as methodological choice would also be to 'give away' my identity as the producer of the supposedly anonymous articles sent to journals for peer review. As with so much in academia, the façade of detached objectivity has to be maintained. The overt putting of oneself into one's work (in my discipline at least) might mean sanction in never having research sent out for peer review. In sum, my methodological choice has to be dressed up as a professional decision, detaching me from my work in sometimes difficult ways to address adequately in methods statements.

Conclusion

To draw things to a close, the first conclusion is that my personal experiences of living with colour blindness in academia testify to the accuracy of Thomas Hehir's assertion (2002: 3) that we live in a 'world that has not been designed with the disabled in mind'. Ableist assumptions are at the heart of the multiple forms of discrimination those with colour blindness encounter. They are sometimes tiny impairments, but they are always noticeable, and all the more annoying for being so easy to fix with a modicum of thought. Designing for the colour blind is a 'thing', but is not well known in academia. Its wider take-up will require a number of mutually reinforcing strategies, particularly spreading the understanding that good design benefits everyone, not just the 8 per cent of males and 0.5 per cent of females with colour blindness.

As software designers with experience of catering for colour blindness have argued, everyone – including colour 'normals' – has a slightly different experience of colour in the margins: 'generally, the elements that are favourable for colour blind users are actually considered to be good design practices in the wider sense. So, if your site is well designed, it should already be accessible to all users' (Collinge, 2017). After all, the point of maps, graphs and charts is to convey information, not look nice – save that for art. Through poor design you might prevent an important figure in your field from noticing your work and citing it, and/or you might expunge from your discipline a committed younger researcher who cannot access the relevant data.

The second conclusion, therefore, is that future research could systematically investigate responses to the raising of disability issues in academia. It would certainly be a good way of shedding light on the ways in which ableist assumptions work to minimise, delegitimise, distort the arguments of, and/or silence altogether, the disabled and impaired. Practically, such a research programme would encourage thought about how to reduce prejudice against those with all forms of disability in higher education by challenging such discourse and altering associated practices, which turn the highfalutin words into ableist reality (Bialka et al, 2017). Only by challenging the narrative hegemony of ableism, which manifestly limits opportunities and the empowerment of those with disabilities and impairments such as colour blindness, can every individual flourish and meet their full potential in education systems.

Reflective questions

- Do you know anyone who is colour blind and have you ever spoken to them about how it affects their daily life?
- When someone tells you they are colour blind what do you understand them to be saying?
- Why is it important to cater for people with colour blindness when designing software, products, maps, graphs and charts?
- If someone were to tell you that they could not interpret an image you had put together, such as a graph, would you take it personally?

- Would you like it if your son or daughter or another member of your family was held back in education not because of a lack of effort but because of a physical impairment?

Recommendations

Show some empathy. Take a few minutes to *listen* to my experiences to help you become more cognisant of what colour blindness is and how it impacts my daily life and work. Merely to feel like one is being heard is a comfort: ask me questions about colour blindness if you wish. It is entirely natural that you might not know what it is or how it affects the routine tasks I perform at work. None of us can understand everything about impairments and disabilities that are not familiar to us. However, if you listen to what I am telling you will be able to empathise a lot more with the condition and the real challenges it poses, minute after minute, hour after hour and day after day. Improving your awareness will help you to help me counter forms of visual and design discrimination that cause me the biggest problems. Oh, and when you find out I have colour blindness please don't ask me the colour of the sky or your jumper.

Please do not tell me to rely on technological solutions. Modern technology has improved our lives and connected us in so many ways it has become something of an orthodoxy that we are better with it than without it (although that liberal optimism has faded slightly in recent years). Poor data visualisation and software design works against me in multifarious ways. A common response you give when I raise colour blindness issues is 'use an app', which assumes I see through the world only through a mobile phone screen. An app will not help me spot the green circle on the toilet door; it will not help me distinguish ripe from unripe bananas; it will not help me unravel sports kit clashes; it will not help me see different plants in the garden against the earth. Do not let your predilection for technology as a panacea confuse you as to the broader impact of colour blindness in my daily life. There is also a broader principle in play, covered next.

The burden of reasonable adjustment is on you not me. The UK's Equality Act 2010 has it that 'Some people or organisations like employers, shops, local authorities and schools must take positive steps to remove the barriers you face because of your disability. This is to ensure you receive the same services, as far as this is possible, as someone who's not disabled' (Citizen's Advice, 2018). What, however, counts as a 'reasonable adjustment'? The Act states that a judgement on whether or not the adjustment is 'reasonable' should be rooted in a reflection on: the nature of the disability; how practicable the changes are; if the change I ask for would overcome the disadvantage I experience; size of the organisation; available resources; and the cost of making the changes (Citizen's Advice, 2018). So ask yourself: would *any* of the changes I ask for in this chapter be unreasonable on these grounds? Is requesting that a graph on a socially important or academically interesting subject conform to accessibility guidelines be too much to ask? Is it unreasonable to ask a publicly funded broadcaster such as the BBC to design graphics that I as well as you can read? We both pay the same licence fee, for a start. At the moment all the burdens fall on me to 'adapt' or face exclusion from public dialogue and debate based on colour-based images and information. The burden of reasonable adjustments should fall on you as producer not me as consumer.

Education and training. We need to find out why there is such a limited understanding of colour blindness and its effects in society. An obvious place to begin is in our schools and universities. However, we should also ask where colour blindness 'fits' into the training for everyone in professions where catering for it is required (not many will be omitted). For example, how it is that in 2018 you, the school curriculum authorities, produce learning resources and assessments that are not colour blind friendly? How is it that you, as university scholars and administrators, continue to design learning and administrative materials that discriminate against me? How is that you, the public and private broadcasters, software designers and product designers can forget integral visual needs of millions like me? How is it right that in 2018 my impairment can be laughed at as if I am an idiot? You need to upgrade the place of colour blind awareness in training and professional development courses at all levels of the institutional hierarchy. Training in how to make simple, cost-free adjustments to our product, software and graphic design will help me and millions like me who live with the world's most common genetic condition.

Notes
[1] I have opted for 'colour blind' as opposed to the technical label 'colour vision deficiency' throughout this chapter because it is how I refer to my impairment: 'I am colour blind'.
[2] And if an image is not accessible on a mobile phone, why bother putting it out in the first place when most people will probably be accessing it that way?

Acknowledgements
I am extremely grateful to Marta Olea de Cardenas, Kathryn Albany-Ward and Nicole Brown for their helpful comments on earlier drafts of this chapter.

References
Bialka, C.S., Brown, K.S., Morro, D., & Gregory, H. (2017). On their LEVEL: How participation in a university student group shapes members' perceptions of disability. *Journal of Diversity in Higher Education*, 10(2), 117–135.

Citizen's Advice (2018). *Duty to Make Reasonable Adjustments for Disabled People*. Available from: www.citizensadvice.org.uk/ law-and-courts/discrimination/what-are-the-different-types- of-discrimination/duty-to-make-reasonable-adjustments-for- disabled-people/ [Accessed 29 October 2018].

Colblindor (2018). *Ishihara 38 Plates CVD Test*. Available from: www.color-blindness.com/ishihara-38-plates-cvd-test/ [Accessed 24 October 2018].

Collinge, R. (2017). How to design for color blindness. *Usabilla*, 17 January. Available from: https://usabilla.com/blog/how- to-design-for-color-blindness/ [Accessed 26 October 2018].

Colour Blind Awareness (2018a). *Colour Blindness*. Available from: www.colourblindawareness.org/colour-blindness/ [Accessed 23 October 2018].

Colour Blind Awareness (2018b). *Types of Colour Blindness*. Available from: www.colourblindawareness.org/colour- blindness/types-of-colour-blindness/ [Accessed 23 October 2018].

Daddow, O. (2011). *New Labour and the European Union: Blair and Brown's Logic of History*. Manchester: Manchester University Press.

Daddow, O. (2015). Interpreting the outsider tradition in British European policy speeches from Thatcher to Cameron. *Journal of Common Market Studies*, 53(1), 71–88.

Harding, L. (2016). BBC 'failed colour blind viewers' during its general election coverage. *Mirror*, 28 July. Available from: www.mirror.co.uk/tv/tv-news/bbc-failed-colour-blind-viewers-8514843 [Accessed 26 October 2018].

Hehir, T. (2002). Eliminating ableism in education. *Harvard Educational Review*, 72(1), 1–32.

Johnson, J. (2010). Tips for designing for colorblind users. *Design Shack*, 28 July. Available from: https://designshack.net/articles/accessibility/tips-for-designing-for-colorblind-users/ [Accessed 27 October 2018].

McLean, M. (2011). Getting to know you: The prospect of challenging ableism through adult learning. *New Directions for Adult and Continuing Education*, 132(Winter), 13–22.

National Eye Institute (2015). *Facts about Colour Blindness*. 15 February. Available from: https://nei.nih.gov/health/color_blindness/facts_about [Accessed 23 October 2018].

Penketh, C. (2017). 'Children see before they speak': An exploration of ableism in art education. *Disability and Society*, 32(1), 110–127.

Public Health England (2018). *Cardiovascular Disease Prevention: Return on Investment Tool: Final Report*. September. Available from: https://assets.publishing.service.gov.uk/government/uploads/system/uploads/attachment_data/file/749866/CVD_ROI_tool_final_report.pdf [Accessed 26 October 2018].

Scope (2018). *Colour Vision Deficiency*. Available from: www.scope.org.uk/Support/Families/Diagnosis/CVD-overview [Accessed 29 October 2018].

Stafford, E. (2017). *Can Colour Blindness Amount to a Disability for the Purposes of the Equality Act?* 17 November. Available from: www.harpermacleod.co.uk/hm-insights/2017/november/can-colour-blindness-amount-to-a-disability-for-the-purposes-of-the-equality-act/ [Accessed 29 October 2018].

6

Stammering in academia: voice in the management of self and others

Robert H. Mann and Bryan C. Clift

Introduction

Scene 1: The interview

Having accepted an interview opportunity to augment his research capacity, Robert found himself sitting in a generic meeting room opposite a panel of three interviewers. Trying to settle into his new surroundings, he awaited their first question.

Interviewer 1:	Please can you provide us with a brief overview of your PhD research?
Robert:	Yes. N-n-n-not a p-p-prob problem. My reeee-search is in-v-v-v-v-est [pause]. In-v-v invest [intake of breath]. In-v-v [pause]. Investigating thh the [intake of breath].
Robert's internal dialogue:	Why did I bother coming to this interview? It was obvious that I would spend the whole time 'blocking' – interviews always make my stammer worse. Anyway, I have made it this far, so they must be interested in what I could

111

bring to the position. Just remember to smile, maintain eye contact and, if you do stammer, make sure that you stammer to the best of your ability!

Interviewer 2: Is there anything that we can do to help?

This opening excerpt depicts an experience of the first author, Robert, during a recent exchange with a funding body interview panel. To augment his research capacity, he applied for a Policy Fellowship Scheme and secured an interview for the opportunity. His area of research and the intricacies of the scheme are relatively unimportant here. Rather, it is his experiences as an academic who stammers, how he makes sense of these experiences and the response that he receives from his academic peers – either implicitly or explicitly – that are fundamental to cultivating an academic voice and identity, which are the focus of this chapter.

Voice is a foundational aspect of developing the necessary agency for academic success. Voice can be generated in a variety of forms: from our speech and communication with peers, to our internal dialogue, electronic communication, what others say about us, and our writings and publications. One's voice in its myriad forms facilitates participation in the many activities of professional academic life: delivering conference presentations, teaching responsibilities and workshops; discussing research ideas with peers; carrying out clerical duties; contributing to meetings; and providing a succinct and coherent account of yourself when pursuing career opportunities, such as interviews, academic positions, and promotions. Although each form of voice is interconnected and important for developing the various roles and responsibilities that we take on as academics, the spoken word (speech) is one that is undeniably significant. Therefore, having a stammer can make navigating the academic environment and fostering a preferred academic identity challenging.

What is stammering?

Stammering is a common speech fluency disorder that can significantly affect an individual's ability to communicate verbally. It is a neurological disorder (Smith and Weber, 2017) that the International Classification of Diseases (2019) stated is 'characterised by persistent and frequent or pervasive disruption of the rhythmic flow of speech'. While every stammer is unique, this 'disruption' can involve involuntary repetition of sounds, syllables or words, prolongations, word breaks, blocks, excessive use of interjections and/or rapid short bursts of speech. The prevalence of stammering is reported to be around 1 per cent of the adult population (Craig et al, 2002). In contrast, the incidence of stammering is typically reported as 5 per cent (Månsson, 2000; Yairi and Ambrose, 2012).

The terms *stammer* and *stutter* are interchangeable. However, *stammer* is the most frequently used term in the United Kingdom (UK), with *stutter* being used more often in the United States (US). Typically, stammering begins during childhood as a neurodevelopmental disorder that affects up to 5 per cent of young children (Yairi and Ambrose, 1992a; 1992b). In the majority of cases, this disorder is resolved before adulthood, either spontaneously or from successful speech and language therapy. However, when the stammer continues over a number of years it is likely to persist into adulthood. Similar to other neurodevelopmental disorders, such as autism, stammering affects more males then females (Bloodstein and Ratner, 2008) and is genetically heritable (Frigerio-Domingues and Drayna, 2017). Although far less common, it is also possible to acquire a stammer as an adult, known as a neurogenic stammer, which results from or is produced by neurological pathology changes in the brain (Ward, 2010). This is often caused by, for example, stroke, drug (mis)use, or severe head injury.

Regardless of the underlying cause (that is, neurodevelopmental or neurogenic), stammering often meets the legal definition of disability. In the UK, according to the Equality Act 2010, one can be classified as having a disability if possessing 'a physical or mental impairment that has a *substantial and long-term* [emphasis added] negative effect on your ability to do normal daily activities'. In Robert's case, his stammer has remained present since early childhood. Although he does not stammer in all situations, his stammer does disrupt his speech patterns considerably more frequently than those who do not stammer. By definition, Robert's case meets the legal definition of disability as both 'substantial' and 'long-term'.

Like many who do stammer, however, the full presence and effect of his stammer is disguised through the application of avoidance strategies. These strategies include removing himself from (in)formal departmental discussions and developing an overreliance on electronic forms of communication. Therefore, the true extent − it's 'substantial' effect − of his stammer is not fully acknowledged by colleagues and friends. Within the wider stammering community, this avoidance often results in a situation where identification as disabled is not necessarily the preferred option. Indeed, the popularist social perception of disability (that is, a visible disability) may not seem to align with the experiences of a person who stammers. This is especially the case when it comes to disclosing a stammer within the workplace, wherein the perceived stigma that surrounds this classification may be seen as a disadvantage (Butler, 2014).

While differences in opinion remain about whether having a stammer should be disclosed as a disability, it is hard to argue against the notion that having a stammer is burdensome, both physically and figuratively (Craig and Tran, 2014). In this chapter we aim to shift the dialogue about stammering and academia beyond that of burdensome or critical self-reflection. Instead, we provide an insight into the assembly of an academic environment that can be more inclusive, works toward equality and equity, that offers insight into the forms of support useful for supporting the success of those with a stammer and those who work with them. Through the experiential view of one person who stammers, and theoretically informed by Goffman's *Presentation of self* (1959), and *Stigma* (1963), we provide a glimpse into a stammering academic's life. Although this chapter provides a forum for Robert's voice, we do not presume to be representative of all other academics with a similar impediment, nor any disability. Every stammer is unique, as is every disability, and specific to the characteristics and identities that modulate the social experience of living with such an impediment (Acton and Hird, 2004; Watson, 2002).

Academic life as a person who stammers

The presence of a stammer imposes a personal attribute that can often impede an individual's attempt to develop their academic voice; an instrumental and vital aspect of an academic's persona and identity. Always developed in relation to those people, scenarios, or scenes in front of us, Goffman (1959) referred to this interactive process – between self, audience and context – as *impression management*: the effort to create specific impressions of ourselves in the minds of others. He understood speech and speech patterns as integral parts in producing a *personal front*. The concept of a personal front was further divided by Goffman (1959) into two different aspects: *appearance* and *manners*. Speech patterns predominantly contribute towards an individual's manners, thereby telling the audience members what to expect during a performance. In this way, a person who stammers does not just experience an involuntary interruption in their speech pattern, but rather several internal and external elements that influence their capacity to craft an academic voice and preferred identity. As Robert's initial account intimated, a stammer can elicit internal dialogue as well as social responses from those around us. It is always present, an inseparable part of everyday experience (Watson, 2002); it is his normal and ontological existence.

Like Scene 1, the following scene illustrates the internal–external dynamics of academic life with a stammer:

Scene 2: The presentation

Invited to present his research at a national conference, Robert hesitantly accepted. He took a painstaking amount of time to write a word-for-word script, both to make sure that he spoke within the allotted time and to assist in managing his stammer. After a full morning of travelling he arrived at the conference. He made his way to the room where he would be presenting and reviewed the conference programme.

Robert's internal dialogue:	That is my name printed in the conference programme. I am not sure how comfortable I am with this. I am on after the first break. Okay. That gives me time to see a few other presentations. Just relax. Hang on, what if I cannot even say my own name: R–R–R–R–R–Robert. Every other presentation that I have tried has been a struggle, even reading aloud in English classes! Why did I dare to think this would be any different? No one here even knows that I have a stammer. That is going to make it even more awkward. Right, I cannot do this. I am unable to do this. I will not do this. It will be less awkward this way. I mean, who wants to watch me choke on my own words for twenty minutes? That is no good for anyone. *At the first break, Robert found the chairperson.*
Robert:	Hello. I am R–R–Robert. I am m–meant to be p–p–p–present [intake of breath]. Speaking after the break. But I do nnn–not thhh–thhh–think that I will be able to do it, because of my st–st–stammer.
Chairperson:	Okay. Are you sure that you do not want to present? Is there anything that we can do to make it easier for you? It would be a shame not to share your research findings. I am sure that everyone would be interested in your work.
Robert:	Yes. I am sure. I w–w–will not be able to d–d–do it.
Chairperson:	Okay. That is fine. I will make a quick note of the change and let everyone know after their break. However, you really should have disclosed this to us before the conference. We could have helped you with alternative arrangements or something.

Like others whose disability is not visible, Robert is consistently caught between whether or not to disclose his stammer. When choosing to disclose his stammer, the preferred situation and timing to do so is neither simple nor straightforward. This tension is referred to as the 'reveal/conceal' dilemma (Lingsom, 2008). Choosing to disclose a disability and be identified as having a disability enables certain forms of support to be accessed (von Schrader et al, 2014; Watson, 2002). Yet, conversely, not disclosing a disability may help an individual avoid discrimination, stigma and their lasting psychosocial effects (Lindsay et al, 2018; Watson, 2002). While more visible disabilities force disclosure through visual cues, less visible forms of disability, such as a stammer, do not immediately manifest themselves until either communication occurs or the choice is made to communicate this prior to meeting. Specific to stammering, it can be very frustrating that the decision to disclose is taken away from an individual through the very act of speaking in front of or with others.

In Goffman's (1959) framing, fostering an academic persona requires convincing others in academia that one possesses the traits of an academic; it is also about crafting one's identity. One's voice, both in written form – which Robert achieved in each scene in order to gain entry to both an interview and presentation – and in spoken form – to be performed at each event – becomes a requisite for convincing others of their quality. In Scene 2, Robert chose not to disclose his stammer prior to attending the conference. This represents his attempt to preserve an academic identity for fear of being undermined by the stigma of the stammer. Yet, in doing so, Robert simultaneously *spoiled* the same academic identity he sought to achieve. Regardless of whether the perception of a stammerer is expressed implicitly or explicitly by academic peers, negative attitudes are often held towards people who stammer (Walden and Lesner, 2018). There remains a general culture of disbelief within universities, and indeed wider society, that it is possible to have both a disability and be an academic (Inckle, 2018). Therefore, a stammer can disrupt the idea of intelligence, coherence of thought, creativity, charisma and problem-solving, all of which are *supposed* characteristics of academics.

A stammer takes on the form of an embodied *unmeant gesture* (Goffman, 1959) to the successful academic persona. In Scene 2, which occurred earlier in his academic career, Robert convinced himself that the awkwardness of his stammer rendered him unable to give a presentation. His interior talk was important. Not only did he tell himself that he could not succeed, he did so through the minds and eyes of others. He silently said to himself, "who wants to watch me choke on my own words for twenty minutes? That is no good for anyone." Goffman (1959: 87) proposed the idea of *self-distantiation* as the process through which a person comes to feel estranged from themselves. In this manner, Robert both preserves and spoils his academic identity. By imagining his audience as stigmatising him in association with his stammer, and then taking action based on that imagining, Robert believed himself unable to convince others of his ability to carry out the tasks of an academic before he has attempted to do so. In his choice not to present, despite his extensive preparation, he felt it better to withdraw and reduce the obtrusiveness (Goffman, 1963) of his stammer. Avoiding the perceived awkwardness that the audience might experience, of watching, listening and engaging with someone who stammers, Robert managed himself through them. Yet, for Robert, if the audience never sees that unmeant gesture, then the integrity of the academic persona could be maintained, even if fleetingly. If, however, the stammer was disclosed unintentionally, then that persona ruptures.

These self-presentational difficulties, regardless of their level of perceived significance, create a formative source of social anxiety, reduced motivation and avoidance of social situations (Tran et al, 2011). In Scene 2, Robert simultaneously spoils and preserves his academic identity. These are scenes of an internalised ableism, what Campbell (2009) referenced as the 'tyranny within'. In a more recent experience, as detailed within Scene 1, Robert began to square up to his stammering reality with formal academic audiences and encounters beyond his advisory team in order to progress. In this instance, he chose to disclose his stammer via email prior to the interview. Rather than manage his anxiety through avoidance and non-disclosure, as he did in Scene 2, in Scene 1 Robert managed himself through similar but less severe internal dialogue. At the moment the stammer occurred in the interview he denigrated himself, "Why did I bother coming to this interview?" Then, through an ironic rhetorical strategy, he quipped, "if you do stammer, make sure that you stammer to the best of your ability!" Not being able to say what you want is an infuriating experience (Crichton-Smith, 2002). However, his interview was successful in that he achieved his desired policy internship, which is definitely a positive moment for confirming an academic identity. Despite this success, Robert remains either unable or struggles to craft and maintain his preferred academic identity.

Both of Robert's experiences (Scenes 1 and 2) illustrate how managing a stammer requires invisible, additional labour contingent for performing academic tasks. A few academics have recently spoken out, through publication (for example, Hannam-Swain, 2018; Inckle, 2018), on the additional labour that those with disabilities must undertake in order to succeed. In relation to stammering, Butler (2014) has also highlighted the aesthetic labour of 'sounding right'. In Robert's case, this work is emotional, physical, social and mental. Although the extent of the additional labour fluctuates, it is evident across a range of academic scenarios, from informal conversations with colleagues, to more formal scenarios, such as conference attendance. Through extensive preparation and effort put into a presentation, despite not giving it, or in other instances where he has pre-recorded talks to his department or faculty, or in the anxiety that currently occupies his mind about completing a PhD viva, Robert must undertake a considerable degree of additional labour. Much like other academics, Robert succeeds in some areas, such as the interview, and not in others, such as the presentation – and indeed has a continued fear and avoidance of presenting. Although self-perceived, Robert's failures are especially challenging to take, as additional labour can be nullified by the practices of self-management. Even the successes, though (his other successes include, for example, progressing well through his degree programme, publishing his first journal article and securing additional funded opportunities), come with labour not needed from, not acknowledged by, and largely invisible to his peers. That additional labour calls into question the ethos of higher education.

As Brown and Leigh (2018) observed, academia prides itself on the quality of its research and teaching output. The moving goalposts of excellence are aligned to a *system of stratification* (Goffman, 1959), whereby, on an individual level, excellence allows access to higher strata, such as job security, career opportunities and the like. 'Proper' academic performances and an academic voice are essential for successful *upward mobility*. Consistently, stammering interferes with an individual's ability to achieve these and therefore become upwardly mobile in academia. Whether it is the self-perceived inability to complete certain tasks, such as the presentation in Scene 2, or the capacity to continue engaging in additional labour practices, those with a stammer are disadvantaged. While universities actively promote inclusivity and equality, the university system (re)produces an ableism with respect to speech and speech patterns. Ableism, following Campbell (2009), consists of those networks of beliefs, processes and practices that produce particular kinds of corporeal standards (the relation between the self and body) that are projected as normal, perfect, species typical and therefore essential for full human recognition. In the university system, this is highlighted by requiring employees to have excellent verbal communication skills (Butler, 2014). Therefore, stammering, through internal and external realities, thoroughly interferes with an individual's ability to be upwardly mobile and gain access to this career trajectory.

The most recent reminder of this academic reality was the recent rejection of alternative PhD viva arrangements meant to accommodate Robert's stammer. A request that was put forward asked for accommodations that gave him additional time to prepare around key issues raised by examiners was rejected. Part of the rationale for this rejection rested on the potential to compromise the ability to assess ownership over the work or requisite working knowledge of a certain standard, because responses could be researched or coached by third parties. At risk here, according to the university concerned, is the entire integrity of the viva. Hannam-Swain (2018) wrote that this form of defence constituted a kind of *sensible say-able* (Titchkosky, 2008: 43), which enables a lack of accessibility to remain ordinary and discourages challenges from the disabled person.

Additional time for the viva, additional bathroom breaks, and a potential pre-recording were deemed acceptable. Admittedly, the pre-recording was a minor gain, but a viva in excess of four hours with more bathroom breaks, as suggested by the university, not only misses the point of accommodating the stammer but instead exacerbates it. Although a more constructive discussion has taken place since this rejection, it demonstrates a clear lack of proactivity from the university, whereby the onus has been placed on Robert to request the necessary changes and challenge institutional norms.

The additional labour invoked through disability also challenges work-life balance, which is more easily managed by those without a disability. The stammer may not be as obvious or extensive as some disabilities, but it very much does require additional labour that must come from somewhere. Often, it is the disabled person that bears this burden. Still, this does not need to be the norm. For Robert, the ability to shift thinking of his stammer as an identifier (Watson, 2002) remains an aspiration, one that perhaps may always remain. Importantly, though, this is not an aspiration that should be his alone, but rather one for all those that make up the institutions in which we work and live. Questions like "Is there anything that we can do to help?" (Scene 1) and, "Is there anything that we can do to make it easier for you?" (Scene 2) should continue to be asked in moments where a stammer is made visible, as a minimum. However, these are reactive starting points. We suggest that the academic environment writ broad should become proactive, rather than reactive.

Reflective questions

- What intellectual, professional and personal assumptions do we carry about those who stammer?
- Recognising that spoken voice is instrumental to academic professional identity and performance, how does a person who stammers achieve academic excellence?
- How do we collectively include a person who stammers in an equal way? How do we collectively include a person who stammers in an equitable way?

- In what ways might we challenge the implicit and explicit attitudes towards people who stammer in relation to academia?
- What would you regard as best practice, in terms of working alongside a person who stammers?

Recommendations

Consideration of working with those who stammer is not isolated to *their* actions, decisions and attentiveness. Instead, if the environment for those who struggle with verbal fluency is going to progress equitably, then its potential lies in *all* of those within academia, those who stammer severely, those who communicate fluently, and everyone in between. The following recommendations speak to those who stammer as well as all who work in the academy.

Disclosure: While every stammer is unique, it is important to take ownership of how this disability is implicitly and explicitly perceived by academic peers. Being upfront with peers or colleagues you trust about how this can impede your ability to complete certain tasks on a day-to-day basis is one way to begin to take ownership. The 'overt' vs 'covert' narrative associated with stammering (Douglass et al, 2018) makes this a challenging personal decision. However, disclosure of a stammer has been shown to improve quality of life (Boyle et al, 2018) and can alleviate some of the additional labour that is created by such an impediment. By doing so, you can begin to shape not just the perceptions of your stammer, but also how peers interact with you, how they contribute to working with you, and your own identity formation. Notably, this is not to say that you have to disclose a stammer as a disability per se, but this approach is certainly one step on that journey.

Institutional support: The burden on those with a disability can be lessened by a proactive institutional presence across its hierarchical structure, from the supervisory team: advisers, staff, fellow academics, directors of studies, department heads, deans and university-level administrative teams. The conversation about how to render the academic environment more equitable can happen everywhere, and indeed should. Legal obligations in relation to the Equality Act 2010 and health and safety at work legislation, or the responsibility to provide reasonable adjustments to accommodate employees with disabilities, may well be the responsibility of those nearer the top of a hierarchy. But each person can enact the ethos of equality, diversity and respect that academic institutions seem to espouse but struggle to practise (Inckle, 2018).

Peer support: Directly related to the previous item, it is important that academic peers provide support for colleagues who stammer. Essentially, this can be in the form of assisting in planning, developing and responding to the numerous challenges faced by academics who stammer. We all need to be advocates within the academic setting. Therefore, having someone to discuss issues with and advocate for you can contribute to developing strategies for working together, raising awareness and fostering a more inclusive, attentive and equitable environment.

Productive difference: Being able to recognise the given benefits of having a stammer allows an individual to maintain productive differences in an academic environment. For example, the presence of a stammer can foster diligence, empathy, determination and an improved writing ability, all of which are highly regarded qualities. It should be seen as best practice to reflect on what academic attributes have been improved as a result of such an impediment – it can be quite a rewarding process!

Resources

Alongside these recommendations, it is worth exploring resources that can be used to support a person who stammers and their colleagues within academia. In the UK, the resources on the British Stammering Association website (www.stamma. org) include advice about speech and language therapy, the recruitment process and employing someone who stammers. Details about stammer-specific discrimination law can be found via the following webpage: www.stammeringlaw.org.uk. In relation to stammering and academia, it may also be helpful to use the services of the Stammerers Through University Consultancy (STUC) and/or actively look to join a stammering support group.

Acknowledgements

Robert would like to acknowledge the ongoing support offered by his PhD supervisory team, including Bryan C. Clift, Craig A. Williams and Alan R. Barker, all of whom provide differing levels of peer support. Rachel Everard, Matthew Hollow, Claire Norman and Lindsey Pike are also acknowledged for providing comments on the first draft of this chapter.

References

Acton, C., & Hird, M. (2004). Toward a sociology of stammering. *Sociology*, 38(3), 495–513.

Bloodstein, O., & Ratner, N. (2008). *A Handbook on Stuttering*. Clifton Park, NY: Thomson Delmar Learn.

Boyle, M., Milewski, K., & Beita-Ell, C. (2018). Disclosure of stuttering and quality of life in people who stutter. *Journal of Fluency Disorders*, 58, 1–10.

Brown, N., & Leigh, J. (2018). Ableism in academia: Where are the disabled and ill academics? *Disability & Society*, 33(6), 985–989.

Butler, C. (2014). Wanted – straight talkers: Stammering and aesthetic labour. *Work, Employment and Society*, 28(5), 718–734.

Campbell, F.K. (2009). *Contours of Ableism: The Production of Disability and Abledness*. London: Palgrave Macmillan.

Craig, A., & Tran, Y. (2014). Trait and social anxiety in adults with chronic stuttering: Conclusions following meta-analysis. *Journal of Fluency Disorders*, 40, 35–43.

Craig, A., Hancock, K., Tran, Y., Craig, M., & Peters, K. (2002). Epidemiology of stuttering in the communication across the entire life span. *Journal of Speech, Language, and Hearing Research*, 45(6), 1097–1105.

Crichton-Smith, I. (2002). Communicating in the real world: Accounts from people who stammer. *Journal of Fluency Disorders*, 27(4), 333–351.

Douglass, J., Schwab, M., & Alvarado, J. (2018). Covert stuttering: Investigation of the paradigm shift from covertly stuttering to overtly stuttering. *American Journal of Speech-Language Pathology*, 27(3S), 1235–1243.

Equality Act (2010). Available at: www.legislation.gov.uk/ukpga/2010/15/contents [Accessed 24 March 2020].

Frigerio-Domingues, C., & Drayna, D. (2017). Genetic contributions to stuttering: The current evidence. *Molecular Genetics & Genomic Medicine*, 5(2), 95–102.

Goffman, E. (1959). *The Presentation of Self in Everyday Life*. New York: Anchor Books.

Goffman, E. (1963). *Stigma: Notes on a Spoiled Identity*. Upper Saddle River, NJ: Prentice-Hall.

Hannam-Swain, S. (2018). The additional labour of a disabled PhD student. *Disability & Society*, 33(1), 138–142.

Inckle, K. (2018). Unreasonable adjustments: The additional unpaid labour of academics with disabilities. *Disability & Society*, 33(8), 1372–1376.

International Classification of Diseases. (2019). ICD-11 for mortality and morbidity statistics. *World Health Organization*. Available at: www.who.int/classifications/icd/en/ [Accessed 12 January 2021].

Lindsay, S., Cagliostro, E., & Carafa, G. (2018). A systematic review of workplace disclosure and accommodation requests among youth and young adults with disabilities. *Disability and Rehabilitation*, 40(25), 2971–2986.

Lingsom, S. (2008). Invisible impairments: Dilemmas of concealment and disclosure. *Scandinavian Journal of Disability Research*, 10(1), 2–16.

Månsson, H. (2000). Childhood stuttering: Incidence and development. *Journal of Fluency Disorders*, 25, 47–57.

Smith, A., & Weber, C., 2017. How stuttering develops: The multifactorial dynamic pathways theory. *Journal of Speech, Language, and Hearing Research*, 60(9), 2483–2505.

Titchkosky, T. (2008). 'To pee or not to pee?' Ordinary talk about extraordinary exclusions in a university environment. *Canadian Journal of Sociology*, 33(1), 37–60.

Tran, Y., Blumgart, E., & Craig, A. (2011). Subjective distress associated with chronic stuttering. *Journal of Fluency Disorders*, 36(1), 17–26.

von Schrader, S., Malzer, V., & Bruyère, S. (2014). Perspectives on disability disclosure: The importance of employer practices and workplace climate. *Employee Responsibilities and Rights Journal*, 26(4), 237–255.

Walden, T., & Lesner, T. (2018). Examining implicit and explicit attitudes toward stuttering. *Journal of Fluency Disorders*, 57, 22–36.

Ward, D. (2010). Sudden onset stuttering in an adult: Neurogenic and psychogenic perspectives. *Journal of Neurolinguistics*, 23(5), 511–517.

Watson, N. (2002). Well, I know this is going to sound very strange to you, but I don't see myself as a disabled person: Identity and disability. *Disability & Society*, 17(5), 509–527.

Yairi, E., & Ambrose, N. (1992a). A longitudinal study of stuttering in children: A preliminary report. *Journal of Speech and Hearing Research*, 35, 755–760.

Yairi, E., & Ambrose, N. (1992b). Onset of stuttering in preschool children: Selected factors. *Journal of Speech and Hearing Research*, 35, 782–788.

Yairi, E., & Ambrose, N. (2012). Epidemiology of stuttering: 21st century advances. *Journal of Fluency Disorders*, 38(2), 66–87.

7

Losing my voice (physically and metaphorically)

Jeanne Barczewska

Introduction

I first experienced professional voice issues as a trainee teacher in 1974 after contracting bronchitis during an extended teaching practice in my second year at teacher training college. Despite struggling to talk, which meant I had to strain in order to project my voice across the classroom, I was reluctant to take any time off as I was really enjoying the school and I did not want to jeopardise my teaching practice grade. The children at this primary school came from deprived backgrounds and were quite challenging with regards to behaviour management, so positive voice projection was essential in order to be heard without actually shouting. In the end, my visiting tutor recognised the potential damage that was occurring, as well as the fact that I was clearly unwell, and advised that I visit the doctor and take time off.

Research into the impact of voice problems in primary school teachers has identified that teachers in this age group 'are particularly at risk as they have little opportunity for voice rest during the working day' (Munier and Kinsella, 2008). This view is supported by Martin and Darnley (2004), who note that teachers are 'professional voice users' and that those working with the younger age groups often display particular disorders by the added necessity to spend time on low chairs or bending down to talk to children. Using the term 'professional voice user' (Martin and Darnley, 2004) implies that within the profession there would be some sort of voice training. Kaufman (1998, cited in Martin and Darnley 2004) identified four levels of vocal usage. We (teachers and lecturers) are classed as: 'Professional Voice Users Level 2', that is 'a person for whom a moderate vocal problem might prevent adequate job performance'. As academics, we would hope to inspire and motivate our students, therefore presenting only an 'adequate' performance is not acceptable. Given also the necessity to gain high levels of student feedback and the importance placed on university rankings one might begin to doubt one's own professional integrity and question the ability to deliver a 'good quality' lecture. In this chapter, I reflect not only on what universities could do to support academics as 'professional voice users', I also consider the wider implications for introducing voice coaching for courses other than, perhaps, drama and music.

Losing my voice

My initial diagnosis was worse than I thought. On top of bronchitis it turned out that I had vocal cord nodules brought on by the incessant coughing. At that time, surgery was recommended as the best option, followed by a period of voice rest and then support from a speech therapist. Nowadays, consultants generally would prefer to start with voice rest to see if the nodules will reduce naturally with the aim of preventing scar tissue which can cause further issues in the future. In my case, it did.

Recovery after surgery was a slow process, as initially there were two weeks of complete voice rest. Voice rest means no talking at all, which is impossible for a teacher who is used to talking all the time. As a student teacher in physical education I was accustomed to using my voice while playing sport as well as for teaching. So, staying quiet was tremendously difficult! However, there were some interesting lessons to be learned from going through an enforced silent period: mainly, that much of what we say is potentially irrelevant and unnecessary. I learned that conversations would not necessarily have been enhanced by what I would have said and that much social conversation is just that. Being sociable, talking for talking's sake.

In the workplace situation, however, as I later learned, going through a silent period or period of voice rest while among colleagues, had a far more disturbing effect, as it caused me to lose confidence and as such question my identity within the team. In 2014, after contracting a chest infection, I once again found myself experiencing difficulty speaking without strain and pain. Nodules had formed on top of the original scar tissue, but this time I also had an ulcer on my larynx. The diagnosis was more severe than the first time. I had laryngopharyngeal reflux along with chronic fatigue and possible fibromyalgia. The illness and recovery had a more significant effect on my life and career, as I was by now a senior university lecturer and programme leader for an Early Years programme. According to Phyllida Furse (n.d.), an academic and voice expert, 'education staff often forget that one of their most important tools is their voice'. This is true until you personally experience issues, or possibly work alongside someone who is presenting the associated symptoms.

Returning to work

Six months' recovery meant time away from work with little contact with anyone due to having to have voice rest. Academically, I was able to do a lot of reading. Articles on sites such as LinkedIn, discussions on Twitter and other forms of social media kept me mentally alert. And I used the opportunity for the development of new thoughts and ideas. However, there was no outlet to share these with colleagues because 'if you're off sick, you're off sick'. This raises the question about policy and perhaps, how one is treated during sick leave needs to be re-evaluated. Some contact with colleagues could be conducive to recovery in addition and prior to the more standard return to work procedures. In my situation, the return to work 'settling in' period was not at all effective, as I will point out later. But some sort of contact time, perhaps similar to the 'keep in touch' (KIT) days afforded to those on maternity leave, might have been conducive to the mental health issues that can develop when absent from work for extended periods of time. I think that the university likes to 'protect' those off sick but in my case, this was possibly misguided. Of course, keeping in touch style communication methods would need to be carefully managed to avoid raising stress levels, as this would be counterproductive. Indeed, any such initiatives would need to be carefully orchestrated and managed. As my problem was a communication issue and not an illness as such, some channel for keeping in touch would have been useful, not only for my wellbeing, but also for those who needed to ask me the occasional question. This would have helped some aspects of the programmes I was leading on to run more smoothly in my absence.

Despite the difficulties (see more on this later), I still count myself lucky to have been offered time off as, legally, voice disorders are not equal to other disabilities and/or chronic illnesses:

> Voice disorders do not automatically qualify as occupational disorders or as a disability. Each case needs to be considered individually and has to meet certain prescribed criteria. Criteria for prescription are laid down by the Industrial Injuries Advisory Council (www.iiac.org.uk). However, in cases where a voice disorder can be considered a disability, employers are required by law to make 'reasonable adjustments' to help employees cope better in the workplace. (The Equality Act, 2010)

This definition begs the question of who gets to decide at which point of the spectrum of voice losses the disorder can be, should be and is a disability. When my return to work was due, several meetings were arranged and a staggered return was planned. This in itself was not an ideal solution due to my 'illness' being voice related. Initially, it was useful because there were no students in, as I returned during the end of the summer break. But this meant that once the students came back, and new students started, I was back to a full timetable and all of the team and wider university meetings were starting to be scheduled in. A team-teaching approach was put in place for me; this was really helpful but as the term progressed, there were more times when one or another of the tutors in the team were pulled away to do other things. So, the 'talking' time increased.

On reflection, I now know that there was a significant impact on me psychologically and emotionally which, initially and for a short time, affected my confidence. Had there been some strategically organised keeping in touch opportunities, this is likely to have been significantly reduced.

During some of the early team meetings I attended it became strangely apparent that I had lost my 'academic voice' on my return. It was more about the fact that I had 'missed' things and that 'things had changed'. As a consequence, my comments apparently came across as more negative than constructive. This was a very difficult phase but again, thankfully through conversations, though sometimes difficult, I seemed to get through it. To me it seemed that unless I was contributing vocally, my views were not necessarily acknowledged and the period of absence seemed to render me invalid: as if my brain must have ceased to function because I was unable to verbalise out loud. Morton and Watson (1998) cite Berry (1990) in recognising the wider perceptions of the 'occupational pressure' vocal problems can create, and it has since been widely acknowledged that 'emotional and environmental strain' can impact on voice quality. The British Voice Association (2015) identified that stress can impact on our vocal tract (vocal folds, larynx and pharynx) and that the muscle tension this produces impacts on the way we project our voices in the same way that other muscles can be affected by tension:

> An occupational voice disorder is one that develops as a result of the amount or type of voice use required to do your job. It may also be related to vocal irritants in the work environment or a combination of these factors. For example, teachers have to speak for hours every day in noisy classrooms, tour guides may be exposed to traffic noise and fumes, or call centre workers who may speak for long periods loudly against background noise and with air conditioning drying their vocal folds. (British Voice Association; Voice Disorders and the Workplace n.d.)

Longer-term impact can affect one's own perception of oneself through embarrassment about what our voices sound like or the inconvenience of perhaps have to constantly drink fluids during a lecture or teaching period in order to maintain a reasonable level of communication with students or colleagues.

I could be doing a disservice to some of my colleagues during this time, but this is how I was made to feel. The fact that I was able to do a great deal of reading while on my enforced 'silent period' did not appear to count for anything at all. An interesting bonus was that by doing more listening than talking, one has more time to reflect on the various conversations going around the table – even if the impact was restricted by either the effort to respond or the growing feeling that my voice was not being heard from an academic perspective.

Developing my voice

I began to experience voice loss at times, which impacted on my teaching and I had to find ways of working, which would enable me to continue my lectures. Fortunately, I work in an area which both allows and actively encourages students' involvement in their learning through group work and practical activities. However, it was necessary to try to develop strategies which would protect my voice and the tiredness which accompanied the strain. Despite using an amplification device, it was still tiring at the time to talk for longer periods. So, I used a lot of group work, which is a big part of the way the programme is taught because of the practice-based nature of the subject area. Early Years practitioners need time to reflect on their practice, explore theories and share ideas as well having opportunities to research and create activities. The format of our sessions meant that I was able to do introductions and plenary sessions but also spend time working with the students in small groups. An additional learning for me was remembering to turn off the device when someone wanted a private conversation with me. And also, where I perhaps needed to offer guidance which I knew they would prefer others not to hear. There was a lot to think about. But it did make me reflect deeply on my teaching style:

> These common strategies, such as "hydration," "speak softly," and "use amplifiers" are primarily passive or conservative ones as they aim at preserving the voice in good condition or preventing deterioration. The clients need to be informed of the rationales behind these strategies so that they understand how and why they should be done in a specific way.
>
> The suggested content of a programme for preventing voice problems in the teaching profession does not present new ideas but addresses the concerns that come directly from the consumers. (Yiu, 2002)

During some breaks and lunch times, I began to take myself off to a quiet space in order to give myself voice rest. I did not wish to be regarded as being anti-social. However, I had to have a balance between chatting to colleagues and protecting my vocal cords. I was very lucky to have a wonderfully supportive team. Suggestions for reducing voice use and additional stress include using emails instead of telephone calls. This contradicts with best practice but also supports the recognition of technology as a way of providing a more equal platform for people with disabilities. This indicates the dichotomy faced by planners of educational establishments with the demands on those delivering face to face teaching as well as participating in team and other meetings. Structural design such as acoustics and air conditioning are equally significant (Morton and Watson, 1998).

Attending speech therapy sessions raised my awareness of vocal health. The original intention was to work on exercises that would reduce the nodules on my vocal cords. However, the sessions also fuelled my interest in professional voice use. It was necessary to maintain the advice given after returning to work. This would mean doing the exercises during teaching breaks and avoiding additional meetings and tutorials over lunch time and immediately after lectures. Time management suddenly took on new relevance.

The voice expert Furse (n.d.) has delivered sessions on voice management on behalf of the university and college union. When I interviewed her in 2018, she explained the prevalence of vocal issues she came across within academic institutions. She also reminded me of the importance of maintaining vocal health through regular voice exercise. In her leaflet (Furse, n.d.), she identifies key strategies for maintaining good voice projection at work and at the same time helping lecturers to retain composure when facing students.

How we stand allows us to breathe efficiently and effectively and presents a manner that shows we are in control. Furse explains that we 'will not feel or convey confidence by standing in a "sag" position'. She also reminds us of the importance of focusing on breathing in order to successfully project our voice. 'Remember to breathe; sometimes, we forget; allow yourself to breathe deeply. Be focused on where you are sending the sound.'

These messages, along with her recommended exercises, are simple and straightforward, but evidence suggests that as professionals we do not train professionally in this area. Most singers and actors, however, report that they practice every day to allow them to be able to provide a polished performance. Of course, they are judged on their vocal performances, whereas as lecturers we perhaps consider the content of lectures more than the quality of the tools we use to deliver that content. This is something to reflect on.

As noted earlier, another strategy to help me rest and protect my voice during teaching days, I use a portable device consisting of an amplifier with microphone (see Figure 7.1), which helps reduce the strain enormously.

Using the device, I noticed an unforeseen knock-on effect. The device enables hard of hearing students to hear me better. And if student chatter reaches an unacceptable level, I am able to turn the volume up and draw them back on task. The device does have its down side, as it is so unusual to see a tutor wearing one that it leads to some very amusing comments. Am I about sing? Am I about to instruct an exercise class? To be honest, initially, I was not upset by this as it was all in fun. However, over time it did dawn on me that it could become tedious and also that someone else in that situation might have been quite upset by it if they had a more serious condition and/or were embarrassed and therefore might not feel in a position to deal

Figure 7.1: Portable amplification device, with microphone

with the jokes. I was quite surprised to find that the university could not offer me something that looked more professional and that there was nothing I could use which would link to the Wi-Fi or room computers. I felt wearing my device (see Figure 7.2), despite being useful, was ungainly, unprofessional looking and quite ugly! Interventions such as voice exercises and, in one instance a suggestion of cognitive behavioural therapy, were options open to me. However, these alone were insufficient as the teaching timetable played a significant role in recovery and future voice maintenance. Team teaching was another solution; on the surface, this seemed like a good idea but in reality, when the university term became busier, staffing did not allow for this to remain consistent. Munier and Kinsella (2007) identified that because a primary school teacher's day was 'characterized

Figure 7.2: Using the amplification device in teaching

by an average of five hours continuous teaching' with only a couple of short breaks they were more at risk of voice issues than secondary school teachers, who had more opportunity for 'vocal rest'. If we translate this into a day at university, this can often involve not only teaching time but in addition there are faculty meetings and student tutorials, which are often squeezed in between lectures or scheduled over coffees and lunches. So, when planning our academic timetable, how can we factor in these essential aspects of university life? In my case, I had to be very focused and try to manage my time between lectures more rigidly, but this was by no means easy. And on days, when the voice seemed to be performing well, possibly after a weekend of voice rest, it was easy to fall back into old ways and agree to the meetings and tutorials. Tutorials are of course a priority, as they are essential to students and an important part of the student experience as well as an enhancement to their learning and development.

Conclusion

It was noted by Morton and Watson (1998) that many teachers persevere with voice issues without seeking assistance, and their research indicated that teachers formed a larger proportion of people being offered therapy than those in other professions. They also identified the positive effect vocal therapy had on those who participated. It was further evident from their study that there is a 'clear under provision' in providing voice training and preventative exercises during training. This is further supported by Munier and Kinsella (2007), who advocate the necessity to review workload and provide periods of 'vocal rest'. They go on to support the argument for vocal training and raising awareness of symptoms and issues of voice disorders, and conclude that 'the medical profession and departments for education need to be aware of the demands put on teachers' voices'.

The research also infers that organisations would be wise to weigh up the consequences of levels of absenteeism, both for the cost to the establishment but also, I would suggest, from the perspective of the student experience in terms of consistency of teaching. There are measures which universities could implement to support a more inclusive, vocally supportive environment. More attention should be paid to voice use, vocal maintenance and the development of appropriate training to teach voice projection strategies. The impact of vocal disorders needs to be more widely recognised and teachers across all sectors should be recognised, as identified by Martin and Darnley (2004), as professional voice users.

Reflective questions

- How much care do you take about your voice as you go about your everyday life?
- When colleagues of yours are absent due to illness or returning to work, how do you support them?

Recommendations

As a result of my personal experience, which occurred over a three-year period with the longest absence being six months,

I reflected on what could be done to make a difference. My conclusion was instantly to support voice enhancement technology in a way that would not marginalise the tutor but which would also benefit students. For example:

- Wi–Fi microphone capability in all teaching spaces – for all lecturers/presenters;
- hand–held microphones or on–table microphones (button controlled) for students (with 'quiet' voices) to enhance interactive feedback;
- sickness and return to work policy considerations in terms of keeping in touch days;
- raising awareness of voice disorders;
- voice management and vocal health introduced to lecturer training and within teacher training routes;
- timetabling – for example, avoiding front-loaded teaching within any one term.

These are small measures which could make a big difference both to our delivery and to our wellbeing.

References

British Voice Association. (2015). When it isn't just physical: The effects of stress and emotion on the voice. www.britishvoiceassociation.org.uk [Accessed 29 December 2020].

British Voice Association (n.d.). *Voice Disorders and the Workplace*. www.britishvoiceassociation.org.uk/downloads/free-voice-care-literature/Voice%20Disorders%20and%20the%20Workplace.pdf [Accessed 29 December 2020].

Furse, P. (n.d.) https://cpd.web.ucu.org.uk/files/2013/07/CPD-factsheet-11.pdf [Accessed 15 December 2019].

Martin, S., & Darnley, L. (2004) *The Teaching Voice*. (2nd edn). London: Whurr.

Morton, V., & Watson, D.R. (1998). *The Teaching Voice: Problems and Perceptions*. Scandinavian University Press.

Munier, C., & Kinsella, R. (2008). The prevalence and impact of voice problems in primary school teachers. *Occupational Medicine*, 58, 74–76.

Yiu, E.M.L. (2002). Impact and prevention of voice problems in the teaching profession: Embracing the consumers' view, *Journal of Voice*, 16(2), 215–228.

8

Deafness and hearing loss in higher education

Nicole Brown

Introduction

June 2019

I am an invited guest speaker talking on the topic of ableism in academia. I have held this talk on several occasions already, I know what I am going to say, and I am so attuned to what comes next, that I can include performative elements. Today, I find myself lingering a little bit longer than usual on the topic of conferences. I have already pointed out how difficult it is to navigate the lunch-time buffet if you have disabilities.

"Let's continue imagining. Here we are now with everyone else eating our food, and we would like to network with other conference delegates. But that won't be possible!"

I pause for effect, and pointing to the person signing furiously to my left, I finally add:

"Because the Sign Language interpreters are on their lunch break. Again, a shift in attitude is required. We tend to see the sign language interpreters to be there for the person who is deaf; but in reality, they are here because people like me cannot sign. The barrier is not the deafness, the barrier is *my* lack of language."

After the entire talk, a number of attendees approach me to have a quick chat, ask questions and to thank me. I am happy talking and explaining. I am in my element; until the deaf delegate and his British Sign Language (BSL) interpreter come up to me. I greet them both, saying hello and thanking the interpreter for his help. I am utterly embarrassed. Apart from hello and thank you, I can say nothing. I had formal education in English, French, Latin and Spanish as foreign languages, so I get by in most European languages comfortably, and because I understand how the structure works, I pick up languages quickly. I manage to hold mini-conversations and order food and so on in foreign languages even if I don't have any formal teaching, like I did in South Korea two years ago. And yet, I cannot speak BSL at all. I do speeches and presentations on ableism in academia, but I cannot communicate in BSL. I can lipread, and I can make sure I speak properly so others can lipread off me, but that is it.

I express my embarrassment and shame, but the deaf attendee and the interpreter are both cheerful. They are just grateful that someone has made it plain and clear in public how challenging it is to be a deaf academic.

According to the World Health Organization (2020), hearing loss and deafness affect more than 5 per cent of the world's population, and they are on the increase. Estimates predict that, by 2050, 1 person in 10 will experience disabling hearing loss (World Health Organization, 2020). The figures should be shocking: they mean that in our children's generation 10 per cent of all children and adults will be having a disabling hearing loss of more than 30 or 40 decibels, respectively (World Health Organization, 2020). For now, it may feel easy to forget or ignore the issues in our anglophone, Euro-Western centric society, as the largest proportion of people with hearing loss live in low- and middle-income countries, especially South Asia, Asia Pacific and sub-Saharan Africa, and are over 65 years of age (World Health Organization, 2020). In our 'bury your head in the sand' attitude, we can push aside any concerns about hearing loss, because we are still young, anyway – until we are directly affected by the consequences. A person with disabling hearing loss as defined by the World Health Organization

(2020), for example, will not hear anything that is quieter than 40 decibels: the level of the sound in a library or the bird calls in your garden. If you do not experience hearing loss, imagine a life without hearing breathing, whispers, rustling leaves, or imagine not hearing the bird calls and nature sounds in a quiet rural area or an ambient urban environment (IAC Acoustics, n.d.). For full disclosure, according to the latest hearing test in January 2019, my hearing loss stands somewhere between 70 and 90 decibels in both ears, with some frequencies being less affected than others, and is defined as somewhere between severe and profound (World Health Organization, n.d.). The 70 to 90 decibels equal the noise levels of a vacuum cleaner, a food blender and a Boeing 737 at one nautical mile before landing (IAC Acoustics, n.d.).

Hearing loss and deafness significantly impact individuals. In this chapter, I draw on my personal experiences as an academic with hearing loss and a researcher of ableism in academia to reflect on what it means to be hard of hearing, deaf and Deaf in higher education. I outline the contentions around the use of language and their importance within and among people with hearing loss and deafness, before exploring in more detail what it means to be a hearing impaired, deaf or Deaf academic. I then reflect on the fluidity and changeability of hearing loss and the impact hearing loss may have on individuals, which leads into a very personal conclusion.

I commence each section with descriptions of a critical incident or situation to locate the theorisations, factual accounts and literature within my personal story. The extracts in this chapter all come from diary and journal entries, which I have kept over the years as part of my endeavours to make sense of my experiences, to practise reflexivity and to use writing as a method of inquiry (Richardson, 2000, 2003). The neatness of the write-up in this chapter is deceiving. In reality, my writing is messy, non-linear and includes sketches, symbols and images. I think with stories (Frank, 2013), not to reduce them to content and then analyse them, but to take them as complete, to let them affect my own life, joining with them, becoming immersed in them. The end goal is to develop empathy and resonance, to truly experience and feel nuances and meanings and to let the story lead in particular directions (Frank, 2013: 22–25, 158–161). My approach to thinking with my own stories is possible because the writing, rewriting and retelling do not happen immediately, but are layered upon the originally recorded story, so that I am distanced enough to experience the stories as new to let them lead my thinking.

Hearing impaired, deaf or Deaf?

January 2019

I sit inside the turquoisy-green sound booth. I don't know if this one has holey walls, or doesn't. The booths are all different, but the same, no matter where you are having the hearing tests done. Having been hard of hearing from birth, I have had so many hearing tests throughout my life, I could actually be an audiologist myself, by now.

We start with the easy one: headphones on and listen out for the beeps. If you hear a beep, you click the button. Over the years, I have become quite adept at making this a reaction game. How quickly can I press the buzzer this time?

Right ear done.

After a while, my concentration span starts to drop, and I am starting to hear beeps, where I am not even sure if they are in my head or in my ears. Again, I am used to that. I am really quite smug about this whole episode.

Left ear done.

Next, it's the bone conduction test. That one is always tricky for me. The audiologist puts that special headset over my head, places the oscillator on the bone behind my ear, and off we go.

I can tell that I am not doing well, but that's ok. Some fluctuations always happen. You just need a lapse of concentration, perhaps be a little more tired than usual, or have a cold. Even if you aren't showing any signs of sneezing or sniffles, your hearing may already be affected. Also, the oscillator wasn't positioned very well.

The audiologist opens the door to the booth and explains that we have finished our test on the right ear. I am surprised. I tell her that I don't think this was the best test, and that the oscillator wasn't placed very well. "It was placed just fine." "I would like to repeat that test." "We do the left ear now."

Beep, buzz, beep, buzz.

The booth door opens and I am done.

But I am not.

I am still confused. I haven't had the bone conduction for my right ear. Maybe the oscillator wasn't positioned very well. In fact, I know it wasn't, because I couldn't feel the pressure I usually feel. And also, if I don't press the button for a specific frequency, then the audiologist just needs to increase the volume. Some back and forth between the audiologist and me follows.

In the end, I get the audiologist to repeat the bone conduction for my right ear. Headset on, oscillator on that bone, booth door closed, we are off again. I wait for the beeps.

There are none.

At one point, I can feel vibration on the bone behind my right ear, but I cannot hear the sound. I know that I should be able to hear that beep, the vibration is there, but the sound is not. The sound just is not there. No matter how much I concentrate, the sound is not there.

It is at this point that I realise I am deaf.

I am in shock.

As the audiologist opens the door to the booth, I break down in tears.

A person who is not able to hear the full range of frequencies and/or sound intensities is described as having hearing loss according to the International Statistical Classification of Diseases and Related Health in its tenth revision (ICD-10, 2019). However, in wider society and among the general public more labels or descriptions are in use to describe the physicality of not being able to hear. The terms most commonly in use are: hearing loss, hearing impairment, being hard of hearing, being deaf and being Deaf. I have had hearing loss since birth, and as such, I always identified as being hard of hearing, not deaf. As a result of medical conditions throughout my life, my hearing loss deteriorated over the years, to the point where by January 2019 I had entered the 'profound' or 'deaf' category. I realised that I would now no longer be hard of hearing, but deaf. For me, hearing loss or being hard of hearing was one thing, being deaf quite another.

Organisations and associations use clearly defined signifiers to differentiate between the labels. The most commonly applicable description of hearing loss is that of the World Health Organization, which categorises hearing at 26 to 40 decibels as slight/mild hearing loss, with hearing at 41 to 60 decibels as moderate, hearing at 61 to 80 decibels as severe, and hearing at 81 decibels and above as profound (World Health Organization, n.d.). Within these broad categories, the World Health Organization uses the terms 'hard of hearing' to describe anyone with a mild to severe hearing loss and 'deaf' for people with profound hearing loss (World Health Organization, 2020). The British charitable organisation, Action on Hearing Loss (formerly called the Royal National Institute for Deaf People) uses the terms 'hearing loss' and 'deafness' (Action on Hearing Loss, n.d.), as does the charity Hearing Link (Hearing Link, n.d.), although it prefers 'hearing loss'. But there are many other organisations that specifically focus on deafness, such as the British Deaf Association (British Deaf Association, n.d.) and the National Deaf Children's Society (National Deaf Children's Society, n.d.). The British Deaf Association uses Deaf with a capital D (British Deaf Association, n.d.).

That apparently minor distinction between using or not using the capital D brings into awareness a veritable gulf of differences between identities and identifications. How hearing loss is described is not linked to the underlying cause and has nothing to do with medical diagnoses or clinical descriptions. It has everything to do with how the person defines themselves. A person who experiences hearing loss may still see themselves as primarily the person, with the hearing loss second. A Deaf person, however, aligns themselves with an entire culture and society with its own values and beliefs. They do not see their deafness as an impairment or disability, but as a different and specific way of life, emphasising the positive aspects and gains which they experience through the fact that they are Deaf (Ladd, 2003). Being born Deaf means to have access to and learn to speak sign language. Using sign language therefore is a particular identifier, and having full command of this embodied way of communicating provides opportunities that ordinary language would not. Despite the localised differences in signs, sign language is considered a global language, where individuals are able to adapt quickly to understand one another, where language barriers would usually prevent internationalised conversations. Identifying as Deaf for many means to escape the deficit-focused interpretation of their experiences. Instead of focusing on the 'deficits' of not being able to hear, on the missing ability of the body and on the social barriers that need to be overcome, which would turn their narratives into a tragedy, Deaf people emphasise and embrace their particular being-in-the world, are proud and joyful of belonging to and being part of the Deaf culture (Ladd, 2003; Holcomb, 2012). There are disputes and contentions within Deaf culture (Padden et al, 2009), especially where support systems like hearing aids or cochlear implants are concerned.

A cochlear implant is a two-part device, of which one part is surgically implanted under the skull and the outside part is worn behind the ear. Despite its invasive nature, cochlear implant surgery is considered a safe and successful intervention with a relative lack of major complications (Kiringoda and Lustig, 2013). For adults who undergo the cochlear implant surgeries, hearing and quality of life improve significantly (Gaylor et al, 2013; Snels et al, 2019). The cochlear implants move a person from a life without any auditory stimulation to a life with sound with variable results, as individuals need to (re)learn how to cope with new sensory inputs and a different way of life (US Food and Drug Administration, 2018). And it is exactly this aspect of the cochlear implant, and indeed hearing aids, that Deaf culture takes issue with. The Deaf community argues that this different way of life and the new sensory inputs invade a person's identity, what is essentially the core of a Deaf person, what makes the Deaf person Deaf (Blume, 2009), and which contradicts the socially constructed sensory experience of the Deaf (Valente et al, 2011). If hearing loss and deafness are such individual experiences, what then does it feel like to (not) hear in higher education?

What it means to (not) hear in the academy

December 2019

It's 10.55 am. The meeting starts at 11, but I am already by the door of the meeting room. I am always the first or among the first to arrive. How many colleagues know or have noticed that I make sure to be early to have a choice of where I will be sitting? I always move into the room to sit with the window to my back. Working with the sun and daylight, rather than against it, means that I can see people's faces to lipread.

The next criterion is a new one. It's got to be the seat that is most centrally located along the side of the table, so that I have roughly equal distances between everybody. Since I've had my Bionic Woman[1] ears this is important, because I can then adjust the settings via the app on my smartphone that will Bluetooth the information to my bionic ears.

Over the years, I've observed colleagues doing things to help their hearing: tilting their heads to one side, or cupping their hands around an ear to guide the sound more closely into the ear, the low-tech and immediate ear trumpet.

I'm grateful for my bionic ears, and certainly wouldn't want to trade places, here.

Embedded in this extract is the question of disclosure of hearing loss in higher education. In response to my own question, many of my colleagues do not know that I have hearing aids. My non-disclosure here is not an issue relating to stigma (Cienkowski and Pimentel, 2001; Erler and Garstecki, 2002; Iler et al, 1982), the fear of being stereotyped, or potentially being faced with ageism (Southall et al, 2011). For me, my hearing loss and the fact that I use hearing aids, just have not ever been important enough to warrant a mention. Deafness has only recently become a concern for me, dating from that dreadful bone conduction test in January 2019.

For others, however, admitting to be hard of hearing or needing hearing aids may well require the kind of personal commitment and a public statement that so many academics are not able or willing to make in relation to their needs, as it would make them appear vulnerable and weak (Brown and Leigh, 2018). The full truth of hearing loss in academia is simply not known. Research confirms the connection between hearing loss and academic achievement, showing that being only minimally hard of hearing has a significant impact on academic performance and behavioural developments (for example, Tharpe et al, 2009; Qi and Mitchell, 2012). Indeed, education and academia are still 'hearing worlds' (Brooks, 2011), and there is a lack of representation of the Deaf in academia, given that 5 per cent of the world's population is categorised as having hearing loss (World Health Organization, 2020).

Although developments in relation to increased equality and inclusion have resulted in more students with disabilities accessing higher education, it is estimated that only 8 per cent of students in higher education in the United States who have hearing loss have disclosed it (Richardson et al, 2004). If such a high percentage of non-disclosure of hearing loss among students is anything to go by, and we compare this to the wider issues of disclosure of disabilities in academia, then we can only assume that there will be many academics who have not yet 'come out of the hard of hearing closet' (Burke and Nicodemus, 2013, n.p., section 2), particularly as social conventions and perceptions of what constitutes a normal self favour non-disclosure (Lingsom, 2008).

The extract also shows that I have clearly developed particular strategies to create an environment that is particularly conducive to my way of working to cope with hearing loss (Tidwell, 2004). Where Deaf people and British Sign Language users in academia are concerned, the reality of academic work is quite different. As I recorded in the initial diary entry from June 2019, the Deaf need the support of a sign language interpreter, because the vast majority of us working in academia do not sign. Based on official statistics, it is estimated that there are only 151,000 British Sign Language users in the entire UK, 58 per cent of whom are Deaf, which leaves us with a meagre 64,000 hearing people able to use British Sign Language (British Deaf Association Sign Language Week, n.d.). Of course, arrangements and adjustments can be made, but booking a sign language interpreter is no easy feat. Then, there are the kinds of informal conversations along corridors, in lifts, on the staircases or over lunches and coffees after formal meetings that are often more important for community building and social networking. In such situations, the hard of hearing struggle, as the background noises make it more difficult to hear and they will worry about appearing less competent when they give 'wrong' answers (Tidwell, 2004). The Deaf will most likely be excluded entirely, because the sign language interpreter will only have been booked for the time of the formal gathering.

The ableist attitude that pervades the academy also means that many academics are insensitive and unreasonable. Generally, these behaviours are genuinely unintentional and not malicious, but just highlight the lack of awareness within the academy. For example, we have all attended that conference talk, where the speaker asked, "You can hear me without microphone, can't you?" This simple question puts the burden of adjustment and arrangements onto the person with the hearing loss. It requires an enormous amount of courage to raise your hand in a room full of strangers to then admit publicly that you actually cannot hear the speaker. The issue of disclosure has already been mentioned, but this puts disclosure at quite a different level.

Finally, the extract highlights my relationship to my hearing aids. For many individuals, the hearing aid is a stigma symbol (Goffman, 1990/1963), which results in individuals avoiding addressing issues of hearing loss. Among those who do use hearing aids, there are different experiences. If more advanced technology is used in a hearing aid, the wearer's overall satisfaction and quality of life improve more significantly than in less advanced devices (Williams et al, 2009). But there are hearing aid users who state that the devices are not helpful for particular situations or that the individuals prefer a quieter and calmer environment with less noise and stimulation (Lockey et al, 2010). I am clearly excited about my latest hearing aids, to such a point that I refer to them as my bionic ears, as I am fully aware of the deficit I experience when I do not have them.

Conclusion

July 2019

Freshly out of the shower, I try to brush my hair. The tangles of my natural curls require more attention that I would like. I cannot put my hearing aids in,[2] so I start brushing without. But as I do, I realise how much I usually rely on hearing the brush pull its teeth through my tangled curls.
Not hearing, I lose my ability to brush my hair.

Most literature and people talk about senses compensating for the loss of one. But not hearing does not suddenly equip me with X-ray vision, or at least 20/20 vision. I don't gain the superpower of smell or taste. The only sense that's heightening is the sense of danger.

With the narrowing of my auditory field, my heartbeat quickens, my body tenses and muscles tighten, I become nervous and agitated.

My body is in fight or flight mode triggering anxiety and panic. And all that in the safety of my bedroom trying to brush my hair without my hearing aids in.

The impact of hearing loss can be significant: being excluded from conversations may result in withdrawal, social isolation and loneliness. Not being able to access aspects of the world, may also result in losses regarding academic achievement. If the hearing loss occurs in early ages, then speech may also be delayed or otherwise affected (World Health Organization, 2020). The stark reality is that the employment rate for those who are deaf or hard of hearing is 65 per cent, which compares to 79 per cent of people with no long-term health issue or disability (Hearing Link, n.d. a). Within academia, being hard of hearing, deaf or Deaf sits alongside other disabilities and chronic illnesses, in that it often does not get reported or that those who are hard of hearing, deaf or Deaf drop out of the academy. It is through my work on ableism in academia that I have realised and recognised the importance of telling the story of the unheard 'unhearing'.

Epilogue

March 2020

Sitting on the sofa in the living room. Bluetoothing Van Morrison's 'These are the days' from his 1989 *Avalon Sunset* album into my bionic ears. I listen intently to the guitar opening, waiting for the drums to come in. Feeling emotional.

I have heard this song many times before, but this is the first time I listen with my bionic ears. This is the first time, that I don't just simply hear the main melody of the guitar, but the accompanying chords. It's the first time that I hear the flam on the drums. I am amazed. I have always liked this song, but here are notes that I have not ever heard before.

"These are the days," Van Morrison's voice rings in my ears. I can actually make out the individual words and understand them.

This clarity of speech, this beauty of sound. I've had my bionic ears for a few months now, and I've been listening to more music and podcasts and I've been watching more films than ever before.

I realise I have a lifetime of music, podcasts and films to catch up on.

Reflective questions

- Are there any hard of hearing, deaf or Deaf colleagues in your professional networks? If not, why do you think this is?
- How do you feel about communicating with the Deaf?
- Which assumptions may you make when you start a lecture or conference presentation? For example, do you automatically clip on a microphone or do you present without one?

Recommendations

Awareness and empathy: The key element for supporting deaf colleagues is to show awareness and empathy. Information is available freely on the internet and also provides insights into what can be done to support communication with the hard of hearing.

Sign language training: As part of increasing awareness of the challenges of the Deaf, learning sign language may be a first step. Most taster sessions and introductory lessons start out with a general overview of the development of British Sign Language, deaf awareness and a brief insight into Deaf culture. Ideally, the burden for sign language training would not lie with individuals but with institutions, offering courses as part of professional development for staff, in order to ensure that we are all able to at least exchange some general pleasantries, when we meet sign language speakers.

Support and encouragement: Many individuals who need hearing aids struggle to come to terms with the situation. Others get aids fitted, but then struggle to get used to the devices. In such cases, the best you can do is to be supportive of these individuals and encourage them to seek advice from their audiologists. Getting new hearing aids and starting to wear them is a significant event, even if you had hearing aids before. Just like every car make and model is different, and has its own quirks, every set of hearing aids is different. The brain needs time to adjust and (re)learn sounds and stimuli. This is why there are often longer gaps between audiology appointments. But that does not mean you cannot ask to be seen in additional appointments, if you need help and guidance. Additionally, just as not every mechanic is equally good at fixing every car and instead may have preferences for specific makes and models, audiologists also vary in technical skills and specialist knowledge about what is available on the market and what would suit particular kinds of 'hearers'. Hearing aids need to be fitted and moulded to the ear, but they also need to be suitable for the wearer's lifestyle. This is why it is vital that there is a good relationship between the audiologist and the hearing aid user. Being supportive and encouraging may therefore take the form of suggesting finding a different audiologist, just as you would suggest finding a new mechanic or plumber. I would like to take this opportunity to thank my own audiologist Nick Hodge from Boots Hearingcare Canterbury, UK, without whom I would have chosen aids that were not the best fit for me.

Basic rules of communication: Some minor behavioural adjustments on your part may make life unbelievably easier for your hard of hearing and deaf colleagues. When you communicate or present, make sure that everyone in the room has a clear view of your face, as many people are lipreading to support their hearing.

Ensure that you use microphones when they are available. Do not assume that nobody will need them. If there is a situation, where you are asked a question by someone who does not have a microphone, repeat the question, before answering it.

If you are aware of someone being hard of hearing, deaf or Deaf, make sure you have their attention before starting to speak.

Give others time to respond. Sometimes, individuals take a little longer to make sense of what was asked of them.

Finally and most importantly, if your conversational partner asks you to repeat what you have just said, continue speaking at the same speed, just louder. Talking at the same volume, just more slowly, does not help at all – they are deaf not stupid.

Notes

[1] *The Bionic Woman* was a TV series in the 1970s, where the protagonist Jamie receives a bionic ear via a cybernetic implant. With that bionic ear, Jamie can hear at low volumes, unusual frequencies and over uncommonly long distances (Wikipedia, n.d.).

[2] My hearing aids have custom-made ear pieces that are inserted into the ear canal. When I have ear infections or colds, the ear canals become swollen, which makes them too narrow to fit the hearing aids.

References

Action on Hearing Loss. (n.d.). *Glossary – Deaf and Hearing Loss*. Retrieved from: www.actiononhearingloss.org.uk/hearing-health/hearing-loss-and-deafness/glossary/ [Last accessed: March 2020].

Blume, S. (2009). *The Artificial Ear: Cochlear Implants and the Culture of Deafness.* New Brunswick, NJ: Rutgers University Press.

British Deaf Association. (n.d.). *What We Stand For.* Retrieved from: https://bda.org.uk/history/what-we-stand-for/ [Last accessed: March 2020].

British Deaf Association Sign Language Week. (n.d.). *BSL Statistics*. Retrieved from: http://signlanguageweek.org.uk/bsl-statistics [Last accessed: March 2020].

Brooks, B.A. (2011). *It Is Still a Hearing World: A Phenomenological Case Study of Deaf College Students' Experiences of Academia.* Doctoral dissertation, Ohio University.

Brown, N., & Leigh, J.S. (2018). Ableism in academia: Where are the disabled and ill academics? *Disability and Society*, 33(6), 985–989.

Burke, T.B., & Nicodemus, B. (2013). Coming out of the hard of hearing closet: Reflections on a shared journey in academia. *Disability Studies Quarterly*, 33(2).

Bury, M. (1982). Chronic illness as biographical disruption. *Sociology of Health and Illness*, 4(2), 167–182.

Cienkowski, K.M., & Pimentel, V. (2001). The hearing aid 'effect' revisited in young adults. *British Journal of Audiology*, 35(5), 289–295.

David, D., & Werner, P. (2016). Stigma regarding hearing loss and hearing aids: A scoping review. *Stigma and Health*, 1(2), 59–71.

Erler, S.F., & Garstecki, D.C. (2002). Hearing loss- and hearing aid-related stigma. *American Journal of Audiology*, 11(2), 83–91.

Frank, A.W. (2013). *The Wounded Storyteller: Body, Illness, and Ethics* (2nd edn). Chicago, IL: University of Chicago Press.

Gaylor, J.M., Raman, G., Chung, M., Lee, J., Rao, M., Lau, J., & Poe, D.S. (2013). Cochlear implantation in adults: A systematic review and meta-analysis. *JAMA Otolaryngology–Head and Neck Surgery*, 139(3), 265–272.

Goffman, E. (1990/1963). *Stigma: Notes on the Management of Spoiled Identity*. London: Penguin Books.

Hearing Link. (n.d.). *Vision and Values*. Retrieved from: www.hearinglink.org/about-us/our-work/vision-values/ [Last accessed: March 2020].

Hearing Link. (n.d. a). *Facts about Deafness and Hearing Loss*. Retrieved from: www.hearinglink.org/your-hearing/about-hearing/facts-about-deafness-hearing-loss/ [Last accessed: March 2020].

Holcomb, T.K. (2012). *Introduction to American Deaf Culture*. Oxford: Oxford University Press.

IAC Acoustics. (n.d.). *Comparative Examples of Noise Levels*. Retrieved from: www.iacacoustics.com/blog-full/comparative-examples-of-noise-levels.html [Last accessed: March 2020].

ICD-10. (2019). *Chapter VIII. Diseases of the Ear and Mastoid Process. (H60-H95)*. Retrieved from: https://icd.who.int/browse10/2019/en [Last accessed: March 2020].

Iler, K.L., Danhauer, J.L., & Mulac, A. (1982). Peer perceptions of geriatrics wearing hearing aids. *Journal of Speech and Hearing Disorders*, 47(4), 433–438.

Kiringoda, R., & Lustig, L.R. (2013). A meta-analysis of the complications associated with osseointegrated hearing aids. *Otology & Neurotology*, 34(5), 790–794.

Ladd, P. (2003). *Understanding Deaf Culture: In Search of Deafhood*. Bristol: Multilingual Matters.

Lingsom, S. (2008). Invisible impairments: Dilemmas of concealment and disclosure. *Scandinavian Journal of Disability Research*, 10(1), 2–16.

Lockey, K., Jennings, M.B., & Shaw, L. (2010). Exploring hearing aid use in older women through narratives. *International Journal of Audiology*, 49(8), 542–549.

National Deaf Children's Society. (n.d.). Vision, mission and values. Retrieved from: www.ndcs.org.uk/about-us/what-we-do/vision-mission-and-values/ [Last accessed: March 2020].

Padden, C., Humphries, T., & Padden, C. (2009). *Inside Deaf Culture.* Cambridge, MA: Harvard University Press.

Qi, S., & Mitchell, R.E. (2012). Large-scale academic achievement testing of deaf and hard-of-hearing students: Past, present, and future. *Journal of Deaf Studies and Deaf Education,* 17(1), 1–18.

Richardson, J.T., Long, G.L., & Woodley, A. (2004). Students with an undisclosed hearing loss: A challenge for academic access, progress, and success? *Journal of Deaf Studies and Deaf Education,* 9(4), 427–441.

Richardson, L. (2000). Writing: A method of inquiry. In: Denzin, N., & Lincoln, Y. (eds). *The Sage Handbook of Qualitative Research* (2nd edn). Thousand Oaks, CA: Sage. 923–943.

Richardson, L. (2003). Writing: A method of inquiry. In: Lincoln, Y., & Denzin, N. (eds). *Turning Points in Qualitative Research: Tying Knots in a Handkerchief.* Walnut Creek, CA: Altamira. 379–396.

Snels, C., IntHout, J., Mylanus, E., Huinck, W., & Dhooge, I. (2019). Hearing preservation in cochlear implant surgery: A meta-analysis. *Otology & Neurotology,* 40(2), 145–153.

Southall, K., Jennings, M.B., & Gagné, J.P. (2011). Factors that influence disclosure of hearing loss in the workplace. *International Journal of Audiology,* 50(10), 699–707.

Tharpe, A.M., Sladen, D.P., Dodd-Murphy, J., & Boney, S.J. (2009). Minimal hearing loss in children: Minimal but not inconsequential. *Seminars in Hearing,* 30(2), 080-093.

Tidwell, R. (2004). The 'invisible' faculty member: The university professor with a hearing disability. *Higher Education,* 47(2), 197–210.

US Food and Drug Administration. (2018). *Benefits and Risks of Cochlear Implants.* Retrieved from: www.fda.gov/medical-devices/cochlear-implants/benefits-and-risks-cochlear-implants [Last accessed: March 2020].

Valente, J.M., Bahan, B., Bauman, H.D., Petitto, L., & Hall, E.T. (2011). Sensory politics and the cochlear implant debates. In: Paludneviciene, R., & Leigh, I.W. (eds). *Cochlear Implants: Evolving Perspectives,* Washington, DC: Gallaudet University Press. 245–258.

Wikipedia. (n.d.). *The Bionic Woman*. Retrieved from: https://en.wikipedia.org/wiki/The_Bionic_Woman [Last accessed: March 2020].

Williams, V.A., Johnson, C.E., & Danhauer, J.L. (2009). Hearing aid outcomes: Effects of gender and experience on patients' use and satisfaction. *Journal of the American Academy of Audiology*, 20(7), 422–432.

World Health Organization. (2020). *Deafness and Hearing Loss*. Retrieved from: www.who.int/news-room/fact-sheets/detail/deafness-and-hearing-loss [Last accessed: March 2020].

World Health Organization. (n.d.). *Grades of Hearing Impairment*. Retrieved from: www.who.int/pbd/deafness/hearing_impairment_grades/en/ [Last accessed: March 2020].

9

Living with collagenous colitis as a busy academic: chronic illness and the intersection of age and gender inequality

Rosalind Janssen

It's easy to become a prisoner in your own home when you have this illness.

(Morrison, 2016)

Introduction

For a busy academic, Nina Morrison's description of collagenous colitis as a disease that imprisons – because of the urgent need to be close to a toilet – presents insurmountable difficulties. Unlike the immaculate female model on the front cover of her ebook, you simply do not have the luxury to be posing in your silk pyjamas while nursing that second cup of tea. Come rain or shine, your task on a Monday morning is to travel on a packed Tube, in order to reach your institution in plenty of time to deliver your regular nine o'clock lecture. Even more importantly, the chances are that while you may well be female you are not going to look very much like that young model anyway. This is a chronic condition which largely affects older women and as such lies at the very intersection of age and gender. What follows is my personal story: an experience of living with the challenges presented by a little known disabling disease while a full-time female academic, albeit one who at the time was rapidly approaching retirement. It is an account which aims to reflect on what having collagenous colitis might mean in relation to an academy already noted for its gendered ageism.

Defining the disease

Only identified four decades ago (Lindström, 1976), collagenous colitis has been afforded far less medical research investment than its important big sisters Crohn's and ulcerative colitis. At the same time, the PubMed search engine provides 11,335 citations for collagenous or microscopic colitis, 19 of which appeared in the first eight months of 2019 (www.ncbi.nlm.nih. gov/pubmed/).

Collagenous colitis constitutes one of the two subtypes of microscopic colitis, the other being lymphocytic colitis. An inflammatory disease affecting the large bowel, its characteristic is watery non-bloody diarrhoea, with urgent incontinence – often nocturnal – and abdominal pain (Hjortswang et al, 2011). Fatigue and weight loss are likely to result.

What we do know is that there are currently 10 cases per 100,000 persons (Hemert et al, 2018: 39). This agrees with incidents of 5.2 to 10.8 per 100,000 inhabitants per year in Northern Europe and North America (Fernández-Bañares et al, 2016: 805), and the 5–10 per 100,000 cited by O'Toole (2016: 32). A meta-analysis of 25 studies (Tong et al, 2015) shows a pooled incident rate of 4.4 per 100,000 person years. A non-Western Korean study similarly detected collagenous colitis in 4 per cent of patents (Park et al, 2011). The conclusion then is that this is a relatively rare disease.

Women have a proportionally greater risk of collagenous colitis at 2.4 to 1 (Boland and Nguyen, 2017: 671). Increasing age is a further risk factor, since collagenous colitis 'classically occurs in middle-aged females' of around 60–70 years of age (O'Toole, 2016: 32). However, Saad et al (2017) give a lower onset, citing women of 55–63.8 years.

As its blanket name of microscopic colitis suggests, it is only possible to identify collagenous colitis by microscopic examination following a colonoscopy. There is no curative therapy for collagenous colitis, and the aim is simply to induce remission. The only proven effective treatment so far has been found to be the steroid Budesonide, which is also used to treat Crohn's disease. However, there is a worrying 61 per cent relapse rate on cessation of the therapy (Miehlke et al, 2013).

Arguing that their Swedish survey of 116 patients with collagenous colitis has generalisability to a Western population, Hjortswang et al (2011: 109) conclude that its symptoms 'can be very disabling and affect the quality of life'. This can be summed up as 'the problem with diarrhoea results in fear of not finding a toilet and restricts social life which in turn affects the well-being negatively' (Hjortswang et al, 2011: 109). By wellbeing the authors are specifically referring to 'vitality and emotional state' (Hjortswang et al, 2011: 109).

Hjortswang et al (2011: 109) cite 'insufficient knowledge about the disease and the unsatisfactory treatment of the disease'. Highlighting that collagenous colitis as a disability which is very poorly understood is the fact that its precise cause is unknown. It is associated with autoimmune disorders, such as celiac disease and thyroid dysfunction. The use of certain medications, particularly nonsteroidal anti-inflammatory drugs (NSAIDs) such as aspirin, may also play a role, as may smoking. However, it is equally possible that none of these associations are a factor, and the trigger may simply be put down to stress or, as in my case, to a bout of gastroenteritis.

Telling my story

Stress may well have been relevant to my first encounter with collagenous colitis. It was 2009 and my husband's first wife had just died, which meant that we had to travel at a moment's notice to the Netherlands for her funeral. After six weeks of acute watery diarrhoea of up to fifteen times a day, I went to my GP, who referred me for an urgent colonoscopy: collagenous colitis mimics the symptoms of colon cancer. The procedure revealed no abnormalities, but when I went to my follow-up outpatient appointment, I was told that the biopsies taken during the colonoscopy had revealed collagenous colitis. The consultant colorectal surgeon, at what was a large London teaching hospital, could tell me very little about the disease, and instead referred me to one of his colleagues, a consultant gastroenterologist specialising in colitis. By this time, I was in remission, which I attributed to relief that I did not have anything too sinister. The specialist performed a large array of blood tests, but everything came back perfectly normal and I was able to forget about this peculiar disease.

But after eight years as asymptomatic, I experienced a sudden, dramatic relapse. On 14 August 2017 – it seems that sufferers can often pinpoint the exact date and moment when they were struck down – I drank a latte and ate a Devon scone in Marks & Spencer. Just half an hour later, as I strolled with my friend down Kensington High Street to visit the Alma Tadema exhibition at Leighton House, I started to experience excruciating stomach cramps. Following six weeks of permanent diarrhoea with cramps, wind and bloating, I this time bypassed my GP and referred myself to the same specialist gastroenterologist from 2009 as a private patient. "I have got collagenous colitis again," I told him. "That's impossible," he said. "It can't come back again after a gap of so many years. We will have to start again from scratch and do another colonoscopy." So, it was back to the NHS for another fairly urgent colonoscopy, aided this time by an extremely valuable direct line to the consultant's helpful PA.

This time the colonoscopy did not go nearly so smoothly. I woke up after half an hour to be told that the team were only half way, slowed down by what a subsequent report describes as 'a large redundant loop of sigmoid colon'. Having already had my sedation topped up to the maximum, and then as a result of my screams and low blood pressure, the procedure had to be rapidly aborted. The lead doctor was able to tell me that the left side of the colon was clear, and that biopsies had been taken. The right side had not been examined. A telephone call to his senior colleague led to the advice that my next stage was to abandon any idea of a further colonoscopy, and to instead have a CT colonoscopy. The first colonoscopy patient to arrive that morning, I ended up being the last by far to leave. My worried friend had even heard my screams from the waiting room. I left feeling as much a failure as what was termed 'a failed colonoscopy'.

Another wait for a CT colonoscopy which, unlike the original colonoscopy, can give no immediate, reassuring answers. Fortunately, the consultant's PA understood that 27 December was not the best day for an outpatient appointment to receive the results, and kindly moved this forward to earlier in the month. The news was that the CT colonoscopy was normal and showed no other lesion in the colon, but those left-colon biopsies from the original colonoscopy had come back with incontrovertible evidence of recurrent collagenous colitis. As the pathology test report reads: 'There is a diffuse increase in chronic inflammatory cells ... with thickening of the subepithelial collagen plate ... the features are in keeping with a microscopic colitis (collagenous subtype) and further clinicopathological correlation is required.' I had made medical history in what the consultant at the time described as 'not fine, but really interesting' and 'I can't explain it'. His subsequent letter described how, 'it is very interesting to see this recurrent collagenous colitis histology come back triggered by a presumed infection'. Proof, if any were needed, that there really is nothing certain about the disease.

By this time, remission was once again occurring very gradually and there was no need to take Budesonide. A follow-up appointment in June 2018, this time with the consultant's senior registrar, produced the news that I will always have collagenous colitis, and that a flare up is possible at any time. A year later, I have now been discharged.

Impacting academic life

Reference has already been made to Hjortswang et al's 2011 study which concludes that having collagenous colitis can severely impair quality of life. This is aptly illustrated by a sketch by Philip Henry delivered for the BBC at the Edinburgh Festival Fringe on 31 August 2018, an edited version of which is available on the BBC website (Henry, 2018). Entitled 'The stomach-churning one-night stand', Henry, who has Crohn's, finds humour in the seemingly overwhelming awkwardness of the disease. Moreover, his sketch specifically highlights how morning is often the worse time for the colitis sufferer. Not surprisingly, this is especially true for an academic who, as alluded to in the Introduction, must often leave the house early in the morning.

My own quality of life issue was that dealing with the major symptoms of the disease coincided with having to teach a weekly class in Oxford. This involved an early morning start, waiting at a London bus stop for a coach, and then repeating the procedure in reverse later the same day. It is now the case that I could write a guide to the toilet facilities along the route. But how much worse for a female academic who has to travel to that important conference abroad, only to find that she is scheduled to deliver her ground-breaking paper at nine o'clock in the morning.

Having to suddenly exit a classroom when in full lecturing flow is a potentially embarrassing experience. The same goes for meetings. How to explain the situation to students and colleagues? Or, more likely, how to follow Philip Henry and come up with a series of acceptable lies. The situation is compounded by the fact that, in the case of collagenous colitis, one is a woman of a certain age, and as such already in a problematic position within the academy.

In their large study of eleven local authorities and three private sector companies in the UK, Itzen and Phillipson (1993, 1995a, 1995b) identified gendered ageism as the double jeopardy faced by women in the workplace. Granleese and Sayer's (2006) smaller qualitative study of 48 employees subsequently confirmed the double jeopardy experience for women academics in the UK's higher education system. Moreover, it added 'lookism' – namely discrimination through physical appearance and attractiveness – as an additional prejudice. Older women felt they were becoming invisible within the academy, which Granleese and Sayer (2006) suggest may have been a metaphor for 'losing their looks'. The end result is that older female academics are at risk of experiencing a triple jeopardy of sexism, ageism and physical appearance.

Once chronic illness or disability are added into the equation, they risk further exclusion. Twelve years ago, the introduction to a World Health Organization report on ageing and health from a gender perspective stated that 'the rights and contributions of older women remain largely invisible in most settings' (WHO,

2007: 1–2). WHO concluded their report by urging academics and policy makers to 'include older women at each stage of the research, and make use of both quantitative and qualitative methods' (WHO, 2007: 48). In an attempt to address this gap, a recent investigation has shed more light on the intersection between ageing, health and gender (Tuohy and Cooney, 2019). Comprising 40 dialogue interviews with 23 older Irish women, designated as co-researchers, this large qualitative study reached the important conclusion that these three factors 'are interlinked and none should be looked at in isolation, as each have an impact on the other' (Tuohy and Cooney, 2019: 9). Part of the problem is that the symptoms of older women are often dismissed as emotionally based (Annadale, 2009). Moreover, the emphasis of medical research is on female reproductive health, thereby largely ignoring the health needs of older women in social policy (Davidson et al, 2011). In the same way that they are rendered invisible in wider society, older women with chronic illness become additionally marginalised within the academy. The result of such ableism is that they are likely to experience an oppressive quadruple jeopardy.

Bronstein's seminal study (2001: 195) confirms that such marginalisation has long existed in US universities. Relating both her own experiences and those of 13 other women aged 50 to 72, she tells us that 'the issues of older women within academia, as in the society at large, remain mostly invisible'. Confirming that 'there is little published information about the experiences of older women in academia', she asserts that 'like older women themselves, age has often gone unnoticed as an important factor in academic life' (Bronstein, 2001: 184).

Despite the fact that age has subsequently formed one of the protected characteristics under the Equality Act 2010, Bronstein's 2001 statements still very much pertain to our own academy and wider society here in the UK, 20 years later. Such invisibility has been particularly relevant in my own case: back in 2016, I had given two years' notice of my intended retirement, greeted at the time by the interesting expression that 'I was moving on'. The end result was that I subsequently found myself becoming more and more invisible within the academy, with a voice that no longer counted. One particularly shocking example was that my annual appraisal in 2017 comprised a five-minute conversation in a student common room, while that of 2018 failed to materialise.

No wonder then that Bronstein's article retains its relevance today, implying that a consideration of her findings will be fundamental as we come to the final framing of four reflective questions and four recommendations for practice.

Reflective questions

- Were you aware that colitis is a chronic disease which sufferers – be they staff or students – may be very reluctant to disclose within a higher education environment?
- Are you now aware that collagenous colitis seriously impacts on quality of life, and how it presents particular challenges to an academic?
- Were you aware that your older female colleagues, together with mature students, may already be feeling marginalised within the academy due to their age?
- Are you now aware that, as a result of chronic illness and its intersection with gender, age and physical appearance, older women with collagenous colitis may experience a quadruple disadvantage leaving them voiceless within the academy?

Recommendations

My first two recommendations are rooted in higher education and the individual institution, while the final two are designed to challenge older women in the academy – both those who may and those who do not consider themselves as having a disability.

First, I recommend that the academy actively promotes awareness of all types of colitis, and that higher education proactively funds research into the condition and into collagenous colitis in particular.

Second, I recommend that university estates increase their provision of accessible toilet facilities. Moreover, they should continue to maintain a balance of female alongside gender-neutral toilets.

Third, I recommend that older women in the academy start to form feminist co-mentoring relationships as an aid to mutual empowerment. Such non-competitive, equal power groupings – which present a challenge to patriarchal hierarchy – were first recommended by Bronstein (1997: 257), who encouraged older women and lesbian academics to 'forge alliances' since both groups might feel marginalised. McGuire and Reger (2003: 66) similarly recommend feminist co-mentoring as 'particularly helpful for underrepresented groups' in order to 'form supportive relationships, decrease their isolation, and obtain help that they might not receive from their traditional mentors'. Drawing on their own co-mentoring experiences, McGuire and Reger (2003: 55) envisage work and home as seamlessly interconnected, meaning that such relationships can help academics 'integrate their emotional, physical, and intellectual lives'. This implies that 'the goal of co-mentoring is the development of the whole person, not simply her/his intellectual side' (McGuire and Reger, 2003: 56). This aspect is obviously significant for our purposes since we have already witnessed the serious emotional and physical impact of living with collagenous colitis as an older female academic. The goal is to choose as a co-mentor 'someone whom you trust … someone with whom you can speak openly about your experiences' (McGuire and Reger, 2003: 63). The end result would be the opportunity to share the fact that one is living with a chronic disability with a supportive colleague.

My fourth and final recommendation is that, as advocated by Bronstein (2001), older women in academia should start to study themselves. She points to the fact that 'older women scholars as a group have not taken up the challenge; there is no burgeoning body of research addressing age as a salient category in women's lives. It appears that they have internalized society's perspective that the meaning and politics of women's lives beyond their reproductive years are not worth examining' (Bronstein, 2001: 195). That this situation has not changed in the last 20 years, is perhaps because older women still 'generally do not have a sense of identity related to their age' (Bronstein, 2001: 195). Furthermore, her interviewees significantly attributed 'any discrimination they had experienced to sexism alone' and totally failed 'to consider that ageism had also played a role' (Bronstein, 2001: 195).

It is therefore hoped that, by relating my own personal story in relation to the academy, this chapter has taken up the gauntlet. Positioning a particularly unpleasant condition, that is not normally spoken about, it has also dispelled the notion that ageing and gender inequality, which lies at the intersection of chronic illness, is a non-issue for the academy. Only by older women uniting to tell such personal stories can we encourage universities to position themselves in the forefront of change by valuing disability.

References

Annadale, E. (2009). *Women's Health and Social Change*, London: Routledge.

Boland, K., & Nguyen, G.C. (2017). Microscopic colitis: A review of collagenous and lymphocytic colitis. *Gastroenterology & Hepatology*, 13(11), 671–677. www.ncbi.nlm.nih.gov/pmc/articles/PMC5717882/

Bronstein, P. (1997). Older women in academia. In: B. Minz & E.D. Rothblum (eds), *Lesbians in Academia. Degrees of Freedom*, New York: Routledge, pp. 350–259.

Bronstein, P. (2001). Older women in academia: Contemporary history and issues. *Journal of Women's History*, 12(4), 184–201. https//:doi.org/10.1353/jowh.2001.0004

Davidson, P.M., DiGiacomo, M., & McGrath, S.J. (2011). The feminization of aging: How will this impact on health outcomes and services? *Health Care for Women International*, 32(12), 1031–1045. www.tandfonline.com/doi/abs/10.1080/07399332.2011.610539

Fernández-Bañares, F., Zabana, Y., Aceituno, M., Ruiz, L., Salas, A. & Esteve, M. (2016). Prevalence and natural history of microscopic colitis: A population-based study with long-term clinical follow-up in Terrassa, Spain. *Journal of Crohn's and Colitis*, 10(7), 805–811. https://doi.org/10.1093/ecco-jcc/jjw037

Granleese, J., & Sayer, G. (2006). Gendered ageism and 'lookism': A triple jeopardy for female academics. *Women in Management Review*, 21(6), 500–517. https://doi.org/10.1108/09649420610683480

Hemert van, S., Skonieczna-Żydecka, K., Loniewski, I., Szredzki, P. & Marlicz, W. (2018). Microscopic colitis – microbiome, barrier function and associated diseases. *Annals of Translational Medicine*, 6(3), 39. https://doi.org/10.21037/atm.2017.03.83

Henry, P. (2018). The stomach-churning one-night stand. Edinburgh Fringe Festival. 31 August. www.bbc.co.uk/news/disability-45045223

Hjortowang, H., Tysk, C., Bohr, J., Benoni, C., Vigren, L., Kilander, A., Larsson, L. Taha, Y. & Ström, M. (2011). Health-related quality of life is impaired in active collagenous colitis, *Digestive and Liver Disease*, 43(2), 102–109. https://doi.org/10.1016/j.dld.2010.06.004

Itzin, C., & Phillipson, C. (1993). *Age Barriers at Work*, Solihull: Metropolitan Authorities Recruitment Agency.

Itzen, C., & Phillipson, C. (1995a). *Age Barriers at Work*, Solihull: Metropolitan Authorities Recruitment Agency.

Itzen, C., & Phillipson, C. (1995b). Gendered ageism: A double jeopardy for women in organizations. In: C. Itzen, & J. Newman, J. (eds), *Gender Culture and Organizational Change: Putting Theory into Practice*, London: Routledge, pp. 84–94.

Lindström, C.G. (1976). 'Collagenous colitis' with watery diarrhoea: a new entity? *Pathologia Europaea*, 11(1), 87–89.

Maye, H., Safroneeva, E., Godat, S., & Schoepfer, A. (2018). P468 Microscopic colitis: Systematic analysis of 200 adult patients with a mean follow-up of 4 years, *Journal of Crohn's and Colitis*, 12(Issue supplement_1), S341. https://doi.org/10.1093/ecco-jcc/jjx180.595

McGuire, G.M., & Reger, J. (2003). Feminist co-mentoring: A model for academic professional development. *National Women's Studies Association Journal*, 15(1), 54–72. www.jstor.org/stable/4316944

Miehlke, S., Hanson, J.B., Madisch, A., Schwarz, F., Kuhlisch, E., Morgner, A., Teglbjaerg, P.S., Vieth, M., Aust, D. & Bonderup, O.K. (2013). Risk factors for symptom relapse in collageneous colitis after withdrawal of short-term budesonide therapy, *Inflammatory Bowel Diseases*, 19(13), 2763–2767. https://doi.org/10.1097/01.MIB.0000438135.88681.98

Morrison, N. (2016). *Living with Microscopic Colitis*. Self-published.

O'Toole, A. (2016). Optimal management of collagenous colitis: A review. *Clinical and Experimental Gastroenterology*, 9, 31–39. https://doi.org/10.2147/CEG.S67233

Park, Y.S., Back, D.II., Kim, W.H., Kim, J.S., Yang, S.-K., Jung, S.-A., Jang, B.I., Choi, C.H., Han, D.S., Kim, Y-H., Chung, Y.W., Kim, S.W. & Kim, Y.S. (2011). Clinical characteristics of microscopic colitis in Korea: Prospective multicenter study by KASID. *Gut and Liver*, 5(2), 181–186. https://doi.org/10.5009/gnl.2011.5.2.181

Saad, R.E., Shobar, R.M., Jakate, S. and Mutlu, E.A. (2017). Development of collagenous colitis in inflammatory bowel disease: Two case reports and a review of the literature. *Gastroenterology Report*, gox026, 1–5. https://doi.org/10.1093/gastro/gox026

Tong, J., Zheng, Q., Zhang, C., Lo, R., Shen, J. & Ran, Z. (2015), Incidence, prevalence, and temporal trends of microscopic colitis: A systematic review and meta-analysis. *The American Journal of Gastroenterology*, 110, 265–276. https://doi.org/10.1038/ajg.2014.431

Tuohy, D., & Cooney, A. (2019), Older women's experiences of aging and health: An interpretive phenomenological study. *Gerontology and Geriatric Medicine* 5, 1–10. www.ncbi.nlm.nih.gov/pmc/articles/PMC6410378/

WHO (World Health Organization) (2007). *Women, Ageing and Health. A Framework for Action*, Geneva: World Health Organization. https://apps.who.int/iris/bitstream/handle/10665/43810/9789241563529_eng.pdf

10

Three cheers for Access to Work partnership: two cheers for Two Ticks and one question about a university-wide self-disclosure scheme

Chris Mounsey and Stan Booth

Introduction

It was only in the mid-19th century that the term 'disabled' became intransitive. That is to say, it was only then that society, following the practices of the army, excluded people like me with impairments from work. Until then we were understood transitively as 'disabled from getting bread' during our transition period from being able-bodied, after which we were expected to pull our weight, however we may. Think of Horatio Nelson, an 'able seaman' who continued on active duty with one eye and one arm. He was not alone in the navy. Many ship's surgeons, for example, John Atkins, have written up cases of named officers and able seamen whom they treated with amputations and for gunshot wounds which might have rendered them 'disabled' in the modern sense but did not stop them from getting their bread. Atkins describes the amputation made of the right arm of Galfridus Walpole (brother of Sir Robert) while he was in charge of HMS Lion, a 60-gun fourth-rate ship of the line. Captain Walpole continued to serve in the navy after the amputation, his last commission being on HMS Peregrine Galley from 1716 to 1720. Atkins also describes the successful treatment of able seaman Alexander Henderson, who lost an eye 'struck out by a splinter'.

After the Equality Act 2010 enshrined in UK law four EU Equal Treatment Directives on pay, sex, race and disability discrimination, I for one, hoped that we would return to the days of transitivity. My transition period had been a long one of denial that I could not concentrate when looking, so I skim read with my hand over my left eye, and only gave up driving after four serious accidents, after which I continued to cycle until I ran into a six-inch kerb that I just didn't see. I had sold my car, and now had to sell my bicycles, but what was I to do about my work? It was 2008, and when I had a meeting with the dean and administrators in my department, it became clear that they were not able to help. This was not because they were unwilling, but more that they expected me to give up work, now that I was disabled. I suppose they thought I could get a miraculously large 'break-down pension' so why would I want to continue to teach and research when I could stay home and ... be blind (?) I suppose, listen to daytime TV and become an alcoholic.

Luckily, after fighting my way through two years to and in work in a fog, literally, the Equality Act 2010 was passed. This was the first time I began to feel safe at work, as I could no longer be asked to resign because of some perceived insurmountable obstacle caused by my inability to see very well. This is not to say that my colleagues were not generally very helpful and kind, but when you feel that people are being helpful and kind to you, you also feel that:

1. they don't believe you have a disability;
2. they don't believe you're pulling your weight.

At a stroke, the Equality Act's demand that employers made 'reasonable adjustments' in my working practice meant that, for example, my concentrating my on-campus hours to two days a week had a legal status, and that my requirement that student assignments could not include hand-written exams was no mere eccentricity. Since then I've implemented many electronic-enhanced practices that students prefer, such as Skype[1] tutorials at their and my convenience – I've even held a couple at 9.30 at night, and at 6.30 in the morning.

But this is all the experience of an established professor who transitioned into being a disabled employee while holding down a full-time job. I never believed that I would stay in the same job all my life, and receive job advertisements every day for positions in which I would thrive were I to pass or even be called to the interview. But I still have the same job I started with, no matter how many applications I make. The downside of the Equality Act is that it has engendered a lot of virtue signalling, which appears usually in the form of a logo on the bottom of the institution's headed notepaper. I know from the experiences of the postgraduate students I've published in essay collections that they suffer the same as I do in being overlooked for interview. I only wish that I could stipulate that the next holder of my job also had some kind of impairment. The fear of people with disabilities is, I believe, the cause of the even worse job situation from which we suffer. I am trying to remedy this in a small way at my own university with a self-disclosure scheme for staff and students. Although there is a notice on the door of the accessible toilet that 'Not all disabilities are visible' (smile from me, how would I know, I just wait in line) it seems to me that if people know that the ground-base for a person with a disability is different from theirs, then there would not be so many altercations and recriminations, especially now that we disabled have the law on our side.

Me and Stan

The original intention of this chapter was to present, using voice to text software, a typical conversation between Stan and me, who are known by our students as Ant and Dec. We are something of a comic duo: I'm from Liverpool and Stan from Manchester, which makes us rivals in everything from football, to music, to accents, to arguing which is the most important North Western UK city. Our opposition also lies in the types of impairments we have: Stan has bilateral hip arthroplasty, which means he has trouble bending down and has more trouble getting up, and I had a brain injury which has affected my sight, balance and makes my hands shake. But impairments and assistive environments are not always 'hurdle and leap': they do produce unthought-of opportunities.

I regularly use text to voice software, and can now read so fast that marking student essays is no longer a chore. I notice most of the mistakes the student makes in spelling, and am used to the voice's peculiarities (such as reading the name Foucault as 'Fa-oo-coo-alt'). I am also well aware of the annoyance of in-text citations, which I discourage students from using because they break up sentences rendering them gobbledegook to a listener. But when Stan and I came to record our conversation in voice to text, the result was – well – also gobbledegook:

> This is a potential love but how to do voice transcription using an audio recording. ... Play conversation between Chris mounsey and stand groove 7th of November 282 in offs 1246 Talk others turn really well because I've known him for on and all the 7 stages for I know all of the 7 stages of whose would you call He called it raged ash this rage From the I rollicks morrow to the 10 posterous and her family and I think its the I think that close knowledge is important On which to found a working relationship based on respect him I jokingly Corley rage what is it just not crush you

It reads like concrete poetry. Translations on a post card, please, in block letter handwriting. Get a grip, you techies!

Returning to Ant and Dec, I can tell you that we get odd looks when Stan drops something, and puts his foot near the thing he's dropped, so I can bend down and pick it up after a bit of scrabbling around on the ground. It's only when people notice my white stick (Stan tells me) that they pretend not to have been staring. We also get odd looks when either of us is having a bad day and loses it, usually in a public place. There's no getting away from having an impairment, and sometimes you just have to shout and yell. The white stick does not help here because people without impairments believe that those of us who do have them are angels with the patience of saints. Stan had his surgery years ago, and taught himself how to be fragile: if he falls and breaks something, he'll be in traction for 6 months. He learned how to be a different person after years hobbling around on crutches. But Stan had to teach me to be fragile when my sight problems became apparent ten years ago. It's because I'm built like a rugby player and used to be the mad cyclist in front of your car who ran the red lights. And no, that's not the reason I got my brain injury.

Despite our differences and our bad days, what is wholly positive about having an Access to Work partnership is that we complement each other, but more than that, we help each other to become more than we might have been if we were alone. I am a research professor of 30 years' standing, and I would not be able to edit the texts I'm writing or research as quickly and effectively without Stan. Nor, probably, would Stan be working for his PhD. Stan does the eye work, we discuss what he's found and I write it up. What is important is that we discuss findings as they turn up, and we always disagree on their significance, so nothing is taken for granted. We have run conferences together, have travelled worldwide to conferences and archives and Stan recognises people we know so we can talk with them. In term time, Stan does the computer work which has become more and more complex; for example, any information disseminated on spreadsheets is illegible to me as they are not amenable to text to voice. Furthermore, our university's website is impenetrable to those with 20-20 vision, and completely impossible for those who have any vision impairment. Stan can find postings that even those who've posted the information fail to retrieve.

If I could wish for anything it would be for perfect OCR (optical character recognition) as I work with 18th-century texts printed in hand carved fonts. It would also be wonderful to have OCRing for manuscripts, where most of my new project on the history of work and disabilities is being carried out. I would also wish for perfect voice to text so I can type without having to listen to what I've written every third word, and dozens of times through to check it. I have no such wish for anything more perfect in Stan – and perhaps the best bit is that he goes home after we've finished working. We work together, however close, we are not conjoined twins: nor are we married.

The theory of Two Ticks

According to the Labour Force Survey, disabled people are now more likely to be employed than they were in 2002, but disabled people remain significantly less likely to be in employment than non-disabled people. In 2012, 46.3 per cent of working-age disabled people are in employment compared to 76.4 per cent of working-age non-disabled people. There is therefore a 30.1 percentage point gap between disabled and non-disabled people, representing over 2 million people (Labour Force Survey, 2015). The gap has reduced by 10 percentage points over the last 14 years and has remained stable over the last two years despite the economic climate. Added to this, disabled people are significantly more likely to experience unfair treatment at work than non-disabled people. The latest figures offered by the government show that, in 2008, 19 per cent of disabled people experienced unfair treatment at work compared to 13 per cent of non-disabled people.

The Two Ticks scheme was set up to help employers to view disabled people as potential employees, rather than as in need of benefits, as transitively rather than intransitively disabled. In 2016, the Two Ticks scheme had a name change to the Disability Confident programme, presumably because no one knew what the former name meant. The government website is hardly more explicit (Disability Confident: how to sign up to the employer scheme, n.d.):

> Being Disability Confident could help you discover someone your business just can't do without.
>
> Whether an employee has become disabled during their working life, or you're looking for new recruits, being Disability Confident can help your people fulfil their potential and contribute fully to your team's success.
>
> By being Disability Confident, you'll also be seen as leading the way in your business sector and beyond, helping to positively change attitudes, behaviours and cultures.

There follows a list of bullet points:

> Disability Confident helps businesses:
> * draw from the widest possible pool of talent
> * secure and retain high quality staff who are skilled, loyal and hard working
> * save time and money on the costs of recruitment and training by reducing staff turnover
> * keep valuable skills and experience
> * reduce the levels and costs of sickness absences
> * improve employee morale and commitment by demonstrating that they treat all employees fairly

Bad teachers use PowerPoints full of bullet points, using information as a substitute for knowledge. The rest of the Disability Confident website is little more than bullet points, reducing the lives of disabled people in work to a few quotes and sometimes not even explaining what the person's disability is. Throughout the site there are multiple buttons to sign up for the scheme. Employers seem to like this sort of virtue signalling, and the website reminds me of the thousands of rainbow signs on shop-fronts and other businesses during the Gay Pride weekend. They had all gone by the end of the week.

The Disability Confident scheme made five commitments. To reach its lowest level, 'Disability Confident Committed', employers had to: 'just agree to the Disability Confident commitments and identify at least one action that you'll carry out to make a difference for disabled people.'

The commitments are:

* inclusive and accessible recruitment
* communicating vacancies
* offering an interview to disabled people
* providing reasonable adjustments
* supporting existing employees
  (Disability Confident: how to sign up to the employer scheme, n.d.)

Higher levels, Disability Confident Employer and Disability Confident Leader, require records of action, although all three levels allow employers, including universities, to add the Disability Confident logo to their websites and job application materials. To meet the middle level employers must 'commit to offer an interview to disabled people who meet the minimum criteria for the job' ('Disability Confident' and guaranteed interviews, 2019).

The reality of the Disability Confident scheme

In the past ten years, since I became registered as partially sighted, I have applied for a number of jobs in universities which displayed the logo and I ticked the box that guarantees me an interview if I 'meet the minimum criteria', and so far I have only once been called for an interview. I am a world leader in the field of disability history. I lead edit a monograph series with a US University Press on the subject, and am rated as an excellent researcher by my university. I offered seven pieces of published research to the 2020 REF (Research Excellence Framework), which are listed in the references. I have won student-led awards for teaching 'The Best Delivered Module' and my dean told me after talking to my students that, "They love you!"

I do not know what the minimum criteria for a job might be. Probably not being blind.

To test why I was not being called for interview, I applied for an academic post advertised under the Two Ticks scheme at a much lower level than I currently hold, and was invited for interview. During the formal section of the day, which I believed was going quite well, the union representative stated to the interview committee that the fact that I said I carried out Skype tutorials with students "would set up an expectation that other tutors could not be expected to match". I told them that Stan's hours meant I could only be on campus for up to 20 hours a week and that Skype worked very well with my current students. There was a silence. I was exasperated. "I'm blind!" I shouted, "What else can I do!" I was told by the union representative, "That was a good answer."

I did not get the job.

I have never felt so demeaned in my life. The university concerned was a Disability Confident Employer and I do not believe that its employees had even heard of 'reasonable adjustments'.

Getting reasonably adjusted

This is not to say that my own colleagues are perfect at reasonable adjustments, although centrally, I have come to a useful working arrangement such that my teaching is all in the room I have designated as best for me to use what sight I have, and consistently timetabled so Stan and I can co-ordinate our working lives. However, every time I ask for adjustments to be made by a colleague who has not interacted with me before, I end up physically and mentally exhausted explaining what should be done and why. I am always treated as though I am making impossible demands, or that I am asking for something special beyond my entitlement. Colleagues ask me impertinent questions and make ridiculous suggestions about accommodations they're willing to make. I believe that if the law states that 'reasonable adjustments' are to be made then, first, I'm the one likely to best suggest what those 'reasonable adjustments' might be, and, second, that although what reasonable might be is negotiable, I have a right to refuse what I deem to be unreasonable. Furthermore, the Equality Act states that 'reasonable adjustments' must be made, there is no question of the largesse of colleagues.

This might sound ungrateful. But I have been at the butt end of a number of email trails (and it is never a single email each way) with colleagues who I believe were only trying to be kind. Kindness is not what I respond to, it's professional behaviour. Kind words have a habit of sounding like threats in text to voice. Try it. The text to voice I use, Apple's Alex, reads brilliantly and clearly, but has no emotions.

It is impossible to give an example of any of the times I've been openly abused without disclosing the abuser, which would be breaking the General Data Protection Regulations. But demands that I perform something I cannot do are regular, and are usually sent in emails that copy in colleagues who have no need to know, despite the fact that I answer to a particular person and ask them not to continue to copy others in. What the abusers do not understand is that it is not just a matter of shrugging off a failure of common courtesy in these situations. I usually spend a number of nights awake with the situation going round and round in my mind, and even writing this down now is bothering me so I'm going to stop.

I have been told the only solution is to make a formal complaint, but I have to continue to work with my colleagues, and I can but imagine what working with people who have been formally reprimanded might be like. One colleague who reduced me to tears was asked to send me an apology for a thoughtless email and has not spoken to me since. That was over a year ago.

In order to draw something positive out of a wholly negative situation, I am currently working on a university-wide self-disclosure scheme, where staff and students with registered impairments can suggest (on the intranet, rather like my university's Out List) the best methods of negotiating 'reasonable adjustments'. Mine will read:

> I am registered partially sighted which means that the Equality Act of 2010 requires that you make 'reasonable adjustments' in your professional interactions with me.
>
> For me to make sense of your emails or attached documents please ensure they are legible by text to voice and contain: no acronyms, tables of information, flow diagrams, or unusual formats that manipulate the presentation of text.
>
> Please remember that it is not polite to ask any details of my impairment or question my conditions of work. The former is private, and the latter have already been agreed with HR.
>
> Please do not copy anyone else into our email conversations unless they are general university or department business. If I reply to you alone, please do not copy others into return emails.
>
> Please do not suggest accommodations to me, I am best able to tell you what I am able to do.

My preferred method of communication is Skype: my Skype name is ★★★★★★★★.

If you are uncertain about any of the above, please send me an email to arrange a Skype. I am usually available on Monday and Friday afternoons.

The idea has been enthusiastically endorsed by a number of committees in my university but has not yet been implemented.

Stan's afterword

Having co-created this piece, Nicole (this volume's editor) suggested that I consider adding a response, which in truth had never occurred to me. My role in this relationship is purely that of facilitator, or am I a co-facilitator? My purpose is not to replace Chris but to support him in achieving the productivity he is renowned for. Do I facilitate, co-facilitate or manage? Good question: it is not one I can answer as my approach to most things in life is – you just get on with it!

One thing I don't do is enable. Enabling creates dependency and how does that help anyone, least of all someone like Chris. I do what I can to support him in his endeavours. The fact I took on a PhD was a natural extension for me. Having done my masters, it seemed like a logical progression. Though maybe not so logical as the masters was in biological sciences and here I am now, in English literature. Perhaps what is important, and probably my own contribution is that I am co-editing a book series with Chris on bioethics: but whatever the path, I have always reflected on my various jobs fondly as I have been doing what I want to do. This is probably my most important statement – that to facilitate is not a passive but an active engagement.

The greatest benefit of our relationship is the intense conversations we have, where anything and everything is discussed. I keep saying I should record them, for they are so diverse and produce such complex analyses. The reason for recording them is quite apparent to me in that we frequently move on to the next problem, get consumed in it and then have trouble remembering the deliberations of the past problems. But what a life to lead when I can claim my mind is consumed by the issues of the world around it and still feel a part of it.

I have a strong sense of self and would take exception to any comparison to being Chris's conjoined twin. Like all relationships ours has grown, and my ambit now includes the wider university. My working relationships have also developed, in that my role could be considered a strange one as I am a student, administrator and an associate lecturer to fill in those other hours when I am not at home or working with Chris. My perceptions of academia are remote as a consequence, as I am never really at one with any of my roles. Thus, I have a more objective view which has made it clear to me that higher academia is not a place I would ever like to hold a single position. A university is comparable to local government where I previously worked, and the business practices and politics often defy logic and drive me mad. Therefore in a way, I am grateful that my role working with Chris has saved me from making a really bad career choice.

But how does our relationship work? Familiarity breeds contempt, as the old adage goes, and frequently it does. I too get tired. I too get bored if the subject under consideration is not sparking my interest. Sometimes I don't want to do the conferences, sometimes I do not want to go to Winchester. But the role is not about me, so I sometimes have to put my life on hold to fulfil the requirements of the job. Fortunately, Chris and I share a similar cultural background and a comparable life progression, and most importantly a similar sense of humour. Our common understanding means we have empathy with each other's needs and desires and we get through it. We argue, we laugh, we cry. I am still here to tell the tale, and able to laugh, I would not change the last seven years for anything!

Reflective questions

For those not disabled

- When you interact with your disabled colleagues, do you think carefully what you should and should not say?

- Do you believe that you are unfairly treated by the Equality Act 2010 because you are not included in its provisions? And what are the implications of your answer to this question?
- Why do you want to know the details of a colleague's disability?

For those disabled

- When you interact with your able-bodied colleagues, do you think carefully what you should and should not say?
- Do you believe that you are fairly treated by the Equality Act 2010 because you are included in its provisions? And what are the implications of your answer to this question?
- Why (or why not) do you want to know the details of a colleague's ability?

Recommendations

- Bring in a self-disclosure scheme to your university.
- Ask a disabled person to write the text for the Disability Confident website, in fact always ask a disabled person to write about disability.
- A nationwide OCR scheme would not only help blind and partially sighted readers but would also help sighted readers. Something like 10 per cent of matches are missed in every word search of a document.

Note
[1]   This chapter was written before the COVID-19 pandemic hit, and so ways of working were different.

References
'Disability Confident' and guaranteed interviews. (2019). Retrieved from www.stammeringlaw.org.uk/employment/recruitment-promotion/disability-confident-guaranteed-interviews/ [Last accessed: March 2020].

Disability Confident: how to sign up to the employer scheme. (n.d.). Retrieved from www.gov.uk/guidance/disability-confident-how-to-sign-up-to-the-employer-scheme#more-information-about-becoming-disability-confident [Last accessed: March 2020].

Labour Force Survey. (2015). Office for National Statistics. Retrieved from www.ons.gov.uk/employmentandlabourmarket/peopleinwork/employmentandemployeetypes/methodologies/labourforcesurveylfsqmi [Last accessed: March 2020].

Mounsey, C. (ed). (2014). *The Idea of Disability in the Eighteenth Century*. Plymouth: Bucknell University Press.

Mounsey, C. (ed). (2015). *Developments in the Histories of Sexualities: In Search of the Normal, 1600–1800*. Plymouth: Bucknell University Press.

Mounsey, C. (2015a). Blind woman on the rampage. In: Fowler, J. & Ingram, A. (eds). *Voice and Context in Eighteenth-Century Verse*. London: Palgrave Macmillan. 230–247.

Mounsey, C. (2015b). Learning from blindness. *Proceedings of the Modern Language Association*, 130(5), 1506–1509.

Mounsey, C. (2016). A manifesto for a woman writer: Delarivier Manley's *Letters Writen* as Varronian satire. In: Hultquist, A. & Matthews, E. (eds) *The Ladies Pacquet Broke Open*. London: Routledge. 171–188.

Mounsey, C. (2017). Edward Rushton, the first British Blind School, and charitable work for the blind in eighteenth-century England. *La Questione Romantica: Special Issue: Edward Rushton's Bicentenary. Cultural History/Legacy, Nuova Serie*, 7(1–2, 7), 89–101.

Mounsey, C. (2018). Henry Crawford as Master Betty: Jane Austen on the 'disabling' of Shakespeare. *Eighteenth-Century Fiction*, 30(2), 265–286.

Mounsey, C. (2019). *Sight Correction: Vision and Blindness in Eighteenth Century Britain*. Charlottesville, VA: University of Virginia Press.

Mounsey, C. & Booth, S. (eds). (2016). *The Variable Body in History*. Oxford: Peter Lang.

11

"I'm not saying this to be petty": reflections on making disability visible while teaching

Emma Sheppard

Introduction

In this chapter, I reflect critically on my experiences of making my disability visible in teaching, through the process of asking students to engage in particular behaviours which improve the accessibility of my role as their lecturer. I use critical and feminist disability studies work to reflect on how this has been – and still is – a difficult, discomforting decision and process. I conclude with some reflective questions for disabled academics, and some recommendations.

This is personal

Before starting, I want to make clear that my experience, and my reflection, is rooted in my embodied identity as a White woman living with a chronic illness; other disabled people will have different experiences depending on their own embodied identities, and how others read and respond to those identities. My disability is broadly regarded as invisible, which is to say that I can pass as non-disabled to an observer who is not looking for signs of my particular disability or its impacts. But I experience chronic pain, fatigue and some brain fog. Brain fog is an experience of cognitive impairment that occurs with pain and/or fatigue, such as struggling to comprehend concepts or conversation that one might otherwise find easily manageable. My own brain fog tends to come with forgetfulness, and an inability to say certain words (noun aphasia), while others might experience slurred speech, or auras similar to that of migraine (see Chen, 2014 for a cripistemological reflection on brain fog). Sometimes I use a walking stick, but infrequently enough that when I do it is remarked upon by those who don't know me well. For this chapter, I am explicitly and deliberately not naming my diagnosis. This is in part because my diagnosis is not particularly useful when it comes to understanding the lived realities of my experience, especially as people with the same diagnosis as myself may have very different capacities and capabilities, and be impacted in different ways. This also reflects my deliberate decision to withhold naming my diagnosis from my students when asking for their cooperation in making my teaching spaces and approaches accessible to myself, choosing instead to identify to them as a disabled person. I want them, and you, as the reader, to focus on disability as a broad experience and socio-political identity, rather than the specifics of a medical diagnosis.

Asking

I make a number of requests of my undergraduate students, which are outlined in the module guide, and which I go through at the start of term, and as and when those requests become relevant again. These requests are concerned with:

- the formatting of written work
- communication
- movement in teaching spaces

I request that students present their essays using a particular format: with sans-serif fonts and wide-spaced lines. I am required by my role to mark student essays by using a particular online programme to provide comments, grades and feedback to students. There is no way for the format to be changed once students upload their coursework. Thus, it is up to students to format their work in ways accessible to me. Students may or may not give any particular consideration to impacts on how their essays are read, and for some my classes may be the first time they have done so.

When it comes to communication, I ask students to be forgiving of my poor short-term memory. This means that I may take a few moments to get back on topic if we diverge, or I may ask them to repeat multi-part questions. I explain that I tend to make text-heavy slides because I need the reminders. I also ask them to follow up conversations in which they ask me to do something with emails repeating the request. I explain to them that this functions as a reminder to me to follow it up.

At the start of each term, I inform students that I will not move around the teaching spaces as I lecture. This is in response to earlier student feedback that took rather a dim view of me sitting down. I follow this up with a request that the students who do need to see my face when I talk sit in spaces where they can do so. I explain that I will reserve seating for them, and ensure the various pieces of technology occupying the lectern do not get in their sightlines.

I also invite students to discuss their needs with me, should they wish to or should they find they need to. I explain that I am more than happy to adjust my teaching style, but that I can only guess at their preferences or needs unless they tell me. In the module guide, as well as in the first lecture, this is presented as a part of making a welcoming environment, alongside considerations of how to discuss complex and dangerous topics, and the importance of my students' wellbeing. I return to this topic at regular points, for example by reminding students that lecture recordings are available if they need to miss a lecture, or think it would help their own access needs or study style.

Whys and wherefores

This making of requests, as well as the deliberate expression of my own willingness to make changes to my teaching, reflects my approach that pedagogy is a social relationship (Ellsworth, 1997). In effect, in trying to make explicit that my openness in declaring my own needs is reflected in my openness to consider others' needs, I am attempting to model to my students my sense of fundamental interdependence (Wendell, 1996) in both teaching and broader social contexts: that my teaching is reliant upon their learning, and furthermore, that we are learning together, that our relationships are more complicated than 'lecturer' and 'student', complicated by our identities as people and as members of communities. Within the context of some of my teaching, this reflects all broader social themes explored within lectures and seminars, as well as an encouragement for students to bring their personal experience into their learning and their reflections. At the same time, in positioning my requests close to my statements about my expectations as a lecturer, I am hoping to encourage students to see the requests as a part of their responsibilities as students, that formatting their coursework in a particular way is on a par with meeting deadlines and reading book chapters.

In designing my teaching, I take an approach that aims for broad accessibility. I aim to be as accessible to as many people with differing needs and capacities as possible (Hamraie, 2016), although I also recognise that I am restricted in the changes I can make by a pair of intertwined structures. First, I am precariously employed. My employment to date has been on fixed-term contracts, which present their own issues in terms of access. Second, I work within the UK university system, which requires a certain amount of compliance with internal and external regulations, and which positions disability as an individual issue requiring individual response and responsibility.

Taking a collective and social approach to disability and inclusion in spaces where individualised approach is the expected norm can be a risky strategy. This, in opposition to normative expectations, recognises that: '[access] ... is tied to the social organization of participation, even to belonging. Access not only needs to be sought out and fought for ... it also needs to be understood – as a complex form of perception that organizes socio-political relations between people in social space' (Titchkosky, 2011: 4).

The riskiness of embodying disability (Campbell, 2009), in academia, as well as in other spaces, is joined by academic elitism, 'which perceives disabled students as less capable intellectually and less able to perform well than those who currently make up the norm' (Madriaga et al, 2011: 902). Elitism and risk are compounded by a peculiar phenomenon, where, in drawing attention to the problem, we become the problem (Ahmed, 2013, 2017). In the case of academia, needing to ask students for my adjustments, ableism, academic elitism and the limits of an individualised 'adjustment' approach to access as a whole are primed to positioning the disabled person as the problem. This is particularly prominent when it comes to teaching large-scale university classes, where a single lecturer may teach thirty or fifty or well over a hundred students at a time, rendering much individual interaction impossible. In order to find a solution, on a collective level, as well as an individual one, it is worth first digging into the problem a little more.

The problem has multiple aspects. First, disclosing disability is an act of ongoing negotiation, rather than a single event (Kerschbaum, 2014; Price et al, 2017). I am negotiating with my students in terms of their own expectations and willingness to change established habits. Students' expectations are shaped by a multitude of ableist discourses about disability, education and academia. This, in and of itself, is a relatively minor complication. Due to the variable nature of my disability, I am used to repeated adjustments and re-stating my needs for those who have grown used to one way of seeing me, and especially if I have gone several weeks without using a visible aid when they have been watching. However, it is tiresome. And each return to negotiating brings back the risk that comes from stating a problem.

When students are open to change, the negotiation is straightforward, but there are plenty of reasons why students resist changes to their established habits, including their own individualised access needs. An example of this: my seated position makes it difficult for a hearing-impaired student to see my face clearly, requiring us both to adjust. It requires them to move seat within the lecture theatre, and me to move the monitor on the lectern and raise my seat higher so as to make my face more visible. Students' resistance is shaped by their expectations of lecturers and disability.

This presents the second part of the problem. Students, particularly those who have gone through the UK school system, as these form the majority of my students, have their expectations around inclusion shaped by the medical-tragedy model of disability (Waterfield et al, 2018). This model positions disability as something to be cured or overcome. It places the responsibility to overcome their disability on the individual. This is the broad discourse around disability that my students have been used to. Exceptions include disabled students, and those who have had disabled people in their lives, although experience of disability, however direct or indirect, is no guarantee of not internalising this discourse. When access takes a medical-tragedy approach, access adaptations, often called 'reasonable adjustments', are provided on an individualised, case-by-case basis, with the explicit aim of normalising the disabled individual. As Mitchell et al (2014) point out, this model of inclusion functions instead as a form of exclusion, wherein the only way to succeed in 'inclusive' spaces is to pass as non-disabled. Inclusion requires 'overcoming'. In addition, disability is equated with receiving professional attention, but not with being a professional (Waterfield et al, 2018), and as a result, the mechanisms of 'making reasonable adjustments' within the spaces of universities are focused on disabled students as receivers of professional attention, but not on disabled academics as professionals themselves. Thus, while students may be aware of adaptations made for themselves or their cohort peers, they do not position lecturers in the category of 'needing provision' as people who have not 'overcome' or as people who are capable. This positioning is reinforced by a lack of disabled academics across universities.

At the same time, discourses of academic elitism result in the belief that those same reasonable adjustments are a form of special treatment and that any truly capable person should be able to meet the normative standards without adjustment. This discourse shapes how academics respond to students' requests for adaptations, often with dismissal and lowered expectations, but also shapes how students regard their own and their peers' adaptations. Students and academics alike internalise academic elitism. They may not recognise when they themselves need adaptations, they become unwilling to ask for adaptations because they do not wish to be seen as weak/less capable and they dismiss others' adaptations as special treatment.

This brings us to the third aspect of the problem. Because the individualised approach means that access is an 'add on' rather than a feature, access requires deliberate deviation from the standard provision, often in ways which mark out the disabled person as obviously different, and which reinforce the perception that this deviation is a form of special treatment. When the access requires a behavioural change or action(s) by others, this 'special treatment' becomes a burden to the others. This is regardless of whether or not they are themselves disabled because the change is not something they themselves benefit from on an individual level. It is an action that is perceived as disadvantaging them and this leads to students and lecturers expecting that making changes to their established routines and behaviours will be burdensome. Invariably, this expectation means that those changes are burdensome to those making them, including when students are making changes in order to make lectures accessible to the lecturer. Just as the individual is responsible for overcoming their disability, the individual is responsible for the burden of their disability, and it is seen as unfair when that burden is passed on to others. This combines with the previously mentioned discourse of adaptation as special treatment. Students without individualised adaptations may regard themselves as at a disadvantage, because not only do they not have special treatment, they are being asked to take on the burden of adapting their behaviour, actions and/or expectations.

Furthermore, in declaring disability, especially when a disability is otherwise invisible, and explicitly asking students to make changes to their established or expected activities, I open myself to a loss of authority. Given that disability is positioned in opposition to authority, in repositioning myself as a receiver of professional attention, I risk losing my authority as a lecturer, an authority already made fragile by my precarity, my gender and my appearance as a fat woman with brightly dyed hair. In compounding this by asking for 'special treatment', I am intensely aware of the risk I take in not only being open about my disability, but in asking students to make adaptations to their routine behaviours.

Awareness of the problems and complications presented by declaring disability and the aforementioned risk is my own internalised ableism and academic elitism. As a student, I experienced being at the receiving end of this, having had requested adaptations ignored, and having other students publicly question why I had been allowed to do something differently to the majority of students. And whenever this story comes up, I also like to mention that the lecturers dealt with this questioning with grace and care, and in a way to make continued public disagreement impossible. These experiences made me determined to provide adaptations and adjustments for my students to the best of my ability, but also mean that I struggle with making my disability visible to students. I worry that rather than being seen as a request for 'reasonable adjustments', they are seen as an unreasonable burden on them, brought about by my own nit-picking and over fussy expectations.

But ...

After considering the problem(s), I nonetheless decided to ask my students to engage in making changes to their behaviours and actions. And I have chosen to continue doing so, although I tweak my approach each time, depending on factors such as the size of the class and the cohort present. In this, I am making what Scott and Herold (2018) describe as a strategic pedagogical decision, a part of the 'opportunity to resist compulsory able-bodiedness' (Scott and Herold, 2018: 8). Being invisibly disabled, I do so in part with what Price et al (2017) refer to as a trickster strategy. I use being initially read as non-disabled to '[disrupt] the status quo through subversive means' (Price et al, 2017: n.p.).

Bringing my disability into the classroom and making it visible is also part of a wider pedagogical approach focusing on social justice, supporting students to develop their critical reflection on knowledge itself, and to consider their learning in wider contexts than that of passing assessments. Given the subject and topic areas I teach in, most of which fall under the umbrella of sociology, as well as my research specialism in embodied disability experience, I find students are interested in personal narratives and respond to the topics at hand with their personal experiences in mind. Rather than dissuading them from using their personal experience, I want to bring that experience into the classroom and, to quote bell hooks (1994), as a part of that practice:

> students are not the only ones who are asked to share, to confess ... When [lecturers] bring narratives of their experiences into classroom discussions it eliminates the possibility that we can function as all-knowing, silent interrogators. It is often productive if professors take the first risk, linking confessional narratives to academic discussions so as to show how experience can illuminate and enhance our understanding of academic material. (hooks, 1994: 21)

Students' responses

I present my requests as a part of my introduction to the module. I present students with a set of clear actions as a part of the adaptation requests. This has a double purpose: first, it uses the unequal power relation between us to frame adjustment requests as a part of my expectations for their conduct, and this means they are more likely to actually do as I need them to. Second, the clear actions are framed in a way that seeks to minimise the load I'm placing on students. By making them a part of my expectations, they can also be read as a part of the course rather than as an additional burden. However, I do make it explicit that these are disability adaptations.

Students have, on the whole, responded well to this approach, although I feel there is also a certain amount of serendipity in this. I am not the only visibly disabled person in my department and I teach in a discipline which addresses inequalities. Explicitly labelling my requests as disability adaptations has, thus far, increased the numbers who make the changes, compared to previous times, when I presented my requests around formatting and communication only as course requirements. Some students do still ignore my requests, and some of them do complain of additional burden, or object to my classroom practices – there is always one – but they are very much in the minority. It is hard to tell if this lack of objection is down to the aforementioned power dynamic, or because students actually support me. However, the outcome is positive enough for me to take it as a positive overall.

Being open about my disability has also had a positive impact on my disabled students. Some have opened up to me about their own disabilities, while others have felt supported and encouraged to ask for their own adaptations, in my classes, and in those of other lecturers. This alone is worth the personal risks.

Reflective questions

These reflective questions may help you personally, but should also be considered if you have line management or supervisory responsibilities for lecturers or graduate teaching assistants.

- How does my teaching practice reflect my standpoints, personal politics or beliefs?
- Am I an academic elitist?[1]
- Is there an adaptation I would benefit from when it comes to classroom teaching or wider academic practice?
- Can this adaptation be phrased in terms of clear action(s) for students to take? If not, how else could it be presented?
- Does the benefit of the adaptation outweigh the risks? If you have a management/supervisory role, could use your power to take on some of that risk yourself?
- How else could I make my teaching and academic practice (on multiple levels) flexibly accessible to incorporate a range of possible needs?

Recommendations

Again, while these recommendations might help you in your teaching, they should also be considered from a line management, supervisory, or mentoring viewpoint.

- Consider your needs as a part of your teaching practice – in the same way you consider your students' needs.
- Consider how you can make your teaching more accessible with the tools you already have at your disposal.

- Disability visibility is great, but only when you feel safe and supported – if you feel the personal/professional costs outweigh the positive impacts (and/or necessity of adaptations), you should not feel pressured into visibility.
- Not everyone can pass. If you can't, you are also not required to put disability front and centre of everything you do.
- Consider how you can do better – by yourself, and by your students and colleagues.

Note
[1] Yes, you are. So how can you do better?

References
Ahmed, S. (2013). Making feminist points. 11 September. Retrieved 27 July 2018, from Feministkilljoys website: https://feministkilljoys.com/2013/09/11/making-feminist-points/
Ahmed, S. (2017). *Living a Feminist Life.* New York: Duke University Press.
Campbell, F.K. (2009). Having a career in disability studies without even becoming disabled! The strains of the disabled teaching body. *International Journal of Inclusive Education*, 13(7), 713–725. https://doi.org/10.1080/13603110903046002
Chen, M.Y. (2014). Brain fog: The race for cripistemology. *Journal of Literary and Cultural Disability Studies*, 8(2), 171–184. https://doi.org/ 10.1353/jlc.2014.0015
Ellsworth, E. (1997). *Teaching Positions: Difference, Pedagogy, and the Power of Address.* New York: Teachers College Press.
Hamraie, A. (2016). Beyond accommodation: Disability, feminist philosophy, and the design of everyday academic life. *PhiloSOPHIA*, 6(2), 259–271. https://doi.org/10.1353/phi.2016.0022
hooks, bell. (1994). *Teaching to Transgress: Education as the Practice of Freedom.* New York: Routledge.
Kerschbaum, S.L. (2014). On rhetorical agency and disclosing disability in academic writing. *Rhetoric Review*, 33(1), 55–71. https://doi.org/10.1080/07350198.2014.856730

Madriaga, M., Hanson, K., Kay, H., & Walker, A. (2011). Marking-out normalcy and disability in higher education. *British Journal of Sociology of Education*, 32(6), 901–920. https://doi.org/10.1080/01425692.2011.596380

Mitchell, D.T., Snyder, S.L., & Ware, L. (2014). '[Every] child left behind': Curricular cripistemologies and the crip/queer art of failure. *Journal of Literary & Cultural Disability Studies*, 8(3), 295–313. https://doi.org/10.3828/jlcds.2014.24

Price, M., Salzer, M.S., O'Shea, A., & Kerschbaum, S. (2017). Disclosure of mental disability by college and university faculty: The negotiation of accommodations, supports, and barriers. *Disability Studies Quarterly*, 37(2). http://dx.doi.org/10.18061/dsq.v37i2.5487

Scott, J.-A., & Herold, K.P. (2018). Almost passing: Using disability disclosure to recalibrate able-bodied bias in the classroom. In: Jeffress, M.S. (ed), *International Perspectives on Teaching with Disability: Overcoming Obstacles and Enriching Lives*. London: Routledge.

Titchkosky, T. (2011). *The Question of Access: Disability, Space, MEaning*. Toronto: University of Toronto Press.

Waterfield, B., Beagan, B.B., & Weinberg, M. (2018). Disabled academics: A case study in Canadian universities. *Disability & Society*, 33(3), 327–348. https://doi.org/10.1080/09687599.2017.1411251

Wendell, S. (1996). *The Rejected Body: Feminist Philosophical Reflections on Disability*. New York: Routledge.

12

#AutisticsInAcademia

Chloe Farahar and Annette Foster

Introduction

Community definition of Autistic experience

Autism diagnostic features are defined by the current Diagnostic and Statistical manual (DSM V5) as 'persistent impairment in reciprocal social communication and social interaction; restricted, repetitive patterns of behaviour, interests, or activities, [where] symptoms are present from early childhood and limit or impair everyday functioning' (American Psychiatric Association, 2013: 53). The DSM goes on to state, 'some fascinations and routines may relate to hyper- or hypo-reactivity to sensory input, manifest through extreme response to e.g. sounds; textures; smell; touch' (54). Autistic people may also be diagnosed with accompanying intellectual disability and/or language impairment. However, it is important to note that these impairments are not core specifiers for an autism diagnosis (American Psychiatric Association, 2013; World Health Organization, 2018). While this is the official DSM definition of 'autism spectrum disorder' – an outsider's perspective – there is utility in presenting the lived experience definition of Autistic experience:

> Autism is a developmental phenomenon, meaning that it begins in utero and has a pervasive influence

on development, on multiple levels, throughout the lifespan. Autism produces distinctive, atypical ways of thinking, moving, interaction, and sensory and cognitive processing. One analogy that has often been made is that Autistic individuals have a different neurological "operating system" than non-autistic individuals. (Walker, 2014b)

From our perspective, and including the perspective of other Autistic people we have worked with, the most important aspect of being Autistic is our sensory processing. The differences in the way we, and other Autistic people, interact and communicate socially can be explained by the way we sensorially experience the world. This sensory experience also explains our affinity for routine and structure. For an Autistic person, the sensory and thus social environment can often be loud, smelly, bright and chaotic, to an extreme that can be painful. Controlling, structuring and making predictable as much of our experiences within this sensorially chaotic and often surprising world helps us regulate what would otherwise be a constant sensory onslaught.

We cannot emphasise enough that most Autistic experiences and behaviours can be explained by our hyper- or hypo-reactive sensory processing. Simply adopting this viewpoint may assist non-autistic people to gain an understanding of our experiences, which can help facilitate interacting, accommodating and working with an Autistic peer, colleague, or employee.

A note on language

We describe ourselves and our community as Autistic people rather than 'people with autism'. Although there are technical reasons for this, it is much easier to explain this with everyday parallel examples. For instance, it is not appropriate or factually accurate to describe a White British woman as a person with Whiteness, Britishness and womanness, and so predominantly Autistic people tend to describe themselves using identity-first language, not describing themselves as a 'person with

Autisticness' (or autism; Gernsbacher, 2017; Identity-First Autistic, 2016; Sinclair, 2013).

To create an empathic relationship with us, we would suggest considering the importance of our Autistic experience with/ of the world and letting go of the notion that the 'diagnosis' has discovered that we have some sort of 'disease' or pathology. The notion that an Autistic person has not been afflicted by some form of pathology is encapsulated in a model known as the neurodivergence paradigm, which refers to the biological fact that all human brains differ from one another (Walker, 2014a), and as such there is no one right or normal brain, or consequently, behaviour (Holmes & Patrick, 2018).

Autistics in academia

Autistic people are found everywhere in academia, from the sciences through to the humanities and all disciplines in between. We are in science fields, lending credence to the stereotypes (Wei et al, 2013), and we are also in the social sciences, humanities and creative disciplines like drama and the arts (Playing A/Part, 2019). Quite simply, we are in all disciplines because we are a diverse population, more so than stereotypes would have us believe. This means that in academia you are most likely working with, alongside, managing, or being managed by Autistic people – whether they have disclosed or not. Indeed, many academics do not disclose their Autistic identity to their institutions for fear of discrimination (Autistic in Academe, 2015; Prior, 2017). We have been privileged to be sought out for conversations and questions from undisclosed Autistics or those suspecting that they are Autistic, colleagues who maintain a concealable and concealed identity for fear of being othered and seen in a different light (Quinn & Chaudoir, 2009).

The understanding of Autistic experience in its numerous forms is evolving and we have been privileged to be able to challenge and contribute towards this development. Historically, the first tranche of research focused on male children and later assumed that autism was the result of an 'extreme male-brain' (Baron-Cohen, 2002; see also Fine, 2010; Jack, 2011; Krahn and Fenton, 2012). However, within 20 years of this research we have realised that this was a narrow picture of the Autistic population. Unfortunately, many stereotypes about Autistic people found in the media remain anchored in these models. However, research is slowly coming to realise that it is not just males who are Autistic – that it is a non-gendered experience. There are male, female, non-binary and trans Autistic people (Dewinter et al, 2017; Walsh et al, 2018), with the male-to-female ratio estimated as 2:1 (Grove et al, 2016; Kim et al, 2011; Mattila et al, 2011), but arguably more likely 1:1.

This means that until very recently both of us would be considered rare people indeed: Autistic academic women. With this growing understanding that Autistic experience is non-gendered and not age-related we are seeing an increase in people discovering their Autistic identity later in life. We have personally experienced this and seen this first-hand with people we work with in the university. For these reasons, we are seeing an increase in the number of Autistic university students, and consequently, an increase in Autistic academic staff. For instance, in 2018 there were 140 disclosed Autistic academic staff in higher education, compared with 65 in 2014 (HESA, 2014). So, with numbers of people disclosing that they are Autistic increasing, what are the challenges to being Autistic in academia?

The challenges of being Autistic in academia

Disclosure

While we are both openly Autistic self-advocates, we know of many people in university who are not prepared to disclose their Autistic status for fear of negative repercussions. Our colleagues cite several reasons for non-disclosure, which include stigmatisation: stereotypes; prejudice; and discriminatory behaviour that includes infantilism, benevolence and being perceived as agentic and cold, or overly emotional. On the whole, our own disclosures have been met with positivity: questioning colleagues wishing to increase understanding and offers of reasonable accommodation by our institutions. Nonetheless, we have also experienced some of the downsides to disclosing our Autistic identity, the same experiences our Autistic colleagues cite as preventing them from disclosing.

Annette's school support officer informed her they had never supported a disabled PhD student before and did not know how to support her. Consequently, Annette's school have been unwilling to provide reasonable adjustment when she has multiple PhD deadlines one day apart. Several disabled postgraduate students must intermit when they need extensions such as these, losing access to the university support they need to continue their PhD while intermitting, when what was required was a two-week extension. Disabled academics are already working hard to adjust to an environment not designed with them in mind: all that is asked is reasonable adjustments to make the academic experience equitable. This should include reasonable adjustment to PhD deadlines.

Chloe had not been prepared for some of the issues that self-disclosure raised for her. Diagnosed in her second year of her PhD she believed that disclosure would lead to understanding and acceptance of her 'weirdness', a word that Chloe was all too familiar with. She was pleased that overall, this is what happened. However, what she had not prepared for was the occasional benevolent stigma and infantilism that also accompanied her disclosure, or colleagues questioning her Autistic identity ("Why do you think you're Autistic?"). For Annette, her diagnosis was her raison d'etre for starting a doctorate, her PhD research based as it is on her disclosure and self-advocacy. However, like Chloe, Annette has also experienced similar instances where her Autistic identity has been questioned ("You are not Autistic: your diagnosis is wrong"; "You don't seem Autistic?"). It has not all been negative of course. Chloe and Annette also received more offers of work, particularly collaborative offers based on their Autistic identity, knowledge and expertise, and Chloe's disclosure had no effect on her relationship with her PhD supervisor, for instance, who continued to treat her as the highly competent candidate that she was.

Institutional challenges

As Autistic people we have both faced challenges from institutional systems and the environment of a university. Our individual sensorial hyper- and hypo-sensitivities have meant that the academic environment can be uniquely challenging for each of us.

Annette's hypersensitivity predominantly relates to visual, auditory and olfactory senses, along with a need for larger personal space around her. These hypersensitivities make the dedicated postgraduate study space in her school challenging, as it is a large glass fronted area, colloquially known as the 'fishbowl'. The design of this space impacted on Annette as the glass walls and door make the space very bright, and activity outside the space is distracting, while noises from outside the space are amplified by the glass walls.

When Annette attempted to access a carrel at the university library none were vacant, and the library did not have a waiting list. It took two months of daily visits before Annette secured an open carrel. Unfortunately, this was on a noisy balcony above an open-plan study area so her daily visits to the desk continued. Some six months later Annette acquired a walled private carrel, but Annette's Disabled Student's Allowance would not cover her carrel rental fees, and to date she continues to have to self-fund this space. These examples demonstrate possible environmental and institutional systems that can negatively impact Autistic academics.

Although as Autistic academics we have both experienced negative interactions and situations due to our neurotype, we would like to focus on the positive experiences we had post-disclosure to provide institutions with a template of what underpins a supportive environment for Autistic people. While we focus predominantly on Autistic experience, much of what we discuss can be applied to other experiences. Social and generalised anxiety, depression (psychological-divergences, typically referred to as 'mental illnesses'; Farahar, 2020) and other neurodevelopmental differences such as dyslexia would derive benefit from the inclusive changes discussed.

What 'good' looks like

The challenge of change: the need for routine

> **Differences and challenges**: repetitive behaviours (and thoughts); need for routine, sameness, and predictability; sensory overwhelm

Chloe struggles to adapt to changes that she lacks control over (due to cognitive processing and 'scripting' conversations; room schematics; and tasks). Chloe's school administration manager, who is aware that she is Autistic, has arranged to let Chloe know as far in advance when there are any changes to offices. Chloe is also involved in the selection of rooms that she knows suit her personal sensory processing capabilities, and is currently in a room where she can control the lights and temperature. This is not typical practice and Chloe remains grateful to the administration manager for accommodating her needs.

Struggling with change applies to other academic situations, such as changes to timetabling and university strike action (which disrupts routine). The take home message is that Autistic people benefit from a sense of agency when any form of change occurs. Where possible, reduce the distress of change by: preparing Autistic colleagues; avoiding change where practical; and informing ahead of time where avoiding change is not possible.

Meetings, presenting, interviews and PhD vivas

> **Differences and challenges**: atypical eye contact; cognitive scripting; difficulty processing in real time; literal, blunt, black and white thinking; need for specificity

Autistic people are typically considered to have deficits in social communication. Recent research has demonstrated that Autistic people can be adept at social interaction *when it is with other Autistic people* (Crompton et al, 2019). The difficulty we face is during cross-neurotype interactions (that is, Autistic and non-autistic), and this is known as the double empathy problem (Milton, 2012). As academics it is possible to avoid cross-neurotype interactions so that our differences listed are less likely to cause us distress – hiding in our offices is one good reason to become an academic! However, there are obviously occasions where we need to attend meetings, reviews, present to a group, attend interviews and deliver PhD vivas and so on.

Chloe requested reasonable accommodations for her PhD viva. The adjustment needs contained in Chloe's 'Guidance for Viva examination of Autistic/neurodivergent PhD Students' (free to access; Farahar, 2019a) is not exhaustive, nor is it necessary to accommodate all suggestions it contains for every Autistic person. For example, Chloe's viva document was sent to her examiners, and some of her requested adjustments and accommodation of needs were as follows:

- **Choice of room**: settling on one that Chloe was familiar with (relating to scripting; need for specificity; cognitive and processing need for planning ahead, otherwise Chloe exhausts herself thinking of every possible scenario, including where she will be in physical space).
- **Atypical eye contact**: Chloe processes information visually, so she does not make eye contact as she cannot 'see' what she is processing. Examiners were informed that Chloe would be unlikely to make eye contact, and she would be likely to look past the examiners; look at a blank wall; close her eyes.
- **Clear and specific instructions**: Chloe received clear instructions on the process of the exam, as well as an explanation of the procedure and method of examination at the start of the viva. This allowed time to process information, which is linked to difficulties processing in real time, a need for specificity, anxiety and cognitive scripting/preparing.

The recommendations made here for viva can easily be adapted for meetings and interview situations, as well as presentations when Autistic people deliver them.

Something that might help Autistic academics in many situations is the ability to 'stim' with an object and/or wear noise-reducing headphones/earphones. Stimming refers to the term self-stimulatory behaviour, which is something that all humans do. Many people fidget with an object or jiggle their leg when nervous or bored, but Autistic people tend to stim to a greater degree and for numerous reasons – when we are sad, happy, anxious, overly energetic – and Autistic people tend to stim more when overwhelmed to help regulate their senses. Sensory overwhelm (sensory overload/difficulty regulating sensory input) can lead to meltdown (emotional explosion/extreme stress reaction); shutdown (emotional implosion/retreating from the world); and/or burnout. Autistic burnout is not to be confused with the typical understanding of burnout. At times Autistic burnout can look like depression (https://soyoureAutistic.com/meltdown-shutdown-burnout/), but differs in that it tends to be episodic, and follows extreme sensory and/or social exhaustion. It is possible to limit or reduce Autistic burnout by saying 'no' to things, and preparing for downtime following activities likely to solicit overwhelm and burnout. Sometimes burnout is unavoidable due to commitments, and the Autistic person needs downtime which may last days, weeks, or sadly even months.

Having attended a meeting at Parliament the previous day and with burnout imminent, Chloe attended a teachers' meeting while sat fiddling with a squishy toy and wearing noise-reducing earphones. In situations like this we are better able to pay attention if we can stim freely without feeling judged, and Chloe's colleagues at the meeting were aware she is Autistic and did not make her feel uncomfortable for regulating her senses.

Networking (urghhhh!), socialising and office politics

Differences and challenges: atypical eye contact; social convention understanding; missing social cues and social communication differences; cognitive scripting; sensory overwhelm; burnout

Networking is the dreaded academic phenomenon for many an Autistic academic, as it pits all our challenges together in one place: cross-neurotype interactions; atypical eye contact and social communication; change to routine and sameness; unpredictability; and sensory overwhelm (as many events are held in large, crowded, noisy spaces). As you can imagine, these challenges create difficulty prior to the event, with many Autistic people mentally preparing for what they should do and say, as well as creating extreme anxiety at the time, followed by social and sensory burnout post-networking (which might mean days in bed). Quite simply, it is exhausting! Both of us have avoided networking situations to prevent extreme anxiety and exhaustion.

There are ways of managing the anxiety and difficulties that arise from networking if an Autistic person really cannot avoid them. Chloe has on several occasions emailed someone she was interested in talking to at conferences and explained her situation – that she is Autistic and would like to discuss X, Y, Z with them, so could they please spare five minutes to talk to the awkwardly hovering, shaven-headed woman? For networking or social events on campus offer to go with your Autistic colleague, perhaps agree with them that you will check in with them throughout the event. You can also offer to be seated near them for staff meals and talk to them about their interests. Chloe's research support officer has a standing offer to attend networking events on campus with her, which she is very grateful for.

It is possible that Autistic colleagues lose out on career opportunities due to missing social engagements such as these, so please remember your Autistic colleagues for projects and collaboration. Remember, there are other ways of networking that suit lots of neurotypes, including neurotypical people who are too busy to attend events or meet face-to-face. Twitter is a great place to network and find other academics, including #AutisticsInAcademia – just remember that some of us will still find lots of online interaction exhausting, but at least not to the same degree as face-to-face.

Teaching, marking and administrative duties

Differences and challenges: perfectionism; Autistic inertia; co-occurring experiences for example. dyslexia; dyspraxia; sensory overwhelm; burnout

Due to differences in executive functioning which can include issues of Autistic inertia (extreme difficulty starting, stopping, or switching tasks) the three-week turnaround of returning student assignments can be incredibly stressful, and a particularly challenging academic task for someone like Annette who is also Dyslexic. For most academics, the first few assignments take longer to mark, and then they get the hang of it. For Annette, all marking takes longer per student due to difficulties reading (dyslexia); traversing the marking systems due to dyspraxia (a neurodevelopmental difference affecting fine and/or gross motor skills, which can affect, for example, typing; time management; planning and organisation, see Dyspraxia Foundation, n.d.); and lack of specific and concise marking guidelines (specificity). Annette has had some better marking experiences where the course convenor has provided clear, concise and detailed marking guidelines and understood that while she may take longer and possibly need a marking extension (particularly when there are multiple marking deadlines), the quality of the marking is consistent and of the same standard as her peers.

When it comes to teaching, similar differences in processing occur, and can affect the time taken preparing, teaching and recovering from teaching, particularly when you factor in numerous room changes in a day; teaching above a kitchen; next to a campus bar with music and so on. When you consider the level of processing many Autistic people perform for tasks, Autistic academics take a greater amount of time preparing for teaching. This relates to processing differences, and for some, relates to co-occurs such as dyslexia and dyspraxia (for example, longer reading preparation time), as well as issues of perfectionism, time management and planning. Given the extra cognitive processing and sensory issues during teaching itself, two hours of teaching is effectively three days of work, spoons,[1] and burnout recovery time. We have adjusted our own teaching environment as much as is feasible, with small things such as having the fluorescent lights off, wearing earplugs to dampen complex group discussion noise, and stimming with an object freely (we also bring stim objects for our students to normalise the practice for both ourselves and other students who are anxious, Autistic, have attention differences and so on).

These are just a few example scenarios of our personal Autistic experiences and how our schools have supported us.

A truly inclusive academia: a starting point

In universities student accommodation needs are written into their digital statements and academic staff must adhere to student Inclusive Learning Plans. An important step forward for neurodivergent people in academia would be staff Inclusive Teaching and Working Plans, where people like us can have our needs recognised and enforced. We attempt this on our own initiative, and hope that colleagues and employers support us, but this may not be suitable for some people to attempt themselves, and quite simply, the Equality Act 2010 makes it clear that the onus is not on the disabled person but the employer to instigate change. Inclusive Teaching and Working Plans would function to support the Autistic person by recording how to accommodate for their needs, and in return the university receives the best staff output, reducing mental wellbeing sick days and/or presenteeism. Everybody wins.

Academia is very much a double-edged sword for many Autistic people, affording us the opportunity to focus on our specialist areas, but also the very real issue of becoming isolated (through no fault of the institution, staff, or Autistic individual). What is sorely needed in universities is a service on campuses for staff who need accommodations, much like students receive. As well as Inclusive Teaching and Working Plans, part of this service would include setting up and maintaining support groups for staff who may benefit from peer to peer support. We suggest this on the back of our highly successful and important Autistic social groups which we run for students, finding that Autistic identity, community, culture and spaces offer protective properties for Autistic wellbeing (Belek, 2019; Davidson, 2008; https://soyoureAutistic.com). Writing basic needs and accommodations into an Inclusive Teaching and Working Plan for staff would set the environment up for effective and inclusive academic institutions.

Conclusion

Student support services are seeing increases in Autistic students enrolling year on year (the University of Kent received 120 Autistic students enrolling in the 2019/2020 intake, a significant increase on the 80 students enrolling in the 2018/19 intake). Logically, there will also be a parallel increase in the number of Autistic staff in universities over the coming years, in part thanks to Autistic self-advocacy, community and culture becoming more widespread and visible. Making our institutions neurodivergent inclusive in their work practices, and social and physical environments will not only better support your Autistic colleagues and employees, but also make a suitable environment for all students and staff.

Being Autistic does not inherently mean that we struggle. However, people's attitudes, behaviour and lack of knowledge about and toward us means that we are often challenged by our physical and social environment (this is the social model of disability; Oliver & Sapey, 1999; Woods, 2017). While some environments are harder to have an impact on (for example, grocery stores), academia is one setting where diversity and inclusion are built into its ethos. We both wish to continue our careers in academia and wish to improve the academic environment for Autistic students and staff. We hope we have given you an insight into our Autistic experience and that the practical suggestions for making your university more inclusive prove helpful.

Reflective questions

- Have you attended any Autistic experience training, and was it led by an Autistic person or persons?
- Consider your sources of information about Autistic experience, does it include Autistic perspectives?
- Scrutinise your internal attitudes about Autistic people – if you learnt a colleague is Autistic after a period of knowing them, did your attitude change? And if so, was it for the better, or worse (for example, before did you see them as competent,

yet awkward/quirky, and after did you seem them as less agentic, less capable and you pitied them)?

- Is your understanding of Autistic experience based largely or solely on the pathological perspective?
- Does your education establishment formally consider the reasonable accommodation that academics with visible and invisible disabilities need?

Recommendations

Consider your Autistic colleague on an individual basis, finding out how we want to identify and disclose to you, our colleagues, and our peers (if at all). Focus on our strengths and accommodate where you can so that we face fewer challenges. Tackle stigma and discrimination where you encounter it, do not stand for stereotyping or throwaway comments, even when they are not directed at your Autistic colleague/member of staff – we hear these comments and sometimes we do not have the confidence or the energy to keep fighting the stereotypes alone. Be our ally, you will have a grateful and hardworking colleague in return. We ask that you do not question our Autistic identity/status, or ask us what makes us Autistic, because we "don't look Autistic" to you. Take our disclosure of our Autistic status at face value and ask respectfully what *you* can do to accommodate us.

Insist on Autistic-developed, led and delivered training – and pay those Autistic trainers. There is an ongoing practice of hosting 'autism' training delivered by organisations and charities, paying non-autistic trainers. This training typically falls short of the lived-experience narrative and practical recommendations for accommodating Autistic people in the workplace. There is a difference between learning about the theory of 'autism' as a pathological concept and learning about neurodivergent experiences and practical recommendations as delivered by seasoned Autistic trainers. Take a look at the training we offer at soyoureAutistic.com.

We encourage you to read up on the double empathy problem by Dr Damian Milton (2012). Autistic people are not deficient in communication ability. When together, Autistic people manage to understand one another due to similar frames of reference and experience of the world. Communication difficulties arise during cross-neurotype interactions – that is between non-autistic and Autistic (Crompton et al, 2019). Quite simply we speak different languages. Autistic people already work incredibly hard to understand the language and experiences of non-autistic people, *we ask that you learn our language and culture so that we can meet one another on a more equitable footing.*

Finally, and importantly, we *challenge universities to develop Inclusive Teaching and Working Plans* with their student support services, human resources and most importantly #ActuallyAutistic personnel and/or trainers. Putting into practice support for your valued disabled academics will lead to a less stressful working environment for us, and you will have enabled colleagues to become the role models students with and without Inclusive Learning Plans need. What better way to learn how to make your institution inclusive of diversity than from the people teaching your students?

Note
1 Spoon theory refers to the disability metaphor defined by Christine Miserandino (2003) who has Lupus. To explain the limited energy a disabled person has compared to a non-disabled person Christine had to hand cutlery – spoons – to demonstrate to a non-disabled friend how much energy she expends in a day, which is considerably more than a non-disabled person. Autistic people use spoon theory, and it is not unheard of for us to say "Sorry, I don't have the spoons today" when asked to do something we do not have the energy for.

Acknowledgements
We give thanks to Dévan Rajendran and Louis Bishopp-Ford for their comments on earlier drafts of this chapter.

References
American Psychiatric Association. (2013). *Diagnostic and Statistical Manual of Mental Disorders (DSM-5®).* Arlington, Virginia: American Psychiatric Publishing.
Autistic in Academe. (2015). Retrieved December 2019, from Conditionally accepted: A search for scholars on the margins of academia. https://conditionallyaccepted.com/2015/03/17/autism/

Baron-Cohen, S. (2002). The extreme male brain theory of autism. *Trends in Cognitive Sciences*, 6(6), 248–254. doi:10.1016/S1364-6613(02)01904-6

Belek, B. (2019). An anthropological perspective on autism. *Philosophy, Psychiatry, & Psychology*, 26(3), 231–241. doi:10.1353/ppp.2019.0038

Crompton, C.J., Fletcher-Watson, S., & Ropar, D. (2019). Autistic peer to peer information transfer is highly effective. *OSF Preprints*. 24 September. doi:10.31219/osf.io/j4knx

Davidson, J. (2008). Autistic culture online: Virtual communication and cultural expression on the spectrum. *Social & Cultural Geography*, 9(7), 791–806. doi:10.1080/14649360802382586

Dewinter, J., De Graaf, H., & Begeer, S. (2017). Sexual orientation, gender identity, and romantic relationships in adolescents and adults with autism spectrum disorder. *Journal of Autism and Developmental Disorders*, 47(9), 2927–2934. doi:10.1007/s10803-017-3199-9

Dolmage, J. (2017). *Academic ableism: Disability and higher education*. Michigan: University of Michigan Press.

Dyspraxia Foundation. (n.d.). *Dyspraxia at a Glance … What is Dyspraxia?* https://dyspraxiafoundation.org.uk/about-dyspraxia/dyspraxia-glance/

Farahar, C. (2019a). *University Reasonable Adjustments.* Retrieved December 2019, from So, You're Autistic? https://soyoureAutistic.com/university-reasonable-adjustments/

Farahar, C. (2019b). *The Importance of Language: What's in a Name?* 29 March. Retrieved from So, You're Autistic? https://soyoureAutistic.com/the-importance-of-language-whats-in-a-name/

Farahar, C. (2020). Stigmaphrenia: Reducing mental health stigma with a script about neurodiversity. In D. Milton (ed), *The Neurodiversity Reader: Exploring Concepts, Lived Experience and Implications for Practice.* UK: Pavilion.

Fine, C. (2010). *Delusions of Gender: How Our minds, Society, and Neurosexism Create Difference.* London: Icon Books.

Gernsbacher, M.A. (2017). Editorial perspective: The use of person-first language in scholarly writing may accentuate stigma. *Journal of Child Psychology and Psychiatry*, 58(7), 859–861. doi:10.1111/jcpp.12706

Grove, R., Hoekstra, R.A., Wierda, M., & Begeer, S. (2016). Exploring sex differences in Autistic traits: A factor analytic study of adults with autism. *Autism*, 21(6), 760–768. doi:10.1177/1362361316667283

HESA. (2014). Who's working in HE? Personal characteristics by academic employment function. www.hesa.ac.uk/data-and-analysis/staff/working-in-he/characteristics

Holmes, A.J., & Patrick, L.M. (2018). The myth of optimality in clinical neuroscience. *Trends in Cognitive Sciences*, 22(3), 241–257. doi:10.1016/j.tics.2017.12.006

Identity-First Autistic. (2016). *Welcome to Identity-First Autistic.* www.identityfirstAutistic.org/

Jack, J. (2011). 'The extreme male brain?' Incrementum and the rhetorical gendering of autism. *Disability Studies Quarterly*, 31(3), 14.

Johnstone, L., & Boyle, M. (2018). *The Power Threat Meaning Framework: Overview.* Leicester: British Psychological Society.

Kim, Y.S., Leventhal, B.L., Koh, Y.J., Fombonne, E., Laska, E., Lim, E.C., . . . Grinker, R.R. (2011). Prevalence of autism spectrum disorders in a total population sample. *American Journal of Psychiatry*, 168, 904–912. doi:10.1176/appi.ajp.2011.10101532

Krahn, T.M., & Fenton, A. (2012). The extreme male brain theory of autism and the potential adverse effects for boys and girls with autism. *Journal of Bioethical Inquiry*, 91(1), 93–103. doi:10.1007/s11673-011-9350-y

Mattila, M.-L., Kielinen, M., Linna, S.-L., Jussila, K., Ebeling, H., Bloigu, R., ... Moilanen, I. (2011). Autism Spectrum Disorders according to DSM-IV-TR and comparison with DSM-5 draft criteria: An epidemiological study. *Journal of the American Academy of Child & Adolescent Psychiatry*, 50(6), 583–592. doi:10.1016/j.jaac.2011.04.001

Milton, D. (2012). On the ontological status of autism: The 'double empathy problem'. *Disability & Society, 27*(6), 883–887. doi:10.1080/09687599.2012.710008

Miserandino, C. (2003). *The Spoon Theory written by Christine Miserandino*. But you don't look sick. https://web.archive.org/web/20191117210039/https://butyoudontlooksick.com/articles/written-by-christine/the-spoon-theory/

Oliver, M., & Sapey, B. (1999). *Social Work with Disabled People* (2nd ed). Basingstoke: Palgrave Macmillan.

Playing A/Part. (2019). *Presentations and Resources*. https://playingapartAutisticgirls.org/inside-out-conference-2019/presentations-and-resources/

Prior, M. (2017). Autistic academics give their thoughts on university life. 10 February. http://theconversation.com/Autistic-academics-give-their-thoughts-on-university-life-72133

Quinn, D.M., & Chaudoir, S.R. (2009). Living with a concealable stigmatized identity: The impact of anticipated stigma, centrality, salience, and cultural stigma on psychological distress and health. *Journal of Personality and Social Psychology*, 97(4), 634–651. doi:10.1037/a0015815

Sinclair, J. (2013). Why I dislike 'person first' language. *Autonomy, the Critical Journal of Interdisciplinary Autism Studies*, 1(2), 1–2.

Walker, N. (2014a). *Neurodiversity: Some Basic Terms & Definitions. Notes on Neurodiversity, Autism, and Cognitive Liberty*, 27 September. http://neurocosmopolitanism.com/neurodiversity-some-basic-terms-definitions/

Walker, N. (2014b). *What is Autism?* 1 March. neurocosmopolitanism. https://neurocosmopolitanism.com/what-is-autism/

Walsh, R.J., Krabbendam, L., Dewinter, J., & Begeer, S. (2018). Brief report: Gender identity differences in Autistic adults: Associations with perceptual and socio-cognitive profiles. *Journal of Autism and Developmental Disorders*, 1–9. doi:10.1007/s10803-018-3702-y

Wei, X., Jennifer, W.Y., Shattuck, P., McCracken, M., & Blackorby, J. (2013). Science, technology, engineering, and mathematics (STEM) participation among college students with an autism spectrum disorder. *Journal of Autism and Developmental Disorders*, 43(7), 1539–1546. doi:10.1007/s10803-012-1700-z

Woods, R. (2017). Exploring how the social model of disability can be re-invigorated for autism: In response to Jonathan Levitt. *Disability & Society*, 32(7), 1090–1095. doi:10.1080/09687599.2017.1328157

World Health Organization. (2018). *ICD-11: International Classification of Diseases for Mortality and Mobidity Statistics* (Vol. 11). Geneva: World Health Organization.

13

"I've always wanted to be a nurse ...": challenging academic ableist assumptions

Jo Sullivan

Introduction

Western capitalist ideology has greatly influenced the emphasis on making graduates 'corporate-ready' (Eley, 2010), although it is argued that the point of education is for individuals to identify the dominant work-based ideology and resist becoming indoctrinated (Brookfield and Holst, 2010). Despite this, higher education organisations have embraced the corporate message readily, with an almost anxious emphasis on work-based learning. A university education is no longer limited to the acquisition of knowledge, assisting intellectual enquiry and the attainment of critical thinking skills; even in the context of neoliberal educational opportunity, everyone must graduate ready to enter a professional workforce (Olssen and Peters, 2005).

University provides opportunity for individuals to develop, grow and realise ambition. Organisations such as these pride themselves on equality. All those who have reached 'the standard' are welcome, regardless of gender, age, social class, race or disability. This has been created from a neoliberalist political agenda of equity (Davies and Bansel, 2007). Individuals from any part of society should be able to access the transformational power of education, increasing social mobility and economic status (Dearing, 1997). For undergraduates identified as autistic, policy dictates that there is no discrimination against your disability. For many, university life offers an opportunity to immerse themselves in an area of expertise and reconsider themselves after what is likely to have been a stressful and difficult journey through compulsory education (Petrina et al, 2017).

This chapter challenges all higher education organisations to examine their selection, recruitment and crucially, support, of students identified as autistic undertaking a professional degree. A direct example will be demonstrated using the pathway for student nurses undertaking graduate study who are identified as autistic.

Perceptions of autism in academia

Traditional undergraduate education can lend itself to a narrative of self-management and self-directed study. Students have relative freedom in attendance and how they approach their particular chosen area of study. Students wanting to undertake a professional degree leading to a formal professional qualification experience a very different journey. Although recruitment policy does not actively discriminate against them, the odds are already stacked. Potential students will undergo a value-based recruitment process (Cavendish, 2013, Department of Health, 2015) that is latent with ableist assumptions on what meaningful communication looks like and which personal attributes are required to become a successful professional. As individuals progress, they will be exposed to aggressively busy work-based areas where the acquisition of skills is essential and a direct assessment of professional communication is ongoing (Melincavage, 2011). Central to the whole process of success is the ongoing scrutiny of a student's professional suitability.

Although legislation exists to protect and support students with disability, it is not subtle enough to address and challenge the entrenched ableist beliefs organisations may hold regarding individuals with autism (King, 2018). Universities may hold an unconscious absolutist view about what a potential student beginning their undergraduate career should represent. Despite the belief that the process of study itself will transform, influence and ultimately lead to the professional 'birth' of a student, a non-conformist presentation will be considered too high risk or misinterpreted as lacking the capability to make those transformations necessary to become the professional universities they hope to create (Goode, 2007).

Within professional study there is a latent expectation that when undergraduates join work-based placements they will develop a professional identity which totally adheres to that of the status quo. There exists profound pressure to conform to societal norms, therefore repressing elements of disability in order to be viewed as employable (Cunnah, 2015). Employability has an even more significant meaning for disabled individuals as it may be viewed as a vindication of multiple destructive concepts of themselves (Jolly, 2000). To undertake placement, they will be required to conform and embrace the culture of existing teams. Indeed, any deviation from this is viewed negatively and students may be viewed as suspect.

Furthermore, students undertaking professional degrees are subjected to further organisational governance. The level of surveillance that a professional suitability policy imposes has huge impact for a student with autism. All aspects of conduct are considered. There is no part of a student's life that is not subject to scrutiny. A misunderstanding in living accommodation can directly lead to a dismissal. This is even more of a risk if a student is undiagnosed with autism or has chosen not to make a disclosure (Gurbuz et al, 2019). The additional burden that this scrutiny brings needs to be carefully considered, as it is likely to directly impact on new students' anxiety levels. The fear of reprimand or dismissal following a difficulty may disproportionately affect a student identified as autistic, therefore directly influencing their capacity to successfully manage a university career (Wessel et al, 2009).

Elements of ongoing scrutiny include self-conduct, negotiation of communal living areas and leisure activities. There is an inherent assumption that individuals can negotiate their own inclusion with peers and have the capacity to navigate systems should they need support (Ward and Webster, 2018). This may not be the case. Furthermore, a student with autism may have a contrary view regarding what leisure activities are and what purpose they serve. Students arriving at university may have encountered a long history of poor experiences at 'joining in'. Lifelong experiences of being ignored, made to feel unwelcome and letting a team down during a competitive activity can leave new students reluctant to try new social situations and highly avoidant of any social overture (Reeve, 2004). Neurotypical students are likely to struggle with a useful social response to this dilemma and may well judge a situation with ableist assumptions, such as that an individual with autism is not capable of making meaningful social relationships.

Higher education organisations have begun the commitment to integrating students with disabilities but full inclusivity is still lacking. In order to fully meet the challenge of inclusion, universities need to radically re-think how they organise social space and support. Within the confines of academia, adjustment and facilitation is possible, although arguably much more collaboration is needed with students as to how this should look, and what would be most beneficial (Fabri et al, 2013).

The challenges of autism and undergraduate nurse study

Students who undertake a nursing degree will come into contact with a variety of staff during the three years of their study. Lecturers on nursing undergraduate programmes will have a clinical background in nursing (NMC, 2018). Due to breadth of professional experiences, there is often a diverse professional approach from academic staff. Experiences with difference and disability will be varied, with staff attempting to embrace an inclusive ethos when supporting students with difference (Smith, 2010). Conflicts arise as it is likely there will be a strong, subliminally held belief in the medical model of disability. Medical education specifically nurtures a paradigm of 'clinical gaze' (Pedersen, 2010) compounded by individual clinical experiences and exposures (Wilkinson et al, 2017).

The concept and ethos of the NHS[1] Constitution is introduced to students at the pre-interview stage as they are advised to scrutinise the document prior to university interview. The introduction of the Constitution influenced the development of a values-based recruitment process for all applicants to NHS-funded healthcare programmes (Miller and Bird, 2014). Although recent changes to funding mean that student nurses have been temporarily non-bursaried, there has been no re-imagining of recruitment processes. The publication of the NHS Constitution has directly influenced how higher education establishments advertise, interview and recruit potential student nurses. Value-based recruitment is an attempt to identify and recruit students who hold the same behaviours, beliefs and values as the organisation they are hoping to join (Waugh et al, 2014).

This is likely to present many challenges for an individual with autism undertaking the recruitment process: first, the emphasis on group work and subsequent demonstration of leadership skills. This has its limitations as traditionally only the most confident and extrovert candidates are likely to feel able to contribute to this part of the process (Braathen and Sørensen, 2017). This limits the information gained by recruiters. Although these qualities may have their place, they are not essential in becoming a successful care giver. Culturally, society appears to value greatly attributes such as assertiveness, single-mindedness, self-confidence and a generally powerful personal presentation (Awadh and Alyahya, 2013). Individuals may even be dazzled by them, finding them attractive and charismatic. There is little evidence, however, that these personal qualities translate into excellent professionals (Van der Heijde and Van der Heijden, 2014; Hogan et al, 2013; Poropat, 2014). Furthermore, individuals who have a social and communication challenge, or are even just introverted, may be overlooked. They may possess excellent ideas and creativity but they will be invisible in this situation. Undertaking group work with a group of strangers just provides confident individuals with a platform. It tells would-be recruiters little else regarding the values and beliefs of other participants.

In order to be considered for any nursing degree, applicants must make a 'declaration of good character'. As a part of this, they are organisationally obliged to declare any existing disability (NMC, 2015). This cannot be legally enforced and the Nursing and Midwifery Council explain that any such declaration will not exclude individuals from entering a nursing degree course. Arguably, without a declaration, organisations have no point of reference for individuals' needs and this makes it impossible for reasonable adjustments to be made for potential candidates (Cameron et al, 2019). Furthermore, disclosure can nurture a dialogue of openness and ownership of individual challenges. It can put students with a disability in control at the start of their academic journeys, affording both parties the opportunity for discussion and partnership (Santuzzi et al, 2014).

Should an individual choose confidentiality, the Nursing and Midwifery Council makes it clear that, where no such disclosure is made, if a student then encounters professional challenges, the decision as to whether an individual can remain on the course will be directly influenced by their lack of initial disclosure (NMC, 2015). The implication is that a lack of disclosure is directly related to an individual's level of honesty, integrity and suitability (Charmaz, 2010). A student with autism may view this very differently. Past experiences regarding how organisations have received and processed their challenges may have been extremely negative. Approximately 40 per cent of people with autism will report being bullied in educational settings (Rowley et al, 2012). It is unsurprising that individuals identified as autistic may take the opportunity to begin their higher education careers anonymously. Although best practice within an institution may exist, bias and ignorance may be prevalent in individual teaching staff. Not everyone will subscribe to an inclusive stance with strongly held personal beliefs that some disabilities are too insurmountable to produce appropriate professional people (Riddell and Weedon, 2014). Finally, students are entering a new environment already identified as 'different'. There is no opportunity to influence the thoughts, feeling and opinions of peers. The first thing others perceive is impairment and 'otherness', and some individuals may never be able to move a relationship on from this interpretation.

Much societal currency is given to empathy but a strong empathetic response produces a highly charged emotional response. This can impair judgement and lead to deeply prejudicial decisions being made (Prinz, 2011). It is therefore worth considering its place at the centre of policy and nurse recruitment. It appears to have limited useful application as part of professional competency; it provides a potent response that may lead to poorly rationalised decisions being made. How empathy is viewed in the context of care delivery will depend on individual interpretations of its meaning. The NHS Constitution uses empathy and compassion interchangeably. This unhelpful framing promotes ableism within the policy; this may be inadvertent but the impact is profound for those individuals with autism. It will perpetuate the narrative of 'otherness' and imply that those identified as autistic will find it impossible to reach an acceptable professional standard recognised by others.

Careful consideration needs to be given to organisational interpretations of 'compassion' and 'care'. Much has been written and debated regarding an individual with autism's capacity to show empathy and compassion (Baron-Cohen and Wheelwright, 2004; Jones et al, 2010; Montgomery et al, 2016). The display of empathy is considered a basic human attribute. An inability to demonstrate it is considered a cause for alarm in general populations. In nurses, it is seen as abhorrent and highly unprofessional. Society appears to value empathy in carers above most things (Ward, 2016). However, there is a wealth of growing academic evidence that argues against the 'usefulness' of empathy in individuals. Paul Bloom (2017) argues that we feel empathy mostly for those who are like ourselves and those we find attractive. Empathy therefore is heavily biased towards individuals we know and identify with, while disregarding the anonymous. Empathy can be more powerful than fairness and being empathetic does not enhance situations, rather it leads to poor decisions and bad outcomes (Bloom, 2017). Lack of empathy does not make an individual unkind or lacking in morality. Furthermore, using reasoning and compassion as a guide to making professional decisions can prove more equitable and well-balanced, wholly appropriate to a heightened clinical situation (Decety et al, 2010).

Research into how nurses identified as autistic manage in clinical settings is virtually non-existent (Wood and Marshall, 2010). Individual mentorship is key in the successful acquisition of clinical skills (Jack et al, 2018); yet there is no institutionalised process of training potential clinical assessors in how a student with autism thinks, feels, learns and processes the world around them. It is beyond reasonable expectation and blatantly unrealistic to assume that individual mentors will self-educate to navigate the learning requirements of an identified individual. Furthermore, the Nursing and Midwifery Council are clear, the ultimate responsibility for learning environments remains with the university (NMC, 2018).

Student nurses enter busy, dynamic and brutally challenging workplaces after only weeks of university-based orientation. They may find a mixed response in their new clinical settings, with some staff viewing their arrival as burdensome and creating more work for already over-stretched professionals (Last and Fulbrook, 2003). Arguably, student nurses without any additional need face a traditionally held agenda from qualified staff, as the point of their placement is to attain skill that are currently lacking. Some mentors may view this as a positive educational challenge, whereas others may just perceive a deficit. Clinical settings are unlikely to have the opportunity to offer extensive reasonable adjustments to a student with autism; there are so many other perceived priorities that learners' needs are likely to be completely side-lined when situations change and are acutely busy (Jammaers et al, 2016).

More significantly, clinical staff may possess little understanding of how autism will impact on an individual's presentation (Heidgerken et al, 2005). Even if a disclosure is made prior to the student commencing placement, well-meaning clinical assessors can be mystified as to why a learner is not maintaining eye contact or subliminally responding to the needs and demands of new clinical settings. A student may eventually fail placement because of a strong normative value system that can offer no flexibility in the interpretation of professional values. This perpetuates the social construct of usefulness. Students with a disability are excluded because they are deemed as incompetent and unproductive (Oliver, 1990). There is a latent sense of self-protection on behalf of qualified professionals; groupings are formed of similar people to protect the members from 'others'. Cultural practices of exclusion are so embedded that even well-motivated mentors find it impossible to see beyond a perceived deficit and cannot identify potential in an individual with a disability (Kitchin, 1998).

Conclusion

Findings of a survey published by the National Autistic Society claimed that approximately 100,000 adults with autism were unemployed (Staines, 2009). Individuals identified as Autistic can add immense value to working environments, with many of the qualities they innately possess being highly desirable and sought after by employers (Lee and Carter, 2012). The challenge is that public sector and private sector employers may possess an 'awareness' of autism but cannot conceive how it affects individuals or how to provide meaningful, effective support (Lorenz et al, 2016). For real transformation in academia, it will require steadfast support from expertise that understands autism, and an ongoing commitment to responding dynamically to the needs of employees with additional needs.

Reflective questions

- Do you believe we really understand the latent potential of individuals with autism or does academia possess an entrenched idea of 'humanness,' gift and contribution?
- Do you believe that individuals identified as having social and communication difference can become effective nurses? What do you imagine are the barriers to this becoming a reality?
- Do you think that neurodivergent individuals can truly offer compassionate care to communities? Do you believe that this is a skill or an innate state of existence?

Recommendations

Re-think how student recruitment is structured and create an equitable start to the student journey

Beginning with the journey of recruitment, academia needs to re consider how they it assesses student suitability. It is mandatory that every higher education institution offering pre-registration nurse education utilise a value-based recruitment process (Health Education England, 2014). It is absolutely correct that recruiters should be identifying a future workforce that displays emotional integrity, compassion and personal capability, but there is little evidence to suggest that interviews are applying processes with objective rigour (Mazhindu et al, 2016). How useful and objective is it to draw conclusions from body language, eye contact and tone of voice? All of these may be integral to an individual's diagnosis of autism. Value-based recruitment is driven by personal bias, emotional thinking and personal narratives about relatability and meaningfulness (Miller and Bird, 2014). Individual potential deserves scrutiny during the recruitment process. The challenge is how we make this process much less ableist; this particular process is embedded in communication skills, an area unlikely to facilitate a good 'performance' from an individual with a social and communication disability.

We challenge academia to restructure this recruitment process in order to eliminate the inequality it possesses. We need to invent a selection system which highlights all participants' strengths, not just confident neurotypical thinkers: a system, that can assess latent talent and potential in any candidate; that will embrace and nurture difference and not possess formatting that will make it virtually impossible for individuals with difference to succeed.

Create enabling clinical and work-based learning environments

The biggest challenge any student faces is 'belonging' to a team (Brady et al, 2017). Although the development of new skills is a focus, what is likely to drive learners' anxiety is the interpersonal dynamics of an existing clinical team. First placement experience is crucial to building a student's professional identity and self-belief in success (Bakker et al, 2018). These placements need to be chosen carefully and identified as environments that have a genuine capacity to nurture and possess a variety of learning opportunities for students. Consideration needs to be given to condition-specific challenges, such as processing times and executive function. Simple specific changes can make a powerful and transformational difference to learning environments. Once higher education organisations are aware of students' differences, an offer of a differently paced clinical progression needs to be instigated. Academia is likely to make many assumptions about placement staff that are not accurate (Walker et al, 2011). We need to see visible, intensive ongoing support for students while they are continuing their journey in placement.

Reconsider and challenge ableist assumptions on the concept of professionalism

Anecdotally, a student with autism is likely to fail clinical placement due to their inability to demonstrate professional values, such as 'consistently displaying a professional image in behaviour and appearance'. Members of any profession have strongly held belief systems regarding what that behaviour, image and appearance is (Hoeve et al, 2014). Concepts of professionalism are likely to be socially constructed. This, along with an undiluted neurotypical framing of a profession, leads to rigid interpretations of effective and appropriate social interaction. A common issue with students is the misreading of social interaction; these exchanges are highly contextualised and for an individual with social and communication challenges, the subtle difference is hidden and mystifying. This, coupled with preconceptions regarding how individuals with autism apply empathy and compassion, can leave clinical assessors resistant to committing to 'passing' an individual as clinically competent.

An option to redress this is by increasing student's social 'preparedness' before they begin placement through incorporating a bespoke communication module that is highly specific to commonly occurring interactions in clinical settings. This very specific 'exampling' of professional scenarios offers a safe learning environment and can simulate clinical interaction, where individuals can explore their responses and examine their appropriateness or effectiveness (Hope et al, 2011). Practice is about socialising students into professional role. For this to be a successful journey, intensive and appropriate pre-placement work needs to happen with both the organisation and the individual.

Lead the way in innovative thinking and doing the right thing

It is morally reprehensible to offer an expensive university course to students known to have differences, and yet make little to no accommodation for these challenges. The experience is likely to come at a damaging personal cost to the individual.

There are multiple challenges that any student will face when undertaking a course of this calibre; these are more complex with the addition of autism. However, there is everything to play for, individuals develop and grow throughout their time at university, this is one of the fundamental reasons for undertaking further study of any subject. Individuals may come to perceive themselves differently, influenced by manageable challenges, growing success and the competent navigation of complex social interaction.

There is every reason to believe that individuals with autism can have a successful, happy and fulfilling university experience. Furthermore, they possess attributes that the nursing profession would benefit from greatly: attention to detail, a rigorous respect for regulation and commitment to their chosen field. Above all else, for students to have made it as far as higher education has usually taken immense personal courage and means having overcome so many barriers to success in challenging situations (MacLeod et al, 2018). Organisations should embrace and utilise this amount of commitment by continuing to facilitate student progression, encouraging successful and fulfilment while utilising well-structured policy to embed and enhance excellent practice.

A fundamental question should be: what does a successful university experience look like for those on the autistic spectrum? Is it merely about the acquisition of a formal academic qualification, or are higher education organisations going to display more ambition and commitment than this, by possessing a meaningful and inclusive vision of enhancing individuals' lives for the better? In my view, universities should – possibly for the first time – provide a sense of belonging, acceptance and an authentic commitment to understanding the needs, thoughts and wishes of those with autism.

Note

[1]   NHS or National Health Service refers to the public health services of England, Scotland and Wales, the first of its kind.

References

Awadh, A.M. & Alyahya, M.S. (2013). Impact of organizational culture on employee performance. *International Review of Management and Business Research*, 2(1), 168.

Bakker, E.J., Kox, J.H., Miedema, H.S., Bierma-Zeinstra, S., Runhaar, J., Boot, C.R., … & Roelofs, P.D. (2018). Physical and mental determinants of dropout and retention among nursing students: Protocol of the SPRiNG cohort study. *BMC Nursing*, 17(1), 27.

Baron-Cohen, S. & Wheelwright, S. (2004). The empathy quotient: An investigation of adults with Asperger's Syndrome or high functioning Autism and normal sex differences. *Journal of Autism and Developmental Disorders*, 34(2), 163–175.

Bloom, P. (2017). *Against Empathy: The Case for Rational Compassion*. London: Random House.

Braathen, V.M.L., & Sørensen, M.W. (2017). Unconscious bias against introverts in the recruitment and selection process. Master's thesis: BI Norwegian Business School.

Brady, M., Price, J., Bolland, R., & Finnerty, G. (2017). Needing to belong: First practice placement experiences of children's nursing students. *Comprehensive Child and Adolescent Nursing*, 1–16.

Brookfield, S.D., & Holst, J.D. (2010). *Radicalizing Learning: Adult Education for a Just World*. Chichester: John Wiley & Sons.

Cameron, H., Coleman, B., Hervey, T., Rahman, S., & Rostant, P. (2019). Equality law obligations in higher education: Reasonable adjustments under the Equality Act 2010 in assessment of students with unseen disabilities. *Legal Studies*, 39(2), 204–229.

Cavendish, C. (2013). *The Cavendish Review: An Independent Review into Healthcare Assistants and Support Workers in the NHS and Social Care Settings*. London: Department of Health.

Charmaz, K. (2010). Disclosing illness and disability in the workplace. *Journal of International Education in Business*, 3(1/2), 6–19.

Cunnah, W. (2015). Disabled students: Identity, inclusion and work-based placements. *Disability & Society*, 30(2), 213–226.

Davies, B., & Bansel, P. (2007). Neoliberalism and education. *International Journal of Qualitative Studies in Education*, 20(3), 247–259.

Dearing, R. (1997). *Report of the National Committee of Inquiry into Higher Education: Dearing Report*. House of Lords Papers.

Decety, J., Echoles, S., & Correll, J. (2010). The blame game: The effect of responsibility and social stigma on empathy for pain. *Journal of Cognitive Neuroscience*, 22(5), 985–997.

Department Of Health. (2015). *The NHS Constitution*. Retrieved from https://assets.publishing.service.gov.uk/government/uploads/system/uploads/attachment_data/file/480482/NHS_Constitution_WEB.pdf [Last accessed: March 2020].

Eley, D.S. (2010). Postgraduates' perceptions of preparedness for work as a doctor and making future career decisions: Support for rural, non-traditional medical schools. *Education for Health*, 23(2), 374.

Fabri, M., Andrews, P., & Pukki, H. (2013). *Autism and Uni: A Guide to Best Practice in Supporting Higher Education Students on the Autism Spectrum*. Retrieved from www.autism-uni.org/bestpractice/ [Last accessed: March 2020].

Goode, J. (2007). 'Managing' disability: Early experiences of university students with disabilities. *Disability & Society*, 22(1), 35–48.

Gurbuz, E., Hanley, M., & Riby, D.M. (2019). University students with Autism: The social and academic experiences of University in the UK. *Journal of Autism and Developmental Disorders*, 49(2), 617–631.

Health Education England. (2014). *Values Based Recruitment Framework*.

Heidgerken, A.D., Geffken, G., Modi, A., & Frakey, L. (2005). A survey of autism knowledge in a health care setting. *Journal of Autism and Developmental Disorders*, 35(3), 323–330.

Hoeve, Y.T., Jansen, G., & Roodbol, P. (2014). The nursing profession: Public image, self-concept and professional identity. A discussion paper. *Journal of Advanced Nursing*, 70(2), 295–309.

Hogan, R., Chamorro-Premuzic, T., & Kaiser, R.B. (2013). Employability and career success: Bridging the gap between theory and reality. *Industrial and Organizational Psychology*, 6(1), 3–16.

Hope, A., Garside, J., & Prescott, S. (2011). Rethinking theory and practice: Pre-registration student nurses experiences of simulation teaching and learning in the acquisition of clinical skills in preparation for practice. *Nurse Education Today*, 31(7), 711–715.

Jack, K., Hamshire, C., Harris, W.E., Langan, M., Barrett, N., & Wibberley, C. (2018). "My mentor didn't speak to me for the first four weeks": Perceived unfairness experienced by nursing students in clinical practice settings. *Journal of Clinical Nursing*, 27(5–6), 929–938.

Jammaers, E., Zanoni, P., & Hardonk, S. (2016). Constructing positive identities in ableist workplaces: Disabled employees' discursive practices engaging with the discourse of lower productivity. *Human Relations*, 69(6), 1365–1386.

Jolly, D. (2000). A critical evaluation of the contradictions for disabled workers arising from the emergence of the flexible labour market in Britain. *Disability & Society*, 15(5), 795–810.

Jones, A.P., Happé, F.G., Gilbert, F., Burnett, S., & Viding, E. (2010). Feeling, caring, knowing: Different types of empathy deficit in boys with psychopathic tendencies and autism spectrum disorder. *Journal of Child Psychology and Psychiatry*, 51(11), 1188–1197.

King, L. (2018). Link lecturers' views on supporting student nurses who have a learning difficulty in clinical placement. *British Journal of Nursing*, 27(3), 141–145.

Kitchin, R. (1998). 'Out of place', 'Knowing one's place': Space, power and the exclusion of disabled people. *Disability & Society*, 13(3), 343–356.

Last, L., & Fulbrook, P. (2003). Why do student nurses leave? Suggestions from a Delphi study. *Nurse Education Today*, 23(6), 449–458.

Lee, G.K., & Carter, E.W. (2012). Preparing transition-age students with high-functioning autism spectrum disorders for meaningful work. *Psychology in the Schools*, 49(10), 988–1000.

Lorenz, T., Frischling, C., Cuadros, R., & Heinitz, K. (2016). Autism and overcoming job barriers: Comparing job-related barriers and possible solutions in and outside of autism-specific employment. *PloS One*, 11(1).

MacLeod, A., Allan, J., Lewis, A., & Robertson, C. (2018). 'Here I come again': The cost of success for higher education students diagnosed with autism. *International Journal of Inclusive Education*, 22(6), 683–697.

Mazhindu, D.M., Griffiths, L., Pook, C., Erskine, A., Ellis, R., & Smith, F. (2016). The nurse match instrument: Exploring professional nursing identity and professional nursing values for future nurse recruitment. *Nurse Education in Practice*, 18, 36–45.

Melincavage, S.M. (2011). Student nurses' experiences of anxiety in the clinical setting. *Nurse Education Today*, 31(8), 785–789.

Miller, S., & Bird, J. (2014). Assessment of practitioners' and students' values when recruiting. *Nursing Management*, 21(5), 22.

Mitchell, A.E. (2018). Psychological distress in student nurses undertaking an educational programme with professional registration as a nurse: Their perceived barriers and facilitators in seeking psychological support. *Journal of Psychiatric and Mental Health Nursing*, 25(4), 258–269.

Montgomery, C.B., Allison, C., Lai, M.C., Cassidy, S., Langdon, P.E., & Baron-Cohen, S. (2016). Do adults with high functioning autism or Asperger syndrome differ in empathy and emotion recognition? *Journal of Autism and Developmental Disorders*, 46(6), 1931–1940.

NMC (Nursing and Midwifery Council). (2015). *Character and Health Decision – Making Guidance*. Retrieved from: www.nmc.org

NMC (Nursing and Midwifery Council). (2018a) *Realising Professionalism: Standards for Education and Training Part 3: Standards for Pre-Registration Nursing Programmes*. Retrieved from www.nmc.org.uk/globalassets/sitedocuments/education-standards/programme-standards-nursing.pdf [Last accessed: March 2020].

NMC (Nursing and Midwifery Council). (2018b). *Standards Framework for Nursing and Midwifery Education*. Retrieved from www.nmc.org.uk/globalassets/sitedocuments/education-standards/education-framework.pdf [Last accessed: March 2020].

Oliver, M. (1990). *The Politics of Disablement.* Basingstoke: Macmillan.

Olssen, M., & Peters, M.A. (2005). Neoliberalism, higher education and the knowledge economy: From the free market to knowledge capitalism. *Journal of Education Policy*, 20(3), 313–345.

Pedersen, R. (2010). Empathy development in medical education – a critical review. *Medical Teacher*, 32(7), 593–600.

Petrina, N., Carter, M., Stephenson, J., & Sweller, N. (2017). Friendship satisfaction in children with autism spectrum disorder and nominated friends. *Journal of Autism and Developmental Disorders*, 47(2), 384–392.

Poropat, A.E. (2014). Other-rated personality and academic performance: Evidence and implications. *Learning and Individual Differences*, 34, 24–32.

Prinz, J. (2011). Is empathy necessary for morality. *Empathy: Philosophical and Psychological Perspectives*, 1, 211–229.

Reeve, D. (2004). Psycho-emotional dimensions of disability and the social model. *Implementing the Social Model of Disability: Theory and Research*, 83–100.

Riddell, S., & Weedon, E. (2014). Disabled students in higher education: Discourses of disability and the negotiation of identity. *International Journal of Educational Research*, 63, 38–46.

Rowley, E., Chandler, S., Baird, G., Simonoff, E., Pickles, A., Loucas, T., & Charman, T. (2012). The experience of friendship, victimization and bullying in children with an autism spectrum disorder: Associations with child characteristics and school placement. *Research in Autism Spectrum Disorders*, 6(3), 1126–1134.

Santuzzi, A.M., Waltz, P.R., Finkelstein, L.M., & Rupp, D.E. (2014). Invisible disabilities: Unique challenges for employees and organizations. *Industrial and Organizational Psychology*, 7(2), 204–219.

Smith, M. (2010). Lecturers' attitudes to inclusive teaching practice at a UK university: Will staff "resistance" hinder implementation? *Tertiary Education and Management*, 16(3), 211–227.

Staines, R. (2009). Autism Act paves the way for fresh approach to care. *Learning Disability Practice*, 12(10), 6.

Ten Hoeve, Y., Castelein, S., Jansen, G., & Roodbol, P. (2017). Dreams and disappointments regarding nursing: Student nurses' reasons for attrition and retention. A qualitative study design. *Nurse Education Today*, 54, 28–36.

Van der Heijde, C.M., & Van der Heijden, B.I.J.M. (2014). Employability and social innovation: The importance of and interplay between transformational leadership and personality. *Human Resource Management, Social Innovation and Technology*, 14, 55–72.

Walker, R., Henderson, A., Cooke, M., & Creedy, D. (2011). Impact of a learning circle intervention across academic and service contexts on developing a learning culture. *Nurse Education Today*, 31(4), 378–382.

Ward, D., & Webster, A. (2018). Understanding the lived experiences of university students with autism spectrum disorder (ASD): A phenomenological study. *International Journal of Disability, Development and Education*, 65(4), 373–392.

Ward, J. (2016). The empathy enigma: Does it still exist? Comparison of empathy using students and standardized actors. *Nurse Educator*, 41(3), 134–138.

Waugh, A., Smith, D., Horsburgh, D., & Gray, M. (2014). Towards a values-based person specification for recruitment of compassionate nursing and midwifery candidates: A study of registered and student nurses' and midwives' perceptions of prerequisite attributes and key skills. *Nurse Education Today*, 34(9), 1190–1195.

Wessel, R.D., Jones, J.A., Markle, L., & Westfall, C. (2009). Retention and graduation of students with disabilities: Facilitating student success. *Journal of Postsecondary Education and Disability*, 21(3), 116–125.

Wilkinson, H., Whittington, R., Perry, L., & Eames, C. (2017). Examining the relationship between burnout and empathy in healthcare professionals: A systematic review. *Burnout Research*, 6, 18–29.

Wood, D., & Marshall, E.S. (2010). Nurses with disabilities working in hospital settings: Attitudes, concerns, and experiences of nurse leaders. *Journal of Professional Nursing*, 26(3), 182–187.

Wray, J., Aspland, J., Barrett, D., & Gardiner, E. (2017). Factors affecting the programme completion of pre-registration nursing students through a three year course: A retrospective cohort study. *Nurse Education in Practice*, 24, 14–20.

14

Ableism in music academicism

Ben Lunn

Introduction

The topic of ableism in music academicism is gargantuan. In this chapter I highlight at least some of the problems facing disabled people within academic musical environments. Most of my focus is geared towards issues with the conservatoire/music college environment, as I have had most direct interaction with this form of institution in higher education. However, the issues within these institutions relate to all professionals in the music industry, as performers and composers have to interact with this on some level. All musicologists started as musicians, even if only enthusiastic amateurs, meaning all experiences of performing music are directly influencing the musicological environment – even if the means of discourse has changed. What must be considered also is that the field of musicology is an observation of the professional music world, meaning that if the professional world is devoid of disabled people, musicologists will not have any disabled musicians/artists to observe either. There are four key problems within the academic and professional environment that need to be addressed for disabled musicians, composers or musicologists to begin striving for some sense of real equality (McKay, 2013; Kivijärvi, 2012; Cain, 2010; Meekosha, 2000). They are as follows:

- lack of representation;
- lack of historic figures to draw upon;
- lack of aesthetics that encourage disabled creatives;
- lack of general awareness within the musicological environment.

Lack of representation

From a promotional perspective, the lack of representation is symptomatic of a constant rolling problem starting with the question: 'Why are there few disabled musicologists/professional artists?' This then leads onto the question: 'If they are not numerous, why then give a platform specifically for disabled people?' Or conversely, the assumption arises that: 'If there was a more present community, there would be platform.'

In reality, however, disabled people cannot develop their career without support and so disabled musicians just are not heard. This particular loop is a rather troublesome one to tackle, mostly because it is symptomatic of academia and the professional sphere in general. Realistically, this comes from strong, well-celebrated ideas leading the direction academic discourse should take. As a consequence, disabled musicians can either not picture themselves following a musical career or drop out of music-making, unless they find themselves in disabled-led ensembles or special needs orchestras, such as the Bournemouth Symphony Orchestra Resound (BSO Resound, n.d.), the Paraorchestra (Paraorchestra, n.d.) or the National Open Youth Orchestra (National Open Youth Orchestra, n.d.).

This system is a simple but efficient way of furthering certain ideas. I use the word 'certain' because there are occasions where academics are given platforms because of the nature of the idea, rather than the quality. But this makes the solution more complicated. Within the professional world, cultural institutions depend on an artist's image/brand to push them forward. That is to say that if you have professional commissions from one orchestra, another orchestra is likely to support you, whereas if you have not had such an opportunity you rely on other forms of promotion to prove you are worthy of the commission. Aligning yourself with an orchestra or institution, such as the

BSO Resound, the Paraorchestra or the National Open Youth Orchestra therefore builds a particular brand or image, that individuals may not necessarily feel comfortable with. After all, disclosure is a risk-benefit analysis in relation to one's personal experiences (Brown and Leigh, 2018), as well as a public statement and commitment to the disability discourse, requiring emotional labour and investment (Brown, 2020).

Investing more in academia and the arts would allow for diversity, as there is more finance free to allow undersupported voices the chance to work their way up the pecking order. This is simply a more significant way of addressing inequalities across the board (Blau, 1988; Albert, 2006; de Boise, 2019). If you took the more neoliberal shift of keeping the funding the same but forcing a balance of demographics to be supported on a limited budget, you would ultimately just leave many various peoples trying to push through the same tiny door – instead of paying for a wider doorframe to allow more people through.

To return to the key issue, lack of representation, observing the Arts Council's 2018–22 portfolio statistics, out of 828 portfolio organisations in all sectors only 35 'disabled self definition' and 2 'disabled' led organisations gained funding (Arts Council England, n.d.). Even though overall there was a doubling in organisations gaining support in this field, it underlines simply how tiny the disabled arts sector is in England, with approximately 0.25 per cent of organisations being disabled-led. On further investigation, the portfolio statistics show an even more worrisome picture. In their publication *Equality, Diversity and the Creative Case, 2015–16*, the Arts Council highlighted the discrepancy between the percentage of working age disabled people, which was 19 per cent according to the Annual Population Survey quoted in the article, and the percentage of the workforce in the arts who are disabled, which amounted to a mere 4 per cent (Arts Council England, 2016). The arts sector, and particularly the music sector, is reflected in academic musicology. No matter how inclusive an academic or institution is, the material surroundings will impact directly: the fewer professional disabled musicians and composers, the fewer musicians and composers to discuss.

Lack of historic figures to draw upon

The lack of historic figures is intriguing. There have been many composers who became disabled – Beethoven losing his hearing, Gustav Holst's muscular problems, or Smetana's increasing hearing problems, and arguably Arnold Schönberg's heart problems (Straus, 2011). But what makes the discourse of these figures interesting, is that the discussions imply the issues they faced were more linked to the ageing process instead of actually being disabled (Hendricks et al, 2005). The other problem is, would Beethoven have succeeded like he did, if he had been deaf from birth?

When we critically observe these elements, we realise there have been no real description of composers with disabilities before 1945. Straus (2011) tries to address this in his publication *Extraordinary Measures*. However, the core of the discussion suffers the first defect – ageing over disability. This puts disabled people in a curious position today. Where women, LGBT and BAME composers had their history stolen from them – for example, through composers having ideas stolen, being unpublished during their lives, or simply being brushed under the carpet – disabled people just do not have this history. So, in an odd sense disabled people are able to compose without the burden of history. However, this comes back to issues of lack of representation: why support disabled composers if there are not any?

Of course, referring back to the statistics (Arts Council England, 2016), disability disclosures in themselves need to be considered. Although the general public tends to see disability in a binary of either being or not being disabled, the lived experience of those with disabilities shows that matters are not as simple as that. Disability is in itself a spectrum depending on the circumstances one finds oneself in (Deegan, 2010). For example, a person using a wheelchair will feel more disabled at a venue where there is no ramp than at a venue where there is one. The point I am making here is that there may well be disabled composers who perhaps pass as non-disabled and, because they are not comfortable in disclosing their disabilities, hide their needs instead (see Brown, 2020). As a consequence, however, we continue to lack role models.

The issue of lack of historic role models and the connected representation is compounded further: Kim Jong-Il (1971), the former leader of the Democratic People's Republic of Korea (DPRK, also known as North Korea), points to a contradiction when trying to build a tradition separated from a colonial past. As Japan had such a strong hold over Korea, the arts became heavily influenced by colonial Japan. This brought up the question of whether composers in Korea can truly sound Korean. Kim Jong-Il's solution, much like Cornelius Cardew (1974), is to reject all Japanese influence and look at what the Korean people admire. This includes writing almost solely homophonically as it is most akin to what the people sing. Regardless of one's thoughts on the DPRK or Kim Jong-Il, the question of heritage is a difficult one because histories are deeply intertwined. As disabled-ness is not a universal characteristic, national identity is likely to have a stronger pull. So, no matter how 'disabled' a composer is, without a clear separation from the past disabled-ness could take a back seat. It also begs the question if, musically, we can sound disabled at all, or if disability disappears with us.

Lack of aesthetics that encourage disabled creatives

The third point, the lack of a disabled aesthetic, is the one I am most passionate about. It is something I personally deal with as a young composer trying to find my way in the world. But this is a rather crucial step. Drake Music (Drake Music, n.d.), Drake Music Scotland (Drake Music Scotland, n.d.) and other such organisations are working hard to make music education more accessible, and challenge venues and festivals to adapt their approaches, too. However, the movements lack that extra push. Currently, due mostly to the battle being a very young one, the fight is just to be heard, to be seen, but getting disabled musicians on the stage is barely equality.

The African-American community certainly did not become not equal the moment slavery was abolished in the US. We simply need to observe the literary work of W.E.B. Du Bois, Franz Fanon, Ivan Van Sertima, or Zora Neale Hurston. An intellectual and aesthetic void has to be filled to go from simply surviving to flourishing. So, we can observe that ending slavery was the first battle in the war for equality. Access to anything, be it academia, concert stages, education, or theatre spaces, is merely the start.

As mentioned, organisations like Drake Music and Drake Music Scotland have been working since the late 1990s, developing instruments and ways of learning to create for people from various backgrounds and various disabilities. This has included the developing of instruments specifically for individual needs or developing tools for learning. Figurenotes™ (Figurenotes, n.d.) has been one of the key developers of a musical notation that fits more intuitively to alternative ways of learning. Much like John Mclean's *Socialist Sunday Schools* (Gallacher, 2017), access to education allows the individual an opportunity to achieve radical things they would have previously be unable to achieve. This, despite not addressing issues of disability aesthetic, is still a vital platform to be developed and sustained for disabled artists and musicologists alike.

To return to the point of contention, if we compare the world of 'crip-literature' (or crip-lit), in anthologies like *Beauty is a Verb: The New Poetry of Disability* (Bartlett et al, 2011), we can observe a rich tapestry of approaches under the singular banner of 'crip-lit' or 'crip-poetry'. Within this banner, we see the poets and writers tussle with the idea of the form and bring their own responses which further expand the diversity of the aesthetic. Alternatively, in *Disability Aesthetics* Siebers (2010) postulates that modernism's 'degeneracy' ultimately 'disables' aesthetics or is inherently a 'disabled aesthetic'. Siebers (2010) references the parallels between the Nazis' *Entartete Kunst* (degenerate art) and their propaganda of 'degenerates'. The classification disqualified both modernist artists and disabled people, along with Jewish people and culture, ethnic minorities and other disliked groups like communists, as both equally 'evil' or against the interests of the German people or Aryan race. The core argument, the idea that modernism is inherently 'disabled', does give a vibrancy to the disabled arts movement as whole. However, it simply adopts a movement which has very few disabled bodies involved in it.

For disabled composers and musicians to flourish, what is needed is an aesthetic, or at least an artistic ideal for which they can not only strive to achieve, but which forces academics to deal with this tangible idea. The Spectral composers, sprouting from

Messiaen's class, had a vague but open aesthetic based on music being sound and the exploration of sound and timbre as the basis from which they can work. With this central point, academics ultimately have a concrete basis to work from, to be critical or positive about the idea and how it is achieved. Furthermore, another important element of using aesthetics as a point of growth is that it encourages disabled composers and musicians to be as truly radical and ground-breaking as any other composer throughout history, as the strengths and nuance of the innovation is purely down to the aesthetic. This aesthetic, however, has to come from the disabled community itself; it is not something that can, or should, be given. No one will politely remove the glass ceiling; it needs something or someone to smash it.

From this we can understand why adopting modernism as a 'disabled' or 'degenerate' aesthetic or movement does not necessarily help the disabled artist. The other major flaw in Siebers' (2010) assertions is that for an aesthetic idiom to be disabled it has to be perceived to be 'broken'. This is a difficult assertion to hold, but there is a history of using horrendous stereotypes to the benefit of the discriminated community: the African-American community's reclaiming of racial slurs, the homosexual community using the pink triangle, or disabled rights movement using the black triangle are rather well-known examples. However, maintaining the 'disabled as broken' narrative creates a false comparative narrative: namely, that disabled music-making is broken, therefore lesser than abled music-making. If we compare this to the adoption of the black triangle by disabled rights activists, the Nazi use of the black triangle was just a designation of disabled. This means the black triangle on its own is innocuous, it is the aesthetic or ideology behind it that defines it, whereas disabled art as degenerate art risks putting the stereotype front and centre instead of pushing disabled art into a space of esteem.

Lack of general awareness within the musicological environment

The final point, the lack of musicological awareness, has no speedy solution. As can be extrapolated from the previous points, awareness of disabled composers comes when disabled composers have a clear and tangible voice or at least are so insistent that they cannot be ignored. This being said, female composers, BAME composers and LGBT composers still suffer from a lack of general awareness or acceptance from academics. Through increasingly successful activism, organisations like Archiv Frau und Musik (Archiv Frau und Musik, n.d.), Listening to Ladies (Listening to Ladies, n.d.), Chineke! Foundation (Chineke! Foundation, n.d.) and the International Alliance for Women in Music (International Alliance for Women in Music, n.d.) have at least forced the discussion to be opened up. We can also see, with Keychange's push for 50:50 musical representation (Keychange, n.d.), that in the musical profession a major shift is happening for female composers, so that regardless of personal views of academics, female composers will become impossible any longer to ignore.

I am unsure whether disabled composers and musicians are in the same position – yet. BSO Resound (BSO Resound, n.d.), Drake Music Scotland's Digital Orchestra (Drake Music Scotland, n.d.), National Open Youth Orchestra (National Open Youth Orchestra, n.d.) and ParaOrchestra and Friends (Paraorchestra, n.d.) have all made strong platforms which showcase disabled composers and musicians. They are not quite in a position of prestige. However, it would be naïve to think prestige is born overnight. What makes me pessimistic about the circumstances around disabled performance is that fighting to be allowed on stage is frivolous, when we still cannot guarantee we can access the venue as eager listeners. Change is happening, albeit slowly. For example, the BBC Proms have devised 'specialised' events (see Pickard, 2018). These are not without criticism, but they are at least a positive step. This problem does underline the core issue of addressing broader awareness. When discussing the qualities of music by female, BAME or LGBT composers at no point would the possibility of being physically unable to attend concerts be a point in the discussion or come into the equation. Yet, the disabled are not equal as listeners. And if we are not equal as listeners, how can we then be equal as creatives?

In short, a lot of work has to be done, addressing the material problems facing disabled composers and musicians. It must be said there is a hunger to come to terms with this. As the gates begin to widen, discussions of disabled music-making will broaden but will face new barriers. We just need to focus on the fact that over time these barriers and challenges can also be addressed. As time progresses further, and through focused concerted effort, an Alliance of Disabled Composers and Musicians would be a great way to unify and focus the discussion.

Conclusion

I hope the necessity of highlighting these areas and possible solutions has become clear. I also feel that, due mostly to being a very young academic, it was not really my place to discuss the issues of being a disabled academic in any other form of music. If we were to progress from here, the next steps would simply be to investigate more. Within academia, there are visible shifts in discussing and theorising the experience of those who are disabled or chronically ill (see, for example, Brown and Leigh, 2020). If we are truly serious about encouraging a dialogue on the matter in the music industry and musicology, we need to promote actually disabled people to lead the discourse, as it is our music that we share with everyone. We also need to critically analyse what elements of the music environment need to be challenged and how this environment can be improved as, in short, most things that become more accessible to the disabled community make the platform more approachable for everyone.

Reflective questions

- Have you ever contemplated ableism in the music industries in these ways?
- Can musicology instigate positive change in the profession, or is it eternally reliant on responding to the evolving world around it?
- Can the value of music exist outside of its historical surroundings?
- In an artform defined by virtuosity, where do you put disabled musicians?

Recommendations

- Question the narrative behind the composer. For example, reflect on how composers like Beethoven were actually disabled.
- Where possible, allow the disabled artist to define the narrative.
- Avoid stereotypical tropes such as disabled people are depressed, disabled people are tortured souls, or disabled people are broken.

References

Albert, D.J. (2006). Socioeconomic status and instrumental music: What does the research say about the relationship and its implications? *Update: Applications of Research in Music Education*, 25(1), 39–45.

Archiv Frau und Musik. (n.d.). Retrieved from: www.archiv-frau-musik.de/en/ [Last accessed: March 2020].

Arts Council England. (2016). *Equality, Diversity and the Creative Case, 2015–16*. Retrieved from: www.artscouncil.org.uk/sites/default/files/download-file/Equality_diversity_creativecase_2015_16_web_0.pdf [Last accessed: March 2020].

Arts Council England. (n.d.). *Our National Portfolio in Numbers, 2018–22*. Retrieved from: www.artscouncil.org.uk/sites/default/files/download-file/Investment__factsheet_14062019_0.pdf [Last accessed: March 2020].

Bartlett, J., Black, S.F., & Northen, M. (eds). (2011). *Beauty Is a Verb: The New Poetry of Disability*. Cinco Puntos Press.

Blau, J.R. (1988). Music as social circumstance. *Social Forces*, 66(4), 883–902.

Brown, N. (2020). Disclosure in academia: A sensitive issue. In: Brown, N., & Leigh, J.S. (eds). *Ableism in Academia: Theorising Experiences of Disabilities and Chronic Illnesses in Higher Education*. London: UCL Press.

Brown, N., & Leigh, J.S. (2018). Ableism in academia: Where are the disabled and ill academics? *Disability and Society*, 33(6), 985–989.

Brown, N., & Leigh, J.S. (2020). *Ableism in Academia: Theorising Experiences of Disabilities and Chronic Illnesses in Higher Education*. London: UCL Press.

BSO Resound. (n.d.). Retrieved from: https://bsolive.com/news/bso-resound/ [Last accessed: March 2020].

Cain, M.C. (2010). Of pain, passing and longing for music. *Disability and Society*, 25(6), 747–751.

Cardew, C. (1974). *Stockhausen Serves Imperialism*. Latimer New Dimensions.

Chineke! Foundation. (n.d.). Retrieved from: www.chineke.org/ [Last accessed: March 2020].

Davis, L. (1995). *Enforcing Normalcy: Disability, Deafness and the Body*. Verso.

de Boise, S. (2019). Tackling gender inequalities in music: A comparative study of policy responses in the UK and Sweden. *International Journal of Cultural Policy*, 25(4), 486–499.

Deegan, M.J. (2010). 'Feeling normal' and 'feeling disabled'. In: Barnartt, S.N. (ed). *Disability as a Fluid State: Research in Social Science and Disability*, Vol 5. Bingley: Emerald Group Publishing, 25–48.

Drake Music. (n.d.). Retrieved from: www.drakemusic.org/ [Last accessed: March 2020].

Drake Music Scotland. (n.d.). Retrieved from: https://drakemusicscotland.org/ [Last accessed: March 2020].

Figurenotes. (n.d.). Retrieved from: https://figurenotes.org/ [Last accessed: March 2020].

Gallacher, W. (2017). *Revolt on the Clyde*. Lawrence and Wishart.

Hendricks, J., Palmore, E., Branch, L., & Harris, D. (2005). Societal ageism. *Encyclopedia of Ageism*, 292–297.

International Alliance for Women in Music. (n.d.). Retrieved from: https://iawm.org/ [Last accessed: March 2020].

Jong-il, K. (1971). *Let Us Produce Revolutionary Operas That Are High in Ideology*. Pyongyang: Foreign Language Press.

Keychange. (n.d.). Retrieved from: https://keychange.eu/blog/full-list-of-festivals-signed-up-to-keychange/ [Last accessed: March 2020].

Kivijärvi, S. (2012). Project disabled people as musicians: A systemic approach. *Procedia-Social and Behavioral Sciences*, 45, 416–427.

Listening to Ladies. (n.d.). Retrieved from: http://listeningtoladies.com/ [Last accessed: March 2020].

McKay, G. (2013). *Shakin' All Over: Popular Music and Disability*. Ann Arbor: University of Michigan Press.

Meekosha, H. (2000). A disabled genius in the family: Personal musings on the tale of two sisters. *Disability and Society*, 15(5), 811–815.

National Open Youth Orchestra. (n.d.) Retrieved from: http://noyo.org.uk/ [Last accessed: March 2020].

Paraorchestra. (n.d.). Retrieved from: http://paraorchestra.com/ [Last accessed: March 2020].

Pickard, D. (2018). Pioneering sounds and breaking disability barriers: BBC Proms 2018. Retrieved from: www.bbc.co.uk/blogs/aboutthebbc/entries/f36c5781-9dab-4df4-b7ee-e47b9ea10ffc [Last accessed: March 2020].

Siebers, T. (2010). *Disability Aesthetics*. Ann Arbor: University of Michigan Press.

Straus, J.N. (2011). Musical narratives of balance lost and regained: Schoenberg and Webern. In: Straus, J.N. *Extraordinary Measures: Disability in Music*. Oxford University Press. 72–81.

15

Teaching with and supporting teachers with dyslexia in higher education

Jennifer Hiscock and Jennifer Leigh

Introduction

Dyslexia is the specific learning disability that is most often disclosed by students at university. First descriptions of difficulties with reading and writing date back to the mid to late 19th century, with the term 'dyslexia' being first introduced in 1862 (Soler, 2009). At the time, symptoms like difficulties with reading and word blindness were connected to medical conditions like brain lesions or aphasia. In the late 1890s and early 1900s the ophthalmologist and eye surgeon John Hinshelwood recognised a hereditary link, as well as a higher prevalence among boys than girls, and he attributed the difficulties with reading to a deficit in individuals' 'visual word-centre' (Miles and Miles, 1999: 5). In the subsequent decades, dyslexia research and recognition developed only slowly as environmental, biological and genetic dimensions were considered alongside psychological factors and childhood development (Soler, 2009; Richardson, 1992). The understanding that dyslexia is related to more linguistic and phonological differences emerged from the 1970s onwards (Guardiola, 2001). Since the early 2000s, the most commonly accepted definition is that:

Dyslexia is a specific learning disability that is neurobiological in origin. It is characterized by difficulties with accurate and/or fluent word recognition and by poor spelling and decoding abilities. These difficulties typically result from a deficit in the phonological component of language that is often unexpected in relation to other cognitive abilities and the provision of effective classroom instruction. Secondary consequences may include problems in reading comprehension and reduced reading experience that can impede growth of vocabulary and background knowledge. (Lyon et al, 2003)

Despite this seemingly uniform definition, dyslexia varies from person to person, with no individual exhibiting the same combination of strengths and weaknesses. However, many people with dyslexia exhibit strong visual, creative and problem-solving skills, which may be an asset to a teacher within higher education (Griffiths, 2012), but often cause problems relating to the processing and remembering of information (Riddick, 1995).

Our perspective

This chapter takes an autoethnographic approach (Bochner and Ellis, 2016) and combines the personal perspective from Jennifer H of being an academic with teaching responsibilities in higher education with dyslexia, with that of Jennifer L who works within educational development and who has experience of parenting and supporting someone with dyslexia.

Jennifer H is an early career supramolecular chemist who is quickly gaining recognition within her field. Her work is interdisciplinary, and often crosses disciplinary and field specific boundaries as she creatively applies new ideas to existing problems, tackling them from a different perspective. She actively collaborates with bioscientists, physicists, government researchers and defence specialists which in itself is unusual in an academic world of silos (Becher and Trowler, 1989). Jennifer L initially trained in chemistry, and then fell off the wagon gaining qualifications as a yoga teacher and somatic movement therapist before her PhD in education. Her work focuses on embodiment, reflectivity and reflexivity, academic identity and the use of creative research methods, and she has a strong interest in ableism. Our presence in this study and our voices in this chapter create and underlie the narrative that we write (Meerwald, 2013). We are both passionate about and emotive in our responses to this subject, and offer our own reflective autobiographical comments. Our intention here is to invoke Carolyn Ellis's multivocal autoethnography (Ellis, 2004), evoking a descriptive and emotional response from those who read this contribution.

The chapter was borne out of Jennifer H's postgraduate certificate in higher education research (PGCHE), where she first met Jennifer L. As part of her certificate, Jennifer H conducted experiments with student evaluations and a staff survey to both consider the specific issues a dyslexic higher education teacher might face, and to road test a practical toolkit that she had been advised to use in the aim of developing a more effective one. The results from this research can be found in Hiscock and Leigh (2020), as here we reflect on the experiences of dyslexia from personal perspectives to share how it impacts on higher education teaching as an individual, and how new teachers who may or may not have disclosed their disability might be better supported.

Jennifer H

I am a STEM (Science, Technology, Engineering and Maths) lecturer, and have severe dyslexia. I was diagnosed at the age of 6 by the National Dyslexia Institute (UK). As a student at school, I was aware that I had to work harder than my classmates to achieve the same academic success and often felt frustrated as my academic performance never seemed to keep up with my intelligence. I also often felt very confused; I often had no idea why I seemed to have arrived at an end conclusion to an argument a hundred times faster than my classmates, who just couldn't seem to grasp my methods for hypothesis formulation and my ability to justify this with evidence. In the end, I would just scribble down my answers and wait for everyone else to catch up. This led to me being withdrawn from my classmates and spending most of my days in silence, something no one would believe now. I understood the way my brain operated was different, accepted this fact, put my head down, got the work done and stayed quiet. This led to me achieving four A★s at GCSE level in biology, chemistry, physics and art, with A's in English, maths and statistics.

At school and college, I started to come out of my shell but was often misunderstood, underestimated and on occasion I was told I was stupid. Upon commencing my undergraduate and PhD studies within higher education I had gained a stubborn streak and no longer cared for the opinion of others when related to my academic potential. Still, I was asked on more than one occasion if I had registered on the right study programme. I was told that I should not be ashamed if I failed my chosen programme of study, and I was constantly referred to as being disabled. I have never classed myself as disabled, and although I recognise that dyslexia is termed as a disability, this label does not sit right with me. I have maintained a first-class academic record throughout my academic career, and I found the iteration of these comments and their sentiments rather shocking. To date, I have authored 40 publications in peer reviewed chemistry journals, which have been cited over 1,650 times, and since starting my independent career I have won substantial funding, international recognition and prizes for my ground-breaking interdisciplinary work. I was recently promoted two grades in recognition of my success, and currently hold the position of Reader of Supramolecular Chemistry and Director of Innovation and Enterprise for the School of Physical Sciences at the University of Kent.

That said, I am very aware of my dyslexia and how it impacts me. While I feel that it is the differences in my brain that allow me to work creatively and see interdisciplinary answers to problems others get stuck on, certain aspects of my chosen career are challenging, for example: having to 're-learn' teaching material; remembering the teaching material; keeping on task; and spelling and reading under pressure.

As part of my probation at the University of Kent I was instructed to obtain my PGCHE and become a fellow of the Higher Education Academy. A portion of my academic study to obtain these qualifications was supervised by Jennifer L. It was this coincidental meeting that resulted in me discovering for the first time the term neurotypical. It was not until this point in my academic career that I had found a phrase to describe my dyslexia that did not have negative connotations. As a result of my work in this area I have achieved a new level of self-confidence and I am very proud to call myself not neurotypical.

Jennifer L

I am a senior lecturer in higher education and academic practice, and my eldest daughter has severe dyslexia. She is now a Master of Research student with Jennifer H, having achieved a first-class honours degree in biochemistry. My youngest child, aged 5 at the time of writing, has shown early signs of dyslexia and an Irlen's screening test showed that it is likely. Dyslexia runs in my family. As a parent of a child with dyslexia looking for support for my oldest from her school, I was told by my daughter's teacher that if she could read, then she was not dyslexic, and that there was no such thing as high functioning dyslexia. Her school was unwilling to put anything in place to support her, as she was not failing. As she progressed through secondary school, she showed a typical dyslexic pattern in her assessments, in that she was able to express herself very ably verbally, yet her written work let her down. The school would not recommend that she be assessed or given extra time or support as she was still achieving above average marks. She developed coping strategies, one of which was to move away from English and the humanities subjects she had loved as a child, and towards science. It was not until university that she was assessed comprehensively, without a comparison to a neurotypical average, and instead to her own potential.

With my youngest I am finding that the reaction is different. While I live in an area that fails to recognise dyslexia easily, the school itself is willing to support a child even without an official diagnosis. However, my concerns were initially brushed off as my child is doing well above average, until I shared that I already had a child with dyslexia and recognised the signs.

As an academic developer I champion the importance of building in accessibility in a Universal Design for Learning (Bracken and Novak, 2019). One aspect of my higher education research focuses on ableism in academia (Brown and Leigh, 2018; Brown et al, 2018; Brown and Leigh, 2020), the support that institutions can offer and the impact that disclosing a condition can have on a career.

Coping strategies and support tools

In order for a person with dyslexia to achieve a teaching position in higher education, they will have already had to develop their own effective coping strategies concerning reading and writing. While we both strongly believe that dyslexia can be an advantage within academia, we are both very aware that it also presents many challenges. It is for these reasons that we do not focus on the question of whether an individual with dyslexia is capable of or should be teaching at this level, as for us this is a given. The terminology of coping strategies is tricky, as to use the term 'coping' implies a deficit, and yet 'effective working' risks that the extent to which these are used to address challenges specifically for those with dyslexia is minimised. These workplace coping strategies may be developed by an individual, or taught as part of generic educational development courses for new lecturers, which may utilise materials from reports such as those produced by the University of Southampton (2010); they outline four support tools for teachers with dyslexia:

- setting aside extra time to check material;
- getting a colleague to check your work;
- writing down and preparing as much as possible;
- telling the students about your dyslexia and asking for their help.

We will reflect on the practicality, the emotional impact and the effectiveness of each of these strategies.

Setting aside extra time to check material

At first glance, this seems a sensible and practical suggestion. Jennifer H believes that a dyslexic teacher should probably expect to spend extra time checking and preparing material. However, it can also be seen as ableist, if the extra time is not recognised and allowed for in workload planning as part of reasonable adjustments. This ties into a larger discourse around disclosure of an invisible condition (see Finesilver et al, 2020). Without that time allowance, the consequence would be that the extra time needed to check (and prepare) teaching materials takes away from time that is otherwise needed for research and for activities more closely connected with promotion and progression. In our overworked culture of academia (Gill, 2009) there is an assumption that the work never stops, and this recommendation is asking for extra time that has to come from somewhere. As mother of three, I (Jennifer L) have fairly strict boundaries to the amount of time that I can spend on academic work such as teaching preparation. I am limited by childcare, by taxi-ing my girls to music or dancing, by preparing them dinner and wrangling them into bed. My work is, for the most part, flexible, and I can work from home on a laptop (as I am today), or in the office. I see Jennifer H working to a very different schedule as a laboratory-based scientist. For safety reasons, her lab time is restricted to 9–5, Monday–Friday. She has to be on site and present during those hours, as she is responsible for the health and safety of her team and the students working with her. As she is growing in seniority the demands on her time are increasing, and I regularly witness her working until 11pm or later on a weekday. She does not feel that she can take time off. And yet, we are asking her to take more time to check materials that will not, in all likelihood, contribute to her career progression. We both agree that, while it is necessary to allow enough time to prepare materials, this should be in the context of a larger conversation about ableism and support within the academy.

A solution to this may come with the advent of novel technology. Very recently, Jennifer H decided to invest in new tablet and conventional Microsoft Office setup. In her experience, universities typically do not offer the standard of specialised support required to aid the work of a cutting-edge scientist. This software is, however, available to most academics within the university environment. These conventional software packages now offer spoken word to text and text to spoken word facilities as standard. They also monitor document accessibility and even allow you to scribble all over your lecture notes recording your voice notes at the same time. This is a valuable resource not only for the academic teacher, allowing them to revisit their thoughts at any moment in time quickly and easily without having to read anything, but also provides a resource for the students receiving the lecture material, who can revisit a verbal, written, or pictorial explanation at any point in their studies. This reduces the time that is taken in tutorial or one to one sessions to re-explain material to the student cohort. Access to such technology frees up time that could potentially be used to absorb the extra time necessary to plan the course materials.

Getting a colleague to check your work

This recommendation, while also seemingly simple on the face of it, actually contains a large amount of emotional labour for the dyslexic teacher. I (Jennifer H) found that asking a colleague for help in checking work placed extra pressures on my colleagues, who were already overworked. I also found it quite damaging to both my self-confidence and self-efficacy, in that I felt beholden to and potentially judged by my colleagues for needing and asking for such help. As a strategy to help support someone with a specific learning disability such as dyslexia, where often diagnosis is conditional on 'failing' to reach specified standards, it seems that relying on the individual to ask for yet more unpaid labour from colleagues, and placing themselves in a vulnerable situation psychologically, may not be that supportive. A strategy such as this has the potential to disrupt the power relations within the workplace, by putting the teacher with dyslexia in the power of the teacher checking the work. Dyslexic academics may fear that their colleagues' perceptions of the disability will impact on their career. 'Checking work' is different from acting as a 'critical friend' on academic papers and the like, because it implies that the role is one way. Instead, if an individual with dyslexia felt they needed this level of support, it would be more appropriate, in our opinion, for such a role to be performed by a paid individual (perhaps funded by a scheme such as Access to Work within the UK) than a colleague.

We suggest that committing to this strategy should be considered carefully. Tools such as spell-check, grammar check, read aloud software and the like have greatly enhanced the dyslexic's ability to prepare and write material. Peer feedback is important, however, and ongoing general observations relating to the production of one's teaching materials can also help build new coping strategies, encourage self-reflection and allow an insecure teacher to identify their progress. It may therefore be more effective to ensure that academics with dyslexia have additional peer feedback in some form of mentor–mentee relationship.

Writing down and preparing as much as possible

Writing down as much of the lecture material as possible is an important strategy for effective delivery, and is also helpful to the student cohort for independent learning as it can be shared through the virtual learning environment. However, those with dyslexia should be informed about resources that can assist them and kept up to date with them. We noticed that the resources and provision Jennifer H had access to were in some ways different to those that Jennifer L's daughter had received at university. These might include dyslexia-specific fonts that ease reading, applications that can read material out loud, and applications to change colours or tint screens. In addition to writing, pre-recording lectures can save time, is an effective preparation/ revision resource and allows more innovation in the teaching space with more active teaching and learning approaches such as the 'flipped classroom'. Pre-recording lectures can form part of lecture preparation, to refresh knowledge and act as a backup in case of memory failure. An added advantage is that it will also decrease the time needed to relearn material in subsequent years, as you can review the recordings, particularly if used with up-to-date and enabling technology as discussed. This removes all the potential issues around recall, staying on task and making spelling/reading errors and is an effective coping strategy employed by Jennifer H.

Telling the students about your dyslexia and asking for their help

Revealing my (Jennifer H) dyslexia to a full lecture theatre of first-year students who had no idea of my disability was one of the scariest things that I had ever pushed myself to do within the scope of my academic career to date. It was also one of the most positive experiences I have had within a university setting. The student cohort was supportive, and in some cases found my reveal to be inspirational. The experience also enabled me to lecture more effectively as my secret was out and I could just get on with the job. This transparency around disability allowed me to be authentic, and thus increased my credibility, which is important as a teacher in higher education (Leigh, 2019). This in turn increased the quality of the lecture material being delivered to the students and built a positive relationship between the student cohort and me. Once I had disclosed, the students helped me to pick out spelling mistakes, and even now, months after the module finished, these students are still taking it upon themselves to make me aware of innovations that may help to improve my coping strategies. Being more open to disclosing my dyslexia to my students has had the knock-on effect of being open towards my colleagues, human resources and the support available to me from the institution through units such as occupational health.

One consequence of Jennifer H revealing her dyslexia to students was that she was approached by some who made the effort to ask if there was a text that she would prefer them to write in, and another made her aware of dyslexic-friendly fonts such as Dyslexie font (Wainwright, 2014). This font was specially developed for dyslexics, ignoring all typographical rules, to overcome issues commonly associated with reading and learning. This font claims to improve the speed at which dyslexic individuals read and take in written information. In addition, there are tools available to convert the typeface of submitted student reports, website text and journal articles, enabling the dyslexic academic to work at a comparative rate to non-dyslexic co-workers. Although there has been a significant amount of research positively supporting the claims that this typeface removes common limitations experienced by dyslexic individuals (Leeuw, 2010; Pijpker, 2013), some of these claims have been disputed (Marinus et al, 2016), and not all individuals find such fonts helpful.

Through the revealing of my (Jennifer H) dyslexia and my acknowledgement of my neurotypical status, feedback provided by both my colleagues and my students has been overwhelming. In a recent meeting attended by some of the scientific leaders in my field for the first time I did not feel the need to apologise or hide who I was. This freeing experience has allowed me to increase my own self-confidence, which has in turn enabled me to help others achieve the same sense of confidence in their own brains.

Conclusion

The aim for this chapter has been to reflect on the common coping strategies advised for teachers with dyslexia in higher education as a way of sharing experiences with those thinking to implement them and those working as educational developers, so that they can suggest strategies for dyslexic lecturers who may or may not have disclosed their disability. While it can be seen that revealing dyslexia to students can be helpful to them and to the teacher, and that having dyslexia does not negatively affect teaching ability, disclosing dyslexia, like disclosing any other disability carries a certain amount of risk (Brown and Leigh, 2018). Likewise, disclosing to colleagues and asking them to check work may catch some spelling errors, but it adds to the workload of colleagues and can lower the dyslexic lecturers' own self-confidence in their ability to function independently.

In our own experience of collaborating together, there have been times when Jennifer H has asked me (Jennifer L) to look at her work. The first time I did this, I was very conscious of not wanting to step on her toes, or to make her feel as though as I was 'checking her work'. We had to meet face to face for me to have the confidence that Jennifer H was okay for me to edit directly, and for her to have the trust that in doing so I was not judging her and was working to make the proposal better. After that, it was easier for us to throw pieces back and forth in a natural and easy collaborative manner. The work here was not teaching materials, but grant proposals and accompanying papers and journal articles. Although based in different academic schools, we regularly look for opportunities to collaborate. My oldest daughter now works in Jennifer H's lab, and that has also added a dimension to our relationship. Jennifer H is able to mentor and guide my daughter with an understanding of how her brain works and how she processes information in a way unlike any other teacher she has had.

If we enable dyslexic academics to reach their full potential and confidence, then we will produce a better student experience, as we can speak directly from our personal and lived experience with dyslexia and supporting those with dyslexia. Traits associated with dyslexia can be an enormous advantage to a university department, and we should be incorporating dyslexic skillsets openly within the higher education setting to increase the quality of the student learning experience.

Finally, it may be time to realise the world is changing. As we reach to solve evermore complex problems, within academia research requires evermore novel interdisciplinary approaches. It is the need for such approaches that may highlight the incredible utility of those who are not neurotypical with the research and development environment.

Reflective questions

- What are your perceptions of dyslexia?
- Were you aware that it is a neurodivergence with positives and negatives, and that the negatives are not limited to reading and writing?
- How do you react to a colleague asking you for help?
- What do you and could you do in your practice that supports those around with dyslexia?

Recommendations

We suggest that all academics incorporate Universal Design for Learning into all our materials, whether you are aware of others' dyslexia or not. Practically this means ensuring that documents are written in an accessible type face, fonts are not too large, pictures are captioned, and PDFs and all material are accessible to screen readers.

If you are a teacher with dyslexia, pre-recording lectures can form part of lecture preparation, to refresh knowledge and act as a backup in case of memory failure. An added advantage is that it will also decrease the time needed to relearn material in subsequent years, as the teacher can review the recordings. This removes all the potential issues around recall, staying on task and making spelling/reading errors and is an effective coping strategy employed by Jennifer H. Comments such as "the recorded lectures help" and "we love the recorded lectures they make learning so much easier" from students show that they are in favour of having access to recorded and pre-recorded material of this type. I (Jennifer L) have seen my daughter access such material while studying her lecture notes and revising for university exams, as she understands that she processes information both aurally and visually, and this approach simultaneously supports students who struggle to keep up or take notes.

We suggest that academics with dyslexia have access to up-to-date technology and software to support them, complete with regular updates and training if needed.

Our final suggestion is that academics with dyslexia have specific mentoring in place so that they have input from a senior colleague if needed above and beyond arrangements in place for other staff.

References

Becher, T. & Trowler, P. (1989). *Academic Tribes and Territories.* (2nd edn). Buckingham: SRHE & Open University Press.

Bochner, A. & Ellis, C. (2016). *Evocative Autoethnography: Writing Lives and Telling Stories.* London: Routledge.

Bracken, S. & Novak, K. (eds). (2019). *Transforming Higher Education through Universal Design for Learning: An International Rerspective*. Abingdon: Routledge.

Brown, N., & Leigh, J. (2018). Ableism in academia: Where are the disabled and ill academics? *Disability & Society*, 33, 985–989.

Brown, N., & Leigh, J. (eds). (2020). *Ableism in Academia: Theorising Experiences of Disabilities and Chronic Illnesses in Higher Education*. London: UCL Press.

Brown, N., Thompson, P., & Leigh, J. (2018). Making academia more accessible. *Journal of Perspectives in Applied Academic Practice*, 6(2).

Ellis, C. (2004). *The Ethnographic I: A Methodological Novel about Auto-Ethnography* (Vol. 14). Walnut Creek, CA: AltaMira Press.

Finesilver, C., Leigh, J., & Brown, N. (2020). Invisible disability, unacknowledged diversity. In: Brown, N., & Leigh, J. (eds). *Ableism in Academia: Theorising Experiences of Disabilities and Chronic Illnesses in Higher Education*. London: UCL Press.

Gill, R. (2009). Breaking the silence: The hidden injuries of neo-liberal academia. In: Flood, R., & Gill, R. (eds). *Secrecy and Silence in the Research Process: Feminist Reflections*. London: Routledge.

Griffiths, S. (2012). 'Being dyslexic doesn't make me less of a teacher'. School placement experiences of student teachers with dyslexia: strengths, challenges and a model for support. *Journal of Research in Special Education Needs*, 12, 54–65.

Guardiola, J.G. (2001). The evolution of research on dyslexia. *Anuario de Psicologia*, 32(1), 3–30.

Hiscock, J. & Leigh, J. (2020). Exploring perceptions of and supporting dyslexia in teachers in higher education in STEM. *Innovations in Education and Teaching International*, 57, 714–723.

Leeuw, R. (2010). *Special Font for Dyslexia?* Master's thesis, University of Twente, Enschede, Netherlands. Retrieved from: http://essay.utwente.nl/60474/1/MA_thesis_R_Leeuw.pdf [Last accessed: March 2020].

Leigh, J. (2019). Exploring multiple identities: An embodied perspective on academic development and higher education research. *Journal of Somatic and Dance Practices*, 11(1), 99–114.

Lyon, G.R., Shaywitz, S.E., & Shaywitz, B.A. (2003). A definition of dyslexia. *Annals of Dyslexia*, 53(1), 1–14.

Marinus, E., Mostard, M., Segers, E., Schubert, T., Madelaine, A., & Wheldall, K. (2016). A special font for people with dyslexia: Does it work and, if so, why? *Dyslexia*, 22, 233–244.

Meerwald, A. (2013). Researcher|researched: Repositioning research paradigms. *Higher Education Research & Development*, 32(1), 43–55.

Miles, T.R., & Miles, E. (1999). *Dyslexia: A Hundred Years On*. Harlow: McGraw-Hill Education.

Pijpker, T. (2013). *Reading Performance of Dyslexics with a Special Font and a Colored Background*. Master's thesis, University of Twente, Enschede, Netherlands. Retrieved from: http://essay.utwente. nl/63321/1/Pijpker,_C._-_s1112430_%28verslag%29.pdf [Last accessed: March 2020].

Richardson, S.O. (1992). Historical perspectives on dyslexia. *Journal of Learning Disabilities*, 25(1), 40–47.

Riddick, B. (1995). Dyslexia: Dispelling the myths. *Disability & Society*, 10, 457–473.

Soler, J. (2009). The historical construction of dyslexia: Implications for higher education. In: Fletcher-Campbell, F., Reid, G., & Soler, J. (eds). *Understanding Difficulties in Literacy Development: Issues and Concepts*. Sage. 39–50.

The Dyslexia Association. (2016). *What Is Dyslexia?* Retrieved from: www.dyslexia.uk.net/what-is-dyslexia/ [Last accessed: March 2020].

University of Southampton. (2010). *Supporting Dyslexic Trainees and Teachers*. Retrieved from: http://adshe.org.uk/wp-content/uploads/Supporting-Dyslexia-Brochure.pdf [Last accessed: August 2017]. Similar version available at: www. southampton.ac.uk/assets/imported/transforms/content-block/UsefulDownloads_Download/19BF1A7298774C7 0A533FCFAF995661D/Dyslexia_support_guide.pdf [Last accessed: March 2020].

Wainwright, O. (2014). Dyslexie: The chubby-ankled font that makes reading easier for dyslexics. Retrieved from: www. theguardian.com/artanddesign/architecture-design-blog/ 2014/nov/12/dyslexie-new-font-that-makes-reading-easier-with-dyslexia [Last accessed: March 2020].

Depressed academics: building a group blog community

Mikael Vejdemo-Johansson and Ian P. Gent

Introduction

Mental health problems are widespread: close to 1 in 5 American adults experienced mental health problems in 2018 (Substance Abuse and Mental Health Services Administration, 2019a). Among them, unemployment is higher (Substance Abuse and Mental Health Services Administration, 2019b), school dropout more common (Dupéré et al, 2018) and overrepresentation in both the health care system (Owens et al, 2007; Department of Veterans Affairs, 2016) and the penal system (Bronson and Berzofsky, 2017; Skowyra and Cocozza, 2007).

Within academia, the prevalence is worse. A study (Levecque et al, 2017) in Flanders showed PhD students to be over twice as likely to score high on depression screening questionnaires, with relative risks of 2.43 versus highly educated general population, of 2.84 versus highly educated employees and 1.85 versus higher education students, respectively.

As a way to build a community around these issues, and as a stepping stone to further work in mental health advocacy in academia, we have run a group blog for academics with mental health problems since 2013. Over the years, we have slowly managed to build more and more momentum for mental health advocacy in general, and the group blog has played a role in empowering our own visibility and advocacy.

In this chapter, we describe in the section 'Inception' how our work with Depressed Academics started. This is followed by our design choices for the group blog, in the section 'Choices in community building'. The blog has gone through several noteworthy events: a post that resonates very strongly with almost every reader passing by the blog, and a guest blogger whose post was read at the memorial service after she succumbed to her depression. We describe both of these in the section 'Notable events'. We have found aspects of running the community to be difficult, especially given our own personal struggles. We describe our experiences of how mood and executive function spectrum disorders interfere with the work involved in building a community in the section 'Notable struggles'.

One result emerging from our advocacy came about during the spring of 2019, when Mikael organised:

- a panel discussion at the Joint Mathematics Meetings, the largest mathematics conference in the world;
- an article (Vejdemo-Johansson et al, 2019) on mental health in the mathematics profession for *AMS Notices* for the American Mathematical Society, one of the largest community magazines for mathematicians;
- a follow-up panel discussion planned for the 2020 Joint Mathematics Meetings;
- work on building a community effort, backed by the American Mathematical Society is currently ongoing.

Impact and issues

While some mental health issues interfere with the ability to produce reliable output, as depicted inter alia in the play *Proof* (Auburn, 2001), most conditions strike against more benign aspects of the functioning for an academic: motivation, initiative, executive function, emotional stability and the like. At the benign end of the spectrum of consequences, mental health issues impact quality of life, while at the more extreme end people die.

Within academia specifically, there are examples both of death from suicide (Wikipedia: Floer, n.d.) and of prominent and highly productive researchers leaving academia.

Inception

In 2011 the well-known hackers Len Sassaman and Ilya Zhitomirskiy both died from suicide. This spawned a number of reactions (Noisebridge, 2011a, 2011b) from the hacker and hackerspace community, including a panel discussion (28c3, 2011) on *Geeks and Depression* at the 28th Chaos Communication Congress in Berlin. A few years later, Aaron Schwartz died from suicide in early 2013. Following Aaron's demise, a wave of confessionals (Fenwick, 2012; Dalton, 2013) swept through the hacker community. To reduce the feeling of isolation and increase visibility, many posted statements about their own mental health and their own struggles. A member of both the mathematical, the academic and the hackerspace communities, Mikael watched the efforts in the hackerspace community to increase awareness, support and protection of their own community members, with a stark contrast to the corresponding state of support in academia.

Mikael himself was one of many who took part in this wave of visibility confessionals. He posted about his history with bipolar disorder and depression diagnoses (Vejdemo-Johansson, n.d.), including some details of how his mood disorder expresses itself. Immediately after his posting, Ian made contact, and explained that he suffered from clinical depression. The two of us had earlier worked for a year side by side at the University of St Andrews, Scotland, and neither knew that the other one was handling any sort of mental health problems.

The email conversation where Mikael articulated the community groundswell he was observing in the hackerspace community, and the perceived lack of community support in academia, culminated in our joint creation of a group blog, Depressed Academics (http://blog.depressedacademics.org), as a seed point to build a community.

Choices in community building

From the start we had ambitions of creating an inclusive community, with sufficient moderation to avoid the infamous internet comment section atmospheres that often develop. To this end, the comment field at blog.depressedacademics.org includes the following statement on our comment policy:

> We reserve the right to edit all comments. In particular, we will not tolerate phobic content (race, sex, gender, sexual orientation, nationality, religion, mental health status, etc.) nor personal attacks or threats toward another commenter, significantly off-topic, or as an obvious trolling attempt.

We have not had reason to exercise these moderation policies.

We also wanted, from the start, to make this a community with many voices. We sought collaborators and guest authors, both through giving posting rights to additional authors and through posting text submitted to us by email on the blog. Throughout we have held as our policy that the choice in appearing under a pseudonym or a wider known name remains with each person. By no means are we interested in forcing or even too strongly encouraging our collaborators to come out with their mental health problems in an identifiable fashion. The two of us have always been open under our own primary names. Whether or not this has been a wise choice is hard to tell. Ian has a stable permanent position with relatively low risk of running into more or less conscious discriminatory practices, while Mikael at this time was on his fourth year of what would end up being eight years as a postdoc before finding a tenure track position.

Notable events

The two most notable impacts our blog has had both involve Ian: one as the author of the post that resonates most strongly with readers and with passers-by, and the other through a friendship built with a student he invited to contribute to the blog.

The post we just call 'The Post'

In June 2013, Ian wrote a blog post entitled 'I don't necessarily want to kill myself; I just want to become dead somehow'. The post itself articulates some of Ian's thoughts around suicidality and how he deals with it – largely, through napping. This post ended up resonating dramatically. It is our most viewed post of all time by an order of magnitude, as the snapshot from our statistics shows (see Table 16.1).

It is important to emphasise that our most viewed post is not necessarily our most successful. Our most successful post would the one that helped most, whether it be the author of the post, readers of the post, or anybody else. We cannot know what post that is. But 'most viewed' is unarguable. Also, it is the most commented on, again by many, many times.

But the statistical success of that post feels very like a mixed blessing. Somehow it has sparked so many people to express their pain, and the pain seems so overwhelming.

The post title, 'I don't necessarily want to kill myself', comes from this wonderful comic: *Depression Part Two* by the wonderful Allie Brosh (2013). The comic is a long one and expresses a lot about how Ian felt. The title phrase comes from one of the panels from the comic (see Figure 16.1).

The post itself is not massively insightful. So why is it – capital letters – The Post?

Table 16.1: Snapshot of post views, Depressed Academics

Entry	Date	Comments	Page views
I don't necessarily want to kill myself ...	9 June 2013	127	73,218
High Functioning Depressive (4)	21 March 2013	2	4,662
Link: It's not you, it's a disease	22 March 2013	0	4,308
Having a breakdown as an early career researcher	1 March 2018	0	3,055
Why Depressed Academics?	13 January 2013	0	1,652

Figure 16.1: Panel from *Depression Part Two* by Allie Brosh

Source: Brosh, 2013

As time passed and we moderated further comments, we saw more and more painful and deeply pained comments of people it had struck a chord with. If you wish, you can go and find the comments yourself, but here are some excerpts. In fact, to reduce triggers we are only taking some indicative comments, not the worst things people said:

> "Even on a great day, given the choice I would opt out of living."

> "I feel as though my existence is worthless."

> "I hate my existence, I hate the world I live in."

> "Wishing I didn't exist is an everyday thing for me."

> "I completely relate to it and this was almost word for word what I typed into Google."

Those are just quotes from the first five comments, not selected highlights. We have more than 100 comments and many of them are hundreds of words long. The pain is just so immense, and these are people who *do not* want to kill themselves. It is heart-rending to read the comments and there is so little or nothing we can do to help. At the same time, of course, it is humbling to have written something that touches so many people. And we are pleased to have been able to let people speak for themselves on our site.

Being a sounding board like this is part of what we wanted for the site, but most people posting are not academics, or do not say they are. Why? What happened? We believe the clue is in the quoted text of the last comment: "what I typed into Google". We think that searching for something like 'I don't want to kill myself' had a good chance of directing you to The Post. It used to be on the first page of results and is still in the first few pages. At the time of writing, the first hit is now for a counselling service for the suicidal, which is a good match, whether through an automatic process or active intervention by Google.

In summary, it seems that somehow we hit on something that does not get a lot of attention on the back of a great artist's work on the same topic. But the human pain we accidentally uncovered, and are seeing in our comments as we moderate them, is a remarkable thing and I think clearly shows why it is The Post.

The memorial service

As a lecturer, there is no doubt that the best friend Ian ever made among undergraduate students was Madeleine (Madz) Conway or Patrick (Patch) Reynolds. Which one was the best? Choosing between her and him is easy because they are in fact the same person. She and he had many different names and gender identities even in the shortish time Ian knew them, so please do not get confused during the rest of the post. These events have proven difficult to describe with the detachment inherent in academic prose styles. Instead, the remainder of this section is written in the first person by Ian.

I thought of her as a friend long before she died. I call her the best undergrad friend I ever made because I keep a certain distance between me and students: I think this is necessary since I am somebody who is in a position to judge and assess them. I try to be friendly but not become friends at least until after they have finished their courses. But it was different with Patch. She came to university to study computer science (CS). I did not know it at the time but it had been a massive struggle for her to get here, and indeed had included my colleagues showing sympathy towards her unconventional path through school, which had included hospitalisation. I was first-year coordinator, so naturally came across her. She was extraordinarily enthusiastic and interested and had bright yellow hair, and was not shy in coming forward to talk about things. The first memory I have is of her asking if soya milk was available for coffee because she was vegan. A colleague started getting soya milk for her and other students.

I would not have called her a friend at this point, but we did have a lot of friendly contact during her studies. In writing this, I went back to check my emails from the period to remind myself of encounters. And I was stunned how fast things moved. She was incredibly open about her issues from the very start. I remember a conversation on the doorstep of our building, where she showed her incredible enthusiasm for the subject and learning. But looking at my email, I find that I reached out to her because she had mentioned in passing her mental health issues. I mentioned this blog, then just a few months old, and that I had issues, too, and in response she told me a lot about herself. She mentioned her work for BEAT, an eating disorders charity. As somebody with many problems herself, it was typical of her that she worked hard to help others with similar problems.

Emails show how often we engaged, sometimes because she needed to discuss aspects of the course or her work, but often just to discuss things that were on her mind. And many other meetings where she just popped by to say hello would not be recorded in my emails. One sentence in one email caught my eye from this period: "For some reason I trust you as a decent person in CS, and there are a lot of them in this department". Statements like that mean a lot to me.

But still, it was not in her period of study as a computer scientist that I would have called her a friend. We would have discussions about her issues with courses and her mental health.

Just a few weeks into her studies Madz told us she was transitioning from female to male, and using the name Patrick Reynolds or Patch for short. I had no idea what to do as coordinator, but fortunately our university policies seemed to be pretty good and straightforward. Again, Patch talked to me a lot about issues and appointments meaning missing classes, but as a very open person everybody knew what was going on and it seemed to be easily accepted.

This is kind of coming over as just a story about Patch, but it has also covered a young person with a lot going on in their head: serious mental health and eating disorder issues, and gender reassignment, but through all this being incredibly enthusiastic about their course and incredibly outgoing. In fact, at some point she mentioned that she also had an autism spectrum diagnosis, but the stereotyped lack of social skills was in her case exactly reversed.

I must have suggested that she would be welcome to write a post for our blog. At some point, Patch took up the offer and wrote a beautiful blog post (Reynolds, 2014) for Depressed Academics, 'On being the happiest person in the room', of which more later.

One day around this time Patch appeared in my office and told me he was saying goodbye. I did not know what it meant, but it turned out that he was quitting computer science and not coming back. He took a leave of absence for the second semester and came back the following year as a geologist. Perhaps the most remarkable thing was that, after stopping studying the subject, he helped out at open days to tell prospective students how awesome we were as a place to study, and remained as enthusiastic as ever.

It was after this that I started thinking of Patch as a friend unreservedly. There was little chance I would have to assess him and he continued to come by to chat when visiting his CS friends, as he often did. I remember him for example as an early and passionate supporter of Jeremy Corbyn for leader of the UK Labour Party.

In his second year in St Andrews he also changed his mind about study and again had a leave of absence, returning this time as a film studies student, and now self-identifying as a woman. She was still a friend and a visitor in her third calendar year at St Andrews. One memory stands out from that period. I was still first-year coordinator and during the week before teaching started, we had induction events with the new students. At one event, I was talking to new students, who had been in St Andrews less than a week, and I mentioned that our degree has a lot of flexibility, with one of our past students having changed from CS to film studies. Quick as a flash, one of the group said "Do you mean Patch?", which blew my mind since how did they know her and her history? It turned out they were staying in the same hall, which is part of explanation, the rest being that she was Patch and had instantly got to know everyone in the hall.

The other seminal memory is the tragic one. A few weeks later, I got an email from a student asking for an extension because another student in their hall had died: Patch Reynolds. This was heart-breaking. Among other tributes, I wrote a small piece for the blog (Gent, 2015): 'Rest in peace, dear Patch'. There was an outpouring of many other tributes from friends and fellow students, and also people and groups she had helped such as the eating disorders charity BEAT.

There was a family funeral near her home, which I did not attend, but in the new year the university chaplain helped to organise a memorial service for her, for everybody to remember her. Somehow, I got involved and ended up volunteering to speak, and it was agreed that it would be fitting to read out her wonderful Depressed Academics post from two years earlier. Here's what I read:

> Often, I am told that I appear incredibly happy, positive and optimistic. By often, I genuinely mean at least once a week. When I tell people that I am actually a clinically-diagnosed depressive with Asperger's, anxiety and an eating disorder, the response is usually befuddlement. "But you don't act depressed/anxious/socially awkward/etc! Surely it can't be that bad?" they exclaim, "You act happier than I do and there is nothing wrong with me!" they continue, shocked that someone with mental illness can appear to be as happy as a small child who has just discovered how to blow a raspberry. According to many of the people I converse with, having a psychiatric disorder makes me unable to feel joy,

express delight or giggle with glee. They wonder what exactly my secret is. Weed? Copious amounts of alcohol? Mountains of Prozac? Nope. I'm just good at finding things to be happy about.

Currently it's the fact that my Lush products arrived and they are making my flat smell absolutely delicious. It's the fact that the person who packed the products in the box wrote their name on the invoice with a love heart. It's a letter sent to me from a friend in the states. It's another friend promising to start a rock collection in my honour. It's my self-stirring mug. It's the box of tissues I bought with a boat on the front. It's an email from my Geography tutor telling me not to worry that I couldn't get out of bed due to the flu because he also has it. It's my spotty duvet cover, my wind-up Lego torch, my Thor figure, my replica of the ring of power, my mother sending me a picture of my dog, my hair defying gravity. It's the thought that someone has just read Harry Potter for the first time, that someone just laughed so hard they cried, that someone slipped on a banana skin and landed on their arse. The amusement of mishearing song lyrics, the fun of playing a videogame in a way that you don't normally do. It's the little things, and finding humour in everything. (Reynolds, 2014)

There are also parts I did not read out, because she had died by suicide as a result of what her family called a "terminal mental-illness". So, it did not seem appropriate to read her closing comments in that post:

Preparing for the bad days on the good days is one of the best things you can do, and certainly one of the most useful things I have discovered in my 7 year-long battle with mental illness. By planning for the worst and ensuring you have safe ways of improving your condition can save your life – it's definitely saved mine. (Reynolds, 2014)

I wish so much, it could saved her life another time, and another, and another. It was not to be. I have thought of her so often since then. For years, I would constantly see somebody in town and think "Oh there's Patch" before remembering it could not be. When I mentioned this on Facebook more than one of my friends said they had exactly the same thing.

Patch's friendship enriched my life. Her passing greatly saddened it, but did bring one good thing. As well as her friendship, our shared grief brought me into contact with some new friends who I still have, such as her uncle and the film studies lecturer who had got to know her in her period as a student there in the same way I had in computer science.

And one last thing I remember from the memorial. My colleague who had helped her get into St Andrews attended and had previously said he was worried that helping her get here had been the wrong thing to do, as it had ended badly. I was sure the worry was misplaced so I explicitly asked the family and they confirmed that St Andrews had been the "perfect place" for Patch. I am glad she came here to study and glad to have been her friend.

Notable struggles

Community building takes energy and conscious effort. To keep a community alive and active requires activity. While our work with the blog has inspired our advocacy work in other realms, we have not consistently had the energy to keep the blog active at all times. Through the years, the posting frequency has varied widely (see Table 16.2).

Our own interpretation of the difficulties we have had in keeping this community active is in a particularly insidious Catch 22. To keep a community active, requires energy and consistent regular attention, whereas the depression, anxiety, mood disorder spectrum of disorders actively hamper the executive functioning

Table 16.2: Frequency of posting on Depressed Academics

Year	2013	2014	2015	2016	2017	2018
Post count	117	28	51	13	5	14

and the self-confidence needed to provide that exact regular attention and energy.

This exact issue also surfaced when writing this article. As we have worked our way through it, energy and attention from the authors have been flagging, and both episodes and treatment adjustments have come and gone, all of which distracts from working on articulating our experiences and hampers our progress.

Reflective questions

We do not claim to have answers as much as we have questions, among those possibly the most central one being:

- How do you build a community when everyone in the community suffers from energy drains and executive dysfunction?
- The Depressed Academics group blog grew out of a wish to replicate efforts from a different community. How transferrable do you think that advocacy and support network efforts are between distinct communities? How can you tell whether two communities are similar enough for such a transference?
- What does 'success' mean for this or any other community group blog in an area such as mental health? If there is such a measure does it matter if Depressed Academics is successful or not?
- One of the points of the Depressed Academics blog was to be visibly open about mental health issues. How does one reconcile the perceived benefits of this visibility with the possible pressure it might place on others to be open when it is not appropriate for them?
- Many of the most meaningful posts on the blog come out of human pain experienced by the authors of posts or others. Is there a danger in encouraging and glorifying this pain by celebrating those posts?

Recommendations

We will stratify our recommendations from group building to how to actively help colleagues and friends.

To build an online community

While we feel obligated to provide some recommendations in this area, we should emphasise that we do not feel expert given that (given the caveat about the meaning of 'success' listed in 'Reflective questions') we have not been as successful in building an online community as we originally hoped.

Ensure you have a moderator and core contributor team of a critical mass; for a community characterised by executive dysfunction this means even larger than usual, to compensate for the likelihood that any given member might stop contributing for a period of time.

For an online community in a sensitive area such as poor mental health, *allow for different levels of anonymity*. We have always been happy to accept posts under real names, or under self-ascribed pseudonyms, or using pseudonyms we assigned ourselves (to aid readers in following posts by the same author) or completely anonymously.

Setup moderation policies immediately, and enforce them when needed. Nielsen-Hayden (2005) discusses in some detail how to use active moderation to build a community, and we have based our approach on their work. It has been rare for us to delete online comments but occasionally it has been necessary. More commonly, however, we have had to avoid posting spam or marketing comments. This has been enabled by our blog-software but has the unfortunate side effects that there is sometimes a long delay for genuine comments to be posted after one of us has looked at them manually.

Be accepting of different viewpoints and styles in your contributors. We have never attempted to police our contributors' views. Obviously, we would reject posts which crossed some obvious lines such as racism, but it has never been necessary to do so.

Clarify early on expectations on scope and responsibilities.

To help a colleague

Once one becomes known as a mental-health advocate, it is likely that one is going to be a person that colleagues approach for help with their own issues. Indeed, we have found that one of the greatest privileges of being open about our personal issues has been being trusted with the confidences of others.

The most important advice if a colleague does approach you is that one needs to *take their worries seriously*. A colleague who asks for a minute to chat will most likely just be wanting to chat. But also, be aware that if you are concerned about their own safety or that of others, then you should express these concerns and encourage them to seek help.

First off, you are unlikely to be a therapist – and if you are, *you are unlikely to be this colleague's therapist*. If you were, you wouldn't need this advice. This means you need to consider self-care and boundaries for yourself when stepping in and helping. Helping can definitely mean helping someone to seek out qualified help. In the same light, be aware that thoughts or advice that might be most helpful for you may not be the most helpful for your colleague.

That said, between the rampant invisibility and the widespread ableist and performance-focused attitudes in academia, it can well be important to *mark yourself as approachable*. We do that in part by talking openly about our own struggles; this brings people to talk to us about their own struggles.

If you are open about your own struggles, whether through articles like this or talking about it openly, remind people that there is no reason for them to be open just because you are. Many people like their health problems to remain private.

To help yourself

It is very hard for us to accept either as academics or private individuals wanting to help others, but please remember one cardinal rule. *Your own health is more important* than both your academic work and any help you might be able to offer others in the community.

Acknowledgements

We would like to thank many people, including all contributors to the website Depressed Academics (some of whom we cannot name for anonymity reasons). We thank the family of Patch Reynolds for permission to quote her article. We are very grateful to Nicole Brown for her organisation of the workshop on Ableism in Academia and help in the preparation of this manuscript. We have drawn a lot of inspiration for our work with Depressed Academics from efforts in the hacker community, where along several others maradydd and daravinne stand out.

References

28c3. (2011). 28c3: Geeks and Depression Panel. *YouTube*, 31 December. Retrieved from: www.youtube.com/watch?v=QnfOOoTOrDE [Last accessed: January 2021].

Auburn, D. (2001). *Proof: A Play*. London: Faber and Faber.

Bronson, J., & Berzofsky, M. (2017). Indicators of mental health problems reported by prisoners and jail inmates, 2011–12. *Bureau of Justice Statistics*, June, 1–6.

Brosh, A. (2013). *Depression Part Two*. Hyperbole and a half. Retrieved from: https://hyperboleandahalf.blogspot.com/2013/05/depression-part-two.html [Last accessed: March 2020].

Dalton, J. (2013). One geek's guide to clinical depression. *BlueHackers.org*. Retrieved from: https://bluehackers.org/2013/02/13/one-geeks-guide-to-clinical-depression [Last accessed: February 2020].

Department of Veterans Affairs. (2016). *Suicide Among Veterans and Other Americans 2001–2014*. Washington, DC, Office of Suicide Prevention. Retrieved from: www.sprc.org/sites/default/files/resource-program/2016suicidedatareport.pdf [Last accessed: March 2020].

Dupéré, V., Dion, E., Nault-Brière, F., Archambault, I., Leventhal, T., & Lesage, A. (2018). Revisiting the link between depression symptoms and high school dropout: Timing of exposure matters. *Journal of Adolescent Health*, 62(2), 205–11.

Fenwick, P. (2012). I have depression: An open letter by Paul Fenwick. *BlueHackers.org*. Retrieved from: https://bluehackers. org/2012/11/29/i-have-depression-an-open-letter-by-paul-fenwick [Last accessed: February 2015].

Gent, I. (2015). Rest in peace, dear Patch. *Depressed Academics*. Retrieved from: https://blog.depressedacademics.org/2015/11/rest-in-peace-dear-patch.html [Last accessed: March 2020].

Lentz, A., & Dalton, J. (n.d.). bluehackers.org/.

Levecque, K., Anseel, F., De Beuckelaer, A., Van der Heyden, J., & Gisle, L. (2017). Work organization and mental health problems in PhD students. *Research Policy*, 46(4), 868–79.

Nielsen-Hayden, T. (2005). Virtual panel participation. *Making Light Blog*. Retrieved from: http://nielsenhayden. com/makinglight/archives/006036.html [Last accessed: November 2019].

Noisebridge. (2011a). Geeks and Depression Meetup (in San Francisco). *Noisebridge Blog*, 21 November. blog. noisebridge.net/post/137439336718/geeks-depression-meetup-in-san-francisco

Noisebridge. (2011b). Please Reach Out. *Noisebridge Blog*, 19 November. blog.noisebridge.net/post/137439331543/please-reach-out

Owens P.L., Mutter, R., & Stocks, C. (2007). Mental health and substance abuse-related emergency department visits among adults. *Statistical Brief# 92*.

Reynolds, P. (2014). On being the happiest person in the room. *Depressed Academics*. Retrieved from: https://blog. depressedacademics.org/2014/02/on-being-happiest-person-in-room.html [Last accessed: March 2020].

Skowyra, K.R., & Cocozza, J.J. (2007). *Blueprint for Change: A Comprehensive Model for the Identification and Treatment of Youth with Mental Health Needs in Contact with the Juvenile Justice System*. New York: Policy Research Associates.

Substance Abuse and Mental Health Services Administration. (2019a). *Key Substance Use and Mental Health Indicators in the United States: Results from the 2018 National Survey on Drug Use and Health. (HHS Publication No. PEP19-5068, NSDUH Series H-54).* Rockville, MD: Center for Behavioral Health Statistics and Quality, Substance Abuse and Mental Health Services Administration. Retrieved from: www.samhsa.gov/data/sites/default/files/cbhsq-reports/NSDUHNationalFindingsReport2018/NSDUHNationalFindingsReport2018.pdf [Last accessed: March 2020].

Substance Abuse and Mental Health Services Administration. (2019b). *2018 NSDUH Detailed Tables.* Retrieved from: www.samhsa.gov/data/report/2018-nsduh-detailed-tables [Last accessed: March 2020].

Vejdemo-Johansson, M. (n.d.). *Mental Illness.* mikael.johanssons.org/bipolar.html.

Vejdemo-Johansson, M., Curry, J., & Corrigan, J. (2019). Mental health in the mathematics community. *AMS Notices,* 66(7), 1079–1084.

Wikipedia: Floer. (n.d.). *Wikipedia Page for Andreas Floer.* Retrieved from: https://en.wikipedia.org/wiki/Andreas_Floer [Last accessed: March 2020].

17

Cancer, bereavement and work

Nicola Martin

Introduction

Writing this is not without personal risk. Identity is not only internal but also 'exists in the minds of others' (Little et al, 2002: 170). Prior to 2011, cancer did not shape my identity in my eyes or anyone else's. It does now, but I do not want people to see me and think 'cancer'. Socrates is associated with the expression 'an unexamined life is not worth living' (McElwain, 2013). The need to examine all aspects of my life came into sharp focus when cancer made an unwelcome appearance. I resolved to ensure that dignity and compassion would underpin all my actions. Tony Benn said that the most helpful role older people can play in society is to encourage those younger and less experienced (Benn, 2004). I agree. As a senior academic, I am well placed to do this, and I have always subscribed to the principle of usefulness in research. While getting cancer is scary and the loss of a child to cancer is the most frightening thing of all, I felt that writing accessibly about it might help others to understand, hence my contribution to this book. My focus here is on the workplace. Colleagues threw me a lifeline and in writing this I hope to give something back.

Background

John died nearly seven years ago, at twenty-five. Undoubtedly, my grief will last for the rest of my life, but I am functioning. Social and personal reconstruction of my identity and the feeling that my former sense of self is missing colours my engagement with life and work. Having lost a child, I feel like Sleeping Beauty's thirteenth fairy. For the benefit of an international audience, she is the one who spoiled Beauty's christening with a hundred-year sleeping curse.

'Bereaved mum' was bad enough as a label, but three years later I added a dollop of my own cancer. Although I was treated successfully, intersecting traumas have left me with a strong sense of before and after. This feeling is not uncommon post bereavement (Cheung and Delfabbro, 2016; Greenblatt and Lee, 2018; Hastings, 2000; Rosenberg et al, 2012; Scott, 1997). Foucault (1994) describes experiences which place one outside the dominant hegemony as 'othering'. I feel 'othered'. Most people do not get cancer and children are not expected to die before their parents, especially in parts of the minority world not plagued by extreme poverty, preventable disease and conflict.

Throughout John's twelve months of treatment I worked. He died on 12 December and I returned to work on 4 January. My cancer treatment required me to take two eight-week periods of sick leave and I needed a phased return post-surgery. I got off lightly. Advice I would give to anyone else would be to try and avoid finding yourself back at your desk too soon wearing office clothes, superhero lipstick and an unconvincing smile. 'Finding yourself' is a deliberately chosen form of words. There was something passive about my finding myself in the office, particularly after John died. Recalling how I managed then is almost impossible. Shock seems to have wiped my memory. Colleagues were amazingly supportive, and I recall saying to myself, 'Try harder. It's work, not therapy'. These feelings relate more to bereavement than to cancer. My own cancer left me with survivor guilt and hidden impairments and reinforced the sense of disassociation which started when John was diagnosed.

Bereavement leave policies and the Equality Act 2010

Legislation and policies offer the workplace some pointers about what is supposed to happen when an employee is affected by cancer and bereavement. Underpinning the Equality Act 2010 is the contention that diversity is a positive thing (Bebbington, 2009; Martin, 2017). Although I remember feeling that John's death negated everything I had ever done or would ever do, what happened did not actually cancel years of successful work and skills acquired along the way. Without supportive employers, I would not have been able to continue working. Duties under the Equality Act possibly provided some sort of framework, but actually, it was being treated with compassion that made work possible.

Cancer is covered by the Equality Act from the point of diagnosis, under the protected characteristic of disability. Therefore, the requirement for employers to make reasonable adjustments is anticipatory. People indirectly affected by disability are also protected by the Equality Act, so reasonable adjustments around flexible working to care for a family member should be part of the plan. As with any impairment covered by the Equality Act, once anyone at work knows, the institution is deemed to know and therefore expected to adjust reasonably. Confidentiality is not negated by 'deemed to know' and sensitivity is required. Employees do not necessarily want an all-staff email to announce 'the big C'. Human Resources and Occupational Health have specific roles around anti-discriminatory practices and practical adjustments.

Bereavement in itself is not covered by the Equality Act. Institutions tend to vary in arrangements they make for bereavement leave. The Parental Bereavement (Leave and Pay) Act 2018 was timetabled for 2020. Its intention is to entitle eligible employees to two weeks' paid leave following the death of a child up to the age of 18 (Brown, 2018). This would not have done me any good as my son died in early adulthood. It fails to recognise that children become adults, but parents are still parents. Bereavement is frequently associated with mental health problems or post-traumatic stress disorder (White, 2013), both of which are identified as disability and, rather ambiguously, do not have to be 'clinically well recognised' according to the Equality Act. Complicated grief is defined as a mental health concern in the Diagnostic and Statistical Manual of Mental Disorders, updated iteration 5 (2017). Access to medical support or counselling is not a foregone conclusion, but involvement in these systems is likely to result in the acquisition of mental health labels and often medication. Wellbeing is receiving some attention in the workplace, with many organisations advertising counselling for employees (Lomas et al, 2017; Thomson et al, 2018). Usually provision is limited to six sessions and cognitive behavioural therapy. Research exploring the efficacy of cognitive behavioural therapy for bereaved parents is scant (Cohen et al, 2006; Endo et al, 2015). Often, there is nothing else on the table unless the individual is able to pay. However, grief and depression often coexist. Severe depression is covered by the Equality Act, although ordinary rather than 'Complicated Grief' (White, 2013) may not be. Like depression, anxiety commonly accompanies bereavement. When these conditions tip over into mental health concerns covered by the Equality Act is a matter of degree or self or clinical identification. Bereaved parents may be diagnosed or self-identify with complicated grief more often than people who have lost an elderly relative. It is not possible to say that this is definitely so, because research which focuses specifically on people who have lost one or more of their children is sparse (Hastings, 2000; Rosenberg et al, 2012). The Equality Act is apparently woolly around the edges when it comes to bereavement. It really depends on whether the bereaved person has acquired a mental illness label, in which case they are covered. Cancer is less ambiguous.

Applying grief, loss and bereavement theory

Grief and loss are not only about bereavement. Losing a job, for example, can evoke a sense of loss. Grief may follow. Cancer can result in losing one's previous sense of identity as someone without cancer (Cheung and Delfabbro, 2016; Little et al, 2002). Feelings of loss resulting from my own cancer were never something I grasped on a conscious level because I was in the early stages of a far more profound grief. Primarily, I was concerned for my family. Research with people who have had cancer suggests that anxiety, depression and stress are part of the toxic cocktail (Cheung and Delfabbro, 2016; Greenblatt and Lee, 2018; Little et al, 2002).

Symptoms of anxiety include restlessness, a sense of dread, being on edge, difficulty concentrating, irritability, impatience, distractibility and stress. Anxiety is often exacerbated by uncontrollable stress, the symptoms for which include dizziness, drowsiness, pins and needles, palpitations, dry mouth, sweating, shortness of breath, stomach-ache, nausea, diarrhoea, headache, excessive thirst, frequent urinating, period problems and insomnia (Reeves, 2013; Haig, 2015). Anxiety has to be kept consciously under control following cancer treatment. Little niggles can stimulate fear that the monster has returned to finish what it started (Little et al, 2002). Bereaved parents can become extremely anxious about their other children, particularly if there is any genetic component to the cancer death (Rosenberg et al, 2012). Making sure my anxiety does not oppress my surviving children requires effort.

Depression and anxiety often accompany grief and loss (Greenblatt and Lee, 2018; Reeves, 2013). While celebrating remission from cancer, after-effects of treatment can be somewhat depressing (Cheung and Delfabbro, 2016). I was used to being able to keep going like a little pit pony, and it frustrates me that I tire more easily now. Differences between clinical and reactive depression merit more discussion than space allows. Reactive depression can tip into clinical depression, especially if left untreated. Haig (2015: 87) listed symptoms of clinical depression including: 'fatigue, low self-esteem, slowing of movement and speech, appetite disturbance, irritability, introversion, derealisation and anhedonia (which is "the inability to experience pleasure in anything")'. Derealisation as defined by Haig strongly resonated with my own feeling after John died of not being a real person: 'feeling detached from oneself' ... I derealised. The string that holds onto that feeling of selfhood, the feeling of being me, was cut, and it floated away like a helium balloon' (Haig, 2015: 187).

Bereavement is a very tangible cause of depression and anxiety. Being depressed and anxious after successful cancer treatment, although common, is perhaps more intangible (Greenblatt and Lee, 2018). The feeling of having no right to self-indulgent emotions is expressed eloquently by Haig (2015): 'If you feel the same amount of depression as someone would naturally feel in a prisoner of war camp, and are instead in a nice semidetached house in the free world, then you think "Crap, this is everything I ever wanted, why aren't I happy?"' (Haig, 2015: 164). My cancer broke a few windows in my nice home which were easy enough to fix, and John's cancer reduced his house to ashes. Like Haig, I feel that I have no right to bang on about a lesser catastrophe. Of course, I live with survivor guilt and the sad fact that it was not in my power to swap places with my beloved son.

Associated with anxiety, depression and stress is low self-esteem (Haig, 2015: 158). Low self-esteem tips into my work and is easily explained by my sense that I failed at the most important job I will ever have. Mothers are supposed to keep their children safe. Positive feedback is something I find difficult to own and my CV looks to me like it belongs to someone else because of the bashing my sense of self has taken. The Jungian notion of 'individuation' is relevant to conditions which lead to the healthy state of 'a true integrated self' (Jung, 1967; Kotzé, 2014,: 16). Maslow (1998) refers to a 'hierarchy of needs' necessary for self-actualisation. These include physiological requirements, safety, belonging and self-esteem. Disruption of the underpinning processes for individuation or self-actualisation inhibit the achievement of one's full potential. Cancer disrupts feelings of safety (Costanzo et al, 2007; Yaskowich et al, 2003). Disrupted progress towards self-actualisation because of cancer is discussed (Coreil et al, 2012) but research in this field is limited. In 2011, before John's diagnosis, I was flying high professionally, and John was studying at Oxford University. In extremis, it is clearly possible to slide down Maslow's pyramid suddenly and rapidly.

Disrupted earlier attachments and lack of social support can impact on one's ability to cope with trauma (Reeves, 2013; Bowlby, 1969, 1982; Freud and Strachey, 1966). Fortunately for me, I am built on very strong attachment foundations and have extremely supportive family, friends and colleagues. Bourdieu's

(2002) notion of social capital is relevant to my situation in this respect. Some people are less lucky. Financial worries were highlighted as a factor increasing stress on parents of children with cancer (Rosenberg et al, 2012). In Bourdieusian terms, I also have the privilege of economic capital, which eliminates a rich seam of worry.

Having experienced extreme stress while John was undergoing treatment, followed by profound grief when it was all over, workplace stress does not trouble me. While I am committed to doing a good job and welcome the distraction, I am acutely aware that the world will keep turning whether I work or not. The idea that the world is still turning without my son felt completely unacceptable to me for the first few years. Acceptance is identified as a stage in grieving. Although I am moving in that direction, it is a long and winding road.

Kübler-Ross's (1970) *On Death and Dying* is an early influential work which has been updated several times (Field et al, 2005; Klass et al, 2014; Parkes, 1988; Parkes and Prigerson, 2013; Stroebe et al, 2010). Research with terminally ill patients and their families framed her staged model of grieving. The stages are: denial (and isolation), anger, bargaining, depression and acceptance (Kübler-Ross, 1970: 34–138). Guilt and hope are part of the picture and progress is not necessarily linear, time-limited, or identical for everyone. Subsequent staged theorists built on Kübler-Ross's theme. Parkes and Prigerson (2013) describes numbness, pining, disorganisation and reorganisation. Worden (2018) identifies 'the tasks of grief' as acceptance, working through the pain, adjusting to the new situation and emotionally relocating the deceased in the past. 'Continuing bonds' is a contested idea which some theorists regard as symptomatic of complicated grief (White, 2013), especially if accompanied by the sense that the loved one is not really dead (Field et al, 2005; Klass et al, 2014; Scott, 1997; Stroebe et al, 2014). Acute distress lasting over six months and accompanied by intrusive repeated mental pictures, avoidance behaviours, lack of self-care and social isolation is defined by White (2013) as 'complicated grief'.

A systematic review of 121 studies (Rosenberg et al, 2012) concluded that parents who had lost a child to cancer experienced prolonged extreme distress. Studies cited focused on children under 18. Literature about loss of an adult son or daughter is too thin to be called patchy. Irritation does not quite encapsulate how I relate to the idea of complicated grief. White's (2013) research did not treat bereaved parents as a specific category but Bernstein (1997) brings insider perspective to the table as a bereaved mother. Her study involving over fifty bereaved parents was entitled *When the Bough Breaks: Forever After the Death of a Son or Daughter*. 'Forever' may ring alarm bells for clinicians keen to diagnose complicated grief, but parents who have lost their children experience our ongoing grief as simple. It does not make us unemployable, and it is ever-present but there is nothing particularly complicated about a broken heart. Talking about the death of his five-year-old son, Ken Loach, said 'It changes you, you carry a stone inside' (Hattenstone, 2016). Grief feels exactly like that to me and to Bernstein's (1997) participants, who described reaching some sort of accommodation over time but not the slightest expectation of ever really getting over it.

Developing healthy continued bonds which locate the child in the past tense and the love in the present tense is part of the process. My continued bonds with my son are strong and the fact that my colleagues do not cringe when I talk about my three children is a gift. Bereaved parents cannot make new memories but appreciate the opportunity to reminisce about their dead child, otherwise it would feel as if the world was denying their existence (Klass et al, 2014). Nicci French (2019) wrote in a novel: 'No one is ever like anyone else. No one can be replaced. Every death is the end of a world. And they're gone and yet they remain. They walk with us along the secret rivers' (French, 2019: 374). The fact that my memories are easier to bear over time is at least in part due to the supportive reactions of other people. Symptoms of post-traumatic stress disorder were undoubtedly an everyday occurrence for the first few years but now these are fading. Other people have not been so lucky.

Post-traumatic stress disorder can work in tandem with complicated grief (White, 2013). In 2018 Dr Anke Ehlers gave a talk at The Royal Society in London on post-traumatic stress disorder, entitled 'Haunted by memories'. She described 'disassociation' as a common symptom and illustrated the idea with reference to a picture by Frida Kahlo. The artist, after a near fatal bus crash, depicted herself looking at her injured body from the outside. Post-traumatic stress disorder symptomatology, according to Ehlers, includes: derealisation, depersonalisation, intrusive memories, triggers, flashbacks, the feeling that the triggering event is still happening and, in extremis, a sense of just wanting to die. My relationship with these emotions has become more distant with the passage of time. While John was ill, I remember thinking, it was like living in a horror film. Surprisingly, given the prominence of the notion of denial in grief theory, Ehlers associated post-traumatic stress disorder specifically with sudden death. Because I navigated my son's treatment through a thick fog of denial, to me his death was sudden and shocking.

Grief theory cannot be simplistically applied to every bereavement. The loss of a parent or a lifelong soul mate must feel insurmountable, but the sense of a long life well lived may be a comfort. Premature loss of life offends the natural order of things. Charities such as The Compassionate Friends describe the death of one's child as 'the worse loss' but the social scientist in me questions the evidence base for this assertion. Losing a partner at a young age must be devastating. Violent or preventable deaths raise questions, which I did not have to face because I knew that everything that could be done to save my son was done.

It is impossible not to conflate my own cancer with my bereavement because the impacts are cumulative. I appreciate that this may make the narrative confusing, but life does not really happen in isolated little boxes and traumas tend to have a cumulative impact. In the next sections I focus more specifically on assimilating past events and thinking practically about getting on with my life and work.

Getting on with it

My engagement with having cancer is probably atypical because my son died of cancer. Psychologically, I was deeply troubled by the idea that mine was curable. John went through a year of chemotherapy which was extremely gruelling and ultimately pointless. He was originally told that his cancer was inoperable but having had 'spectacular response to chemotherapy' the inoperable became apparently operable. When the surgeon opened him up, they discovered that this was not the case. Longing to swap places with my son preoccupied and distressed me during my treatment. My surgery was extensive and debilitating and involved more than one operation. Recovery was gruelling, painful and left me with residual impairments, which are permanent. Having cancer has frightened me. Not unusually (Yaskowich and Stam, 2003), I feel like a ticking time bomb. Because I have extensive scarring I am often in pain. When my scars hurt, I find it easy to imagine that the cancer has returned.

During my two periods of eight weeks' sick leave, I wrote during breaks between DVD box sets. My identity is tied closely to my academic writing which provides some respite from the imposed othering connotations of my situation. While not a fan of the misery memoir genre, I did write about losing John. My personal cancer story was effectively a postscript to a piece I aimed at medics who treated young adults unsuccessfully for cancer. Gratifyingly the work has apparently proved useful to the intended audience.

Annoyingly, people feel the need to tell me their cancer stories. Despite being empathic and supportive, I do not want to have general circular conversations with third parties about other people affected by cancer. It is not my hobby. I am not an enthusiast. My very strong preference would be to go back to a time, when I was a university lecturer and the mum of three adult children, close in age, including identical twins. My life is in two parts and so is my career. Before was better. Although I am a functional productive person, I feel that, like Sisyphus, I will always have to push a heavy boulder up a steep hill. Sometimes, I just run out of steam.

Meeting new people is awkward. Questions like 'how many children do you have' are a minefield. Recently at a conference, I described a project I had been involved with just before John got sick as the happiest time of my life. A stranger commented that it was sad to hear me say something so negative because no one could ever know what great things could be just around the corner. It was hard to resist the temptation to say, 'Listen, Buster, you don't have to have been Vlad the Impaler in a former life for terrible things to happen'. Once again, I was playing the role

I never would have chosen in a million years, of the thirteenth fairy hovering over the greasy canapés and cheap red wine. I took from this encounter that it is probably best not to offer unsolicited opinions without an understanding of the bigger picture. Because of my deliberate attempts to lead an examined life and conduct myself with dignity and compassion I did not explain. I tend to think before I speak.

During John's treatment my line manager was incredibly understanding and committed to the idea that the Equality Act extends to disability by association. The organisation had a disabled staff network and a group for carers. Counselling for employees was available and I was actively encouraged to take up the opportunity, to the extent that this was arranged for me with my permission. When John was first diagnosed, I took two weeks off then I returned to work with some flexibility built in to enable me to take time as needed. He was attending university and having treatment in Oxford, and I was in London. The requirement for a longer period of leave was 11 months away. Crucially, my line manager listened and facilitated what I needed rather than making assumptions and imposing unworkable arrangements. As my cancer diagnosis occurred in August, I was able to put in place various arrangements for my role to be covered from the start of term. On hearing the news, I did what anybody would have done, I went into work and removed handbags and shoes from my filing cabinet before teaching my class. It would have been so embarrassing if I had died and left an untidy office.

Between November and December, I embarked upon a phased return following a meeting with occupational health which focused mainly on practicalities. Counselling was not part of the package, but I was able to access a bereavement counsellor at the hospital. I was very physically weak and unable to travel during the rush hour because I could not stand, so as far as possible my hours were shifted to reduce the necessity to do so. Fortunately, my teaching timetable did not include too many 9am lectures. Automatic doors were suddenly conspicuous by their absence, as I was unable to push heavy doors open. Sometimes, I walked with a stick, which I also needed for support if I had to stand. The fact that I did not need to use my stick all the time made me feel self-conscious and I was irritable when expected to attend events which involved standing around. Various 'keep in touch' conversations took place, while I was recovering from surgery. While I was away, I felt worried about being made redundant, although there was no tangible reason. Presumably, these feelings were tied up with residual impacts on self-esteem related to the death of my child.

Ongoing contact with kind reassuring colleagues was hugely important each time I was away. Because cancer and the death of one's child are both huge taboos (Lucas, 2017), particularly in the minority world, people can feel uncertain about what to say. Leaving well alone strengthens the sense of otherness and abandonment and is not the answer. Colleagues were and are an important part of the social capital on which my coping strategies are built.

Enablers at work

When John was ill, and after he died, the person-centred counselling my line manager went out of her way to arrange for me was a lifeline. The disabled staff network carers group was helpful during my son's treatment, but I did not feel I could go back after his death. The university chaplain took care of me. Workplace support groups are generally a good thing. Bereaved parents are fortunately a rare breed, but one of my colleagues was in the same boat and we looked out for each other. Flexible working helped me while I was looking after John and when I returned to work post-cancer. Occupational health made useful recommendations, but I had to be fairly assertive about things like reminding people that I could not travel on the tube in the rush hour. An occupational health follow-up would have been useful. Despite the support I received, almost by accident, I left my job a few months after John died and moved to a different university. I transitioned from a management role in disability and wellbeing services to an academic post in education. Derealisation, disassociation and depersonalisation played a major part in this decision, if it was indeed a decision.

Trying to empathise with disabled students and support them to access services to which they were entitled became too difficult because I was feeling so raw about my loss. I felt embarrassed every time I walked into the building because of my newly acquired identity. The strategy I employed to get through the working day was acting. This involved splitting so that part of me was playing the role of Head of Disability and Wellbeing Services and part of me was drowning in grief. Lecturing felt easier because of its inherently performative nature and I spotted an opportunity to escape from a situation in which everyone knew what had happened.

At the interview for my new post I performed well and then self-sabotaged by saying I was not a firm candidate because my son had died five months before. My impressive CV felt like it belonged to someone else because I had done all those things before, when I was a different person. Imposter syndrome (Lewis, 2018) is not uncommon but in my case was working in tandem with a sense of not even feeling like a real person. It never occurred to me that I would actually get the job for which I was being interviewed. I was in no fit state to make a rational decision.

Hastings (2000) discusses motivations underpinning self-disclosure by bereaved parents. In my case, I just blurted it out at interview despite knowing the risk. Examining my motivation was not high on my agenda. Effectively, I made it impossible to escape my new identity but at that time I was not ready to leave my son in the past because of the strength of my continuing bonds. On my first day, I felt awkward because I knew that everyone knew they were taking on the thirteenth fairy. My former colleagues had given me a lovely send off and my new colleagues made me very welcome. Rites of passage are important.

Six years into my new role I am functioning well at work, somehow. I no longer require the reasonable adjustments, which were necessary post-cancer treatment and I have more energy. Encouraging colleagues and students and engaging only in research that is likely to be of practical use characterise my approach. The idea of making a useful contribution is more important to me than status. I am making use of my experience to make a useful contribution and the opportunity to work in a multidisciplinary way helps. In collaboration with health colleagues, for example, I have developed course materials for palliative nursing students, and I have written about working with terminally ill students (Martin, 2015). I can navigate the question 'how many children have you got?' (Three but one is no longer alive). Roulstone and Williams use the term 'glass partitions' (2014: 16) to describe the situation disabled employees often encounter, in which they do not wish to change roles because they have found workable support with their current colleagues. To an extent, I feel this way, but I also know that my colleagues find me supportive, so it is not a one-way street.

Leading an examined life and acting with dignity and compassion is something of a mantra. Self-care is important and I know when I am running out of steam because of post-cancer physical pain and fatigue or ongoing grief. The flexibility to take the occasional day of annual leave when necessary is helpful. In December, I take a week off around John's anniversary which is two days before the birthday he should be sharing with his twin. Nobody minds. On balance, it was not a mistake to be honest at interview. Pretending to be an academic robot would ultimately have been pointless.

Conclusion

It is amazing to me that I am able to function and contribute in the workplace following the death of my child. Cancer treatment felt like a minor interruption in comparison. Because of what happened, I view my career and my life as a before and after story punctuated by a radical and unwanted shift in my own identity. In this chapter, I have tried to provide a useful picture of my experience, punctuated by relevant theory around grief and bereavement. My aim is to help people to think about the dual taboos of cancer and child loss and consider what they might do to help a colleague affected by either or both of these things. The relevance of the Equality Act 2010 and bereavement leave policies is discussed but the focus is on trying to help colleagues to understand. Writing this contribution still feels risky, but I am wearing the armour of my achievements in the workplace. Somehow, I am managing to contribute, and the support of my colleagues is invaluable.

Reflective questions

• How could you support a colleague who has lost a child, of whatever age, and how might you be personally affected by their situation?
• How could you support a colleague affected directly or indirectly by cancer?
• How could the organisation react supportively to these situations?

Recommendations

• We need to be aware of institutional policies and relevant legislation in relation to supporting an employee with cancer or caring for someone with cancer.
• We need to be aware of institutional policies relating to bereavement leave and support of bereaved colleagues.
• We need to recognise our own relationship with the idea of the death of a child and/or a cancer diagnosis, and support each other while trying to be supportive of a colleague who is a bereaved parent and/or has cancer.
• We need to exercise compassion.

References

Bebbington, D. (2009). *Diversity in Higher Education: Leadership Responsibilities and Challenges*. London: Leadership Foundation for Higher Education.

Benn, T. (2004). *Free Radical*. London: Bloomsbury Publishing.

Bernstein, J. (1997) *When the Bough Breaks: Forever after the Death of a Son or Daughter*. Kansas City, MO: Andrews McMeel Publishing.

Bourdieu, P. (2002). The forms of capital. In: Biggart, N.W. (ed) *Readings in Economic Sociology*. Oxford: Blackwell, 280–291.

Bowlby, J. (1969). *Attachment and Loss, Volume I: Attachment*. London: The Hogarth Press and the Institute of Psychoanalysis.

Bowlby, J. (1982). Attachment and loss: Retrospect and prospect. *American Journal of Orthopsychiatry*, 52(4), 664–678.

Brown, R. (2018). *New Bereavement Leave Entitlements.* www. peoplemanagement.co.uk/experts/legal/new-law-on-parental-bereavement-leave [Accessed 8 October 2019].

Cheung, S.Y. & Delfabbro, P. (2016). Are you a cancer survivor? A review on cancer identity. *Journal of Cancer Survivorship,* 10(4), 759–771.

Cohen, J.A., Mannarino, A.P. & Staron, V.R. (2006). A pilot study of modified cognitive-behavioural therapy for childhood traumatic grief (CBT-CTG). *Journal of the American Academy of Child & Adolescent Psychiatry,* 45(12), 1465–1473.

Coreil, J., Corvin, J.A., Nupp, R., Dyer, K. & Noble, C. (2012). Ethnicity and cultural models of recovery from breast cancer. *Ethnicity & Health,* 17(3), 291–307.

Costanzo, E.S., Lutgendorf, S.K., Mattes, M.L., Trehan, S., Robinson, C.B., Tewfik, F. & Roman, S.L. (2007). Adjusting to life after treatment: Distress and quality of life following treatment for breast cancer. *British Journal of Cancer,* 97(12), 1625–1631.

Diagnostic and Statistical Manual of Mental Disorders, Fifth Edition (2017) https://psychiatryonline.org/pb-assets/dsm/update/DSM5Update_October2017.pdf [Accessed 8 October 2019].

Endo, K., Yonemoto, N., & Yamada, M. (2015). Interventions for bereaved parents following a child's death: A systematic review. *Palliative Medicine,* 29(7), 590–604.

Equality Act 2010. London: The Stationery Office.

Field, N.P., Gao, B. & Paderna, L. (2005). Continuing bonds in bereavement: An attachment theory-based perspective. *Death Studies,* 29(4), 277–299.

Foucault, M. (1994). *The Birth of the Clinic: An Archaeology of Medical Perception.* New York: Random House.

French, N. (2019). *Day of the Dead.* London: Penguin.

Freud, S. & Strachey, J.E. (1966). *The Standard Edition of the Complete Psychological Works of Sigmund Freud.* London: Hogarth Press.

Greenblatt, A., & Lee, E. (2018). Cancer survivorship and identity: What about the role of oncology social workers? *Social Work in Health Care,* 57(10), 811–833.

Haig, M. (2015) *Reasons to Stay Alive.* Edinburgh: Canongate Books.

Hastings, S. (2000). Self-disclosure and identity management by bereaved parents. *Communication Studies*, 51(4), 352–371.

Hattenstone, S. (2016). Ken Loach: 'If you're not angry, what kind of person are you?'. *The Guardian*. www.theguardian.com/film/2016/oct/15/ken-laoch-film-i-daniel-blake-kes-cathy-come-home-interview-simon-hattenstone [Accessed 8 October 2019].

Jung, C.G. (1967). *The Development of Personality: Collected Works of C.G. Jung*, Volume 17. London: Routledge.

Klass, D., Silverman, P.R., & Nickman, S. (2014). *Continuing Bonds: New Understandings of Grief.* London: Taylor & Francis.

Kotzé, Z. (2014). Jung, individuation, and moral relativity in Qohelet 7: 16–17. *Journal of Religion and Health*, 53(2), 511–519.

Kübler-Ross, E. (1970). *On Death and Dying*. Oxford: Routledge.

Lewis, L. (2018). *Imposter Syndrome: The Convoluted Phenomenon and its Popularity in the Workplace*. Presentation, Loyola Marymount University. https://digitalcommons.lmu.edu/honors-research-and-exhibition/2018/section-02/5/ [Accessed 8 October 2019].

Little, M., Paul, K., Jordens, C.F., & Sayers, E.J. (2002). Survivorship and discourses of identity. *Psycho-Oncology: Journal of the Psychological, Social and Behavioral Dimensions of Cancer*, 11(2), 170–178.

Lomas, T., Medina, J.C., Ivtzan, I., Rupprecht, S., Hart, R., & Eiroa-Orosa, F.J. (2017). The impact of mindfulness on well-being and performance in the workplace: An inclusive systematic review of the empirical literature. *European Journal of Work and Organizational Psychology*, 26(4), 492–513.

Lucas, C. (2017). Cancer in Tinsel Town. *The Lancet Oncology*, 18(11), 1443.

Martin, N. (2015). Compassionate Balliol. *Journal of Inclusive Practice in Further and Higher Education*, 6(1), 58–61.

Martin, N. (2017). *Encouraging Disabled Leaders in Higher Education: Recognising Hidden Talents*. London: Leadership Foundation for Higher Education.

Maslow, A. (1998). *Toward a Psychology of Being* (3rd edn). New York: Wiley.

McElwain, H. (2013). *Socrates' 'The Unexamined Life is not Worth Living': Exploring the 'Examined Life' Through an In-depth Analysis of the Dominican Virtues of Love/Compassion and Truth/Knowledge.* http://hdl.handle.net/10969/429 [Accessed 7 October 2019].

Parkes, C.M. (1988). Bereavement as a psychosocial transition: Processes of adaptation to change. *Journal of Social Issues*, 44(3), 53–65.

Parkes, C.M., & Prigerson, H.G. (2013). *Bereavement: Studies of Grief in Adult Life.* London: Routledge.

Reeves, A. (2013). *An Introduction to Counselling and Psychotherapy: From Theory to Practice.* London: Sage.

Rosenberg, A.R., Baker, K.S., Syrjala, K., & Wolfe, J. (2012). Systematic review of psychosocial morbidities among bereaved parents of children with cancer. *Paediatric Blood and Cancer*, 58(4), 503–512.

Roulstone, A., & Williams, J. (2014). Being disabled, being a manager: 'Glass partitions' and conditional identities in the contemporary workplace. *Disability and Society*, 29(1), 16–29.

Scott, S.M. (1997). The grieving soul in the transformation process. *New Directions for Adult and Continuing Education*, 74, 41–50.

Stroebe, M., Schut, H., & Boerner, K. (2010). Continuing bonds in adaptation to bereavement: Toward theoretical integration. *Clinical Psychology Review*, 30(2), 259–268.

The Compassionate Friends (2015). www.tcf.org.uk/ [Accessed 26 July 2019].

The Parental Bereavement (Leave and Pay) Act 2018. London: The Stationery Office.

Thomson, P., Chadwick, A., & Hämisegger, L. (2018). Wellbeing and the Workplace. In: Thomson, P., Johnson, M., & Devlin, J.M. (eds). *Conquering Digital Overload.* Cham: Palgrave Macmillan, 117–126.

White, C. (2013). *Living with Complicated Grief.* London: Sheldon Press.

Worden, J.W. (2018). *Grief Counselling and Grief Therapy: A Handbook for the Mental Health Practitioner.* London: Springer Publishing Company.

Yaskowich, K.M., and Stam, H.J. (2003). Cancer narratives and the cancer support group. *Journal of Health Psychology*, 8(6), 720–737.

18

Invisible disabilities and (re)negotiating identity: life after major traumatic injury

Clare Lewis

Prologue

15 September 2015

We twist through the forest festooned in lichen in heavy rain. Wooden steps, slimy with this rain, had been laid over moss covered rocks which have droplets of water suspended motionless on the tiny leaves. The old forest smells of this wet moss combined with damp soil, wet bark and pine needles. I remember this smell. I remember the feel of Raph's walking sticks that I had borrowed. I remember the feeling of breathing and the squelch of my feet on the waterlogged soil and watching water rise to the surface and seep onto my boots. I remember what I was thinking about and my heartbeat. Clear and precise details … We stop to have tea sheltering under the orange bivvy. I sip the hot tea, rolling it around my mouth. We talk and laugh, listening to the sound of the rain on the bivvy. Hearing, feeling, smelling, seeing, talking and tasting before yet another climb … Then complete blackness. Blackness utterly devoid of any senses until I am in Annecy hospital … the doctor tells me I have broken my back in more than one place. I look away and say nothing as he continues to talk about my injuries.

Disclosure: the accident, remembering and forgetting

Some 45 minutes after that tea was drunk and packed away, I fell 30 or 40 metres – depending upon whether you read the police, emergency room, or my climbing companion Raph's accounts – in a rock-climbing accident. The recollection above is drawn from the diary I kept for the year following this accident. I have deliberately not re-edited the words of this entry as I do not want to edit it to represent the 'I' that sits here today, aware that accounts 'written after recovery, or after years of living with a particular disease or disability, lack the authenticity afforded by real-time life writing' (Eckstein, 2013: 463).

I reached for this diary and wanted to recapture the 'authenticity' of the early post-accident self, as I came to write this paper. Giddens (1991: 53) argues that the self is 'reflexively understood by the person in terms of his or her biography' and the overarching theme of my contribution is the story of my identity, and the self-disclosure and concealment strategies I have adopted at various stages as I manage this 'new' body confronted by the ableist world of academia. Hence, recourse to my diary. In this, during that first year, through the medium of life-writing, bewildered, shocked, broken and unable to concentrate, I attempted to make this accident a footnote in my (auto)biography. I endeavoured to restore the narrative to align with my pre-accident self, trying to make sense of what had happened to me, seeking closure and privately venting my anger and frustrations at the lack of concrete answers.

With distance from the events, I now understand that this accident fundamentally changed my (auto)biography and Giddens' (1991: 59) claim later in this same chapter on the self that '[m]ost people are absorbed in their bodies, and feel themselves to be a unified body and self' is written from the perspective of a non-disabled male (see also Watson, 2002: 518–519). In contrast, the disassociation of the self from the body is part of the biographical narrative of physically disabled individuals. Reading the diary in this light, aware of how I now view my body with contempt and as an obstacle, refusing to associate it with 'me', the act of looking away from the doctor as he spoke about my injuries marked the first step in this disassociation process. Now, as I sit in an office in Malet Place in London looking at the words in my diary describing the walk through the forest and experience the hyper-reality of these memories, I am taken back to the 'unified' person I was before the accident and reminded of the life I still mourn for.

Here again, I reach for literature to understand these emotions. Herman (1992) suggests that individuals who suffer trauma are commonly motivated simultaneously to forget and to 'remember', through intrusions, the trauma. This certainly chimes with my experience and my unease at opening this diary. This suggestion in part also resolves my question as to why I am so reluctant to discuss openly my continuing issues with the injuries I suffered on that day and thus how difficult it was to begin to write this chapter. I choose to 'remember' privately, and frequently, but 'forget' publicly. I use quotation marks since, as intimated in the excerpt at the beginning of this chapter, I have pre-traumatic amnesia. I was unconscious for three hours as a result of my fall and the associated head injury, and also experienced post-traumatic amnesia. Indeed, as I write, I can now only remember snatches of the heavily sedated weeks following my injuries – islands in a sea of confusion and pain.

Concealment: returning to academia

My injuries were once so highly and painfully visible that they caused a father to cross the road to avoid me, loudly warning his accompanying young daughter that I was disabled. Now, they are unseen to all but the closest observer. I am truly fortunate. Although sometimes, it is a little difficult to feel fortunate in this now heavily damaged and constantly hurting body. Among other injuries, I had broken my back in two places, and also dislocated it, requiring metal plates and eight screws to be inserted internally and the external use of a body brace, a thoracic lumbar sacral orthosis or TLSO brace. TLSO braces are made out of moulded plastic and are often used to treat and prevent progression of scoliosis.

On release from hospital my spinal surgeon told me and my worried family that only 30 per cent of people who *survive* the spinal fractures I had, carefully emphasising the word survive, ever walk again, warning me never to Google search my injuries for the mental harm this would cause. And this is only one set of numbers, I have defied. The mortality rate for a seven-storey fall, which equals between 26–28 metres, is 90 per cent (Golob and Como, 2015: 3). I fell 30–40 metres. A key rehabilitation goal for major trauma patients, from the perspective of the medical profession, is the opportunity to return to work (Collie et al, 2019: 972). For my combination of injuries, the return to work statistics are not encouraging. Twenty per cent of patients with serious injuries did not return to work, and a further 13 per cent made an unsuccessful attempt to return to work, with those patients who had sustained a spinal cord injury showing the lowest rates of returning to work (Collie et al, 2019: 975). But, since my return to academia, I have been appointed a lecturer (teaching).

With my disabilities now falling under the invisible umbrella (Davis, 2005), one of the first issues I faced upon my return to university a year after my accident was how much to disclose. At the time, I was involved in my PhD research only, and so I was directed to student support. I was confronted with the dichotomy that Brown and Leigh (2018: 987) identify: choosing to disclose a disability and be identified as having a disability, which enables certain forms of support to be accessed, whereas not disclosing the disability would avoid discrimination, stigma and their effects. I decided to be guided in my choices by my appointment with student support and wellbeing officers.

The individual I met in the student support and wellbeing offices had never encountered anyone with the range of injuries, medically classed as major traumatic injuries (Palmer, 2007), or issues that I faced at the time. Incredulous at the idea of anyone surviving a 30–40-metre fall, they only began to believe me and realise I was not exaggerating, when I showed them various medical correspondence, police reports, certificates and X-rays, where many of my bones looked like snapped matchsticks, that are now absorbed as primary sources in my 'new' (auto)biography. Having provided this information, I was told that disabled PhD students were not entitled to support from university without first applying for a government Disability Support Allowance. Hannam-Swain (2018: 138–142) discusses the complexity and problems surrounding this process for PhD students in particular and I, like her, am keen to make clear that this contribution should not be read as a comment on a particular university, as the experience is common across the UK.

I have often wondered what the purpose of meeting me in person was. Given my mobility and pain issues, a Skype session or a phone call would have been more appropriate, empathetic and understanding. Perhaps limited resources and rising demand mean that only a 'one size fits all' approach is possible. But in my case, the only outcome of that meeting was that I was added to a mailing list which repeatedly circulated requests for volunteers for various people's research into disability. This was the inverse of what I had hoped for. Not only was I not provided with any help or support, I was expected to willingly help others, sacrificing the very hard fought for time that at one stage was not at all clear that I would have. Raph later told me that, as he sat next to me waiting for the emergency helicopter that rainy day in France, he was quite sure I was going to die.

My accident was too raw. The life-changing damage was all too real. In all likelihood suffering symptoms of post-traumatic stress disorder (see, for example, Frueh et al, 2012: 71–89 for a discussion of these symptoms), the thought of having to go through the government application process to 'prove' my disabilities and the requirement for the submission of my prognosis, which I had been very careful never to ask my doctors for, triggered a visceral response. I had avoided, and continue to avoid, a prognosis mindful of the doctors' warnings never to Google my injuries and not wanting to know why. On the steps outside the student support and wellbeing offices, I repeatedly vomited. I was highly unstable and wobbly on my feet because of my still healing spinal fractures; passers-by rudely joked about me being intoxicated. No one offered to help me or paused to ask if I was alright.

Equally, there were much more positive experiences. The approach and humanity the Institute of Archaeology have shown towards me has been extraordinary. They have never once questioned my accounts of my health and I know they would do their utmost to accommodate any request for help that I might make. However, my encounter with student support and welfare, at a key transitional moment, over-informed my approach, and I began the (re)negotiation of my public identity in earnest. I meticulously curated it as I continued to heal to display no outward signs of disability despite the significant issues I faced, and continue to face. I have refused any offers of help while simultaneously becoming expert at finding the hidden, unoccupied, dusty corners of UCL, where I can lie flat and still, when sitting simply becomes too unbearable, away from inquiring eyes.

Having carefully curated this public self, the microaggressions I encounter, such as being sworn at for taking the lift one floor, have to be ignored in my view (see Kattari, 2017: 12–16 for discussion of this term relating to invisible disability). I have not disclosed, so I cannot manage or challenge these microaggressions. Indeed, there are positive aspects of these microaggressions. For example, knowing how upsetting they can be and how one cannot presume to know anything about the person standing next to you, I try very hard to be careful in the way I treat others. Here I make no claim of perfection at all, but I hope this heightened sensitivity and empathy also means I am a better personal tutor than the one I would have been prior to the accident. All too aware of the fragility of life, I believe that one of the most important gifts you can give is time, and in that time to really *listen* to what someone says. My ethos is based around integrity and respect. Once more, I make no claims as to perfection, but my approach seems to be validated, as a range of students on the degree programme where I am a lecturer (teaching) and personal tutor seek my advice on a range of aspects and it is a privilege to work with them.

Passing strategies and teaspoons of energy

I have now curated this public image to such an extent that I am unwilling to disclose the full nature and range of all of the injuries I suffered at this juncture, as I believe that this will both stigmatise me and force me to re-connect the public and very private self too completely and too abruptly. For a detailed discussion of the issue of stigma in disability see Brown (2013: 147–160), and for disability in education in particular, see, for example, Watson (2002: 525), Brown and Leigh (2018: 987); Grimes et al (2019: 642). Here, I will reflect primarily on chronic pain that is my (very) loyal and constant companion as the last thing I feel before I go to sleep and the first thing I feel when I wake up.

I have learnt that my 'concealment of the ... impaired self' is what is termed a passing strategy (Lingsom, 2008: 2). This strategy relates to the choices one makes about whether or not to disclose or reveal one's invisible disabilities. Lingsom (2008: 2) suggests that through concealment strategies one can pass for 'normal', and that social conventions support that silence. This statement definitely rings true for me and, through researching this chapter, I discover I am far from unique in adopting this strategy, and my particular chosen form of passing strategy: 'A common passing strategy involves concentration of energies on life-worlds the impaired individual gives highest priority. Concentration of effort is then restricted in space and time. Only part of the day is visible to others' (Lingsom, 2008: 6). I have been very careful to concentrate my energies on teaching to the best of my abilities, and social conventions in the overworked world of the teaching fellow and related expectations of productivity enable, support and reinforce my strategic choice. However, there is only a finite amount of energy and other areas of my life do suffer, as with chronic pain comes chronic fatigue, but the pain interrupts my sleep building on my fatigue. For example, the 'invisible' world of my social life has been compromised to the extent it is almost completely non-existent. By the time I return home at the end of the day I can only lie on the floor. I am spent:

> With Chronic Pain Tired, the recharging time is limited, the electricity keeps cutting out, and the battery won't quite hold a charge. Chronic Pain Tired is a constant weight, a pulling-down of your entire being. It follows everywhere you go, a stalker you cannot shake. A dark force hooked into your spine

that slowly siphons out your already limited energy.
Everything I do, I do while Chronic Pain Tired.
(Mixer, 2017: 9)

Mixer's (2017. 9) metaphor of 16 spoons of energy to get through a day is particularly useful to explain the sapping effect of chronic pain. When occupying my body, everything takes energy. Getting out of bed takes energy. Sitting takes energy. Sitting on an uncomfortable chair takes a lot of energy. I could continue, but these 'normal' activities sap energy that cannot be used for other things, and it is not readily replaced, as alluded to in the quote above. Every day is a negotiation of what is achievable and the associated contingencies.

However, despite these issues I have been included and I do participate, although some days I am less able than others. But while passing strategies have worked for me in the short term, I am beginning to doubt their long-term sustainability. The symptoms of chronic fatigue and pain, among other elements, after over four years of living with them, are harder to fully conceal. For example, the flattening of my voice tone, and associated lack of animation in lectures on a particularly bad day of pain and fatigue, or my failure to contact friends for long periods of time can be misinterpreted, and (mis)assumptions are made that are damaging for all.

Conclusion: Bring my 'whole self' to work

Bring Your Whole Self to Work is the title of a popularist self-help volume (Robbins, 2018). The ableist recommendations in this publication are both superficial and inappropriate for this volume, but I was struck by the title in terms of the discrepancy between my unified sense of self pre-accident and my disassociated self after the accident in terms of first no longer associating my body with me, and having a private and public me. Indeed, negative self-discrepancy between pre-injury and post-injury selves has been identified as an issue in rehabilitation from various illness and trauma (Beadle et al, 2016).

In forming the public self and protecting the private self, I have deliberately 'downplayed the significance of [my] impairments as [I] seek to access a mainstream identity' (Watson, 2002: 525). I was employed as a teaching fellow subsequent to my accident by individuals who were aware of the circumstances of my accident and willing to take a 'risk' in employing me. Indeed, my personal 'risk benefit analysis of disclosure' (Brown and Leigh, 2018: 988) is just that. I have formed my own views of the risk of stigmatisation and I choose not to disclose the full extent of my situation. This is not the fault of my colleagues in any way. I am not comfortable in linking 'my personal and private with the public' (Brown and Leigh 2018: 987), having used the delinking as a coping strategy as I come to terms with this 'new' body to manage my return to university.

Unlike those with visible disabilities, I have the choice about how much to disclose, which may well be seen as a luxury (Inckle, 2018: 1372). However, I am so concerned as to the stigma that I have not allowed myself to even begin to test for its existence. This is an act of self-preservation if you like, I am all too aware of a body of research warning of stigma's presence in the ableist world of academia. 'Passing strategies', part of this concealment, while helpful for me in the short term as I slowly came to terms with my injuries and adjusted, are ultimately difficult to maintain and destructive when faced with chronic pain and associated fatigue.

As Beadle et al (2016) warn, 'persisting negative self-discrepancies may ... lead to maladaptive coping and disengagement' (Beadle et al, 2016: E14). For me, among other elements, they simply spend too many of my sixteen spoons of energy and the associated (mis)assumptions are damaging for all concerned. Therefore, I am choosing to reveal my impairments more, and 'bring my whole self to work', as many others have done before me, in a written, first-person, account. This marks a first step in reuniting myself and finding my post-accident, disabled, unified identity and being confident with that identity. A 'safe space' for this disclosure is vital. Here, I can begin to reunite the public and private space in a way that I can control disclosure, neither forced to hide nor forced to completely disclose, defining my disability in my own terms, under my own terms of reference, to paraphrase Watson (2002: 51).

Publications such as this play a vital role in creating that safe space, away from the ableist world which enables, and promotes, behaviours such as 'passing strategies'. This is the beginning of a discussion for me and a new stage in my journey to find me new 'whole' self. I can only thank Nicole Brown for the opportunity this book has provided in that regard.

Reflective questions

- What do you assume about disability?
- Have you stopped to wonder why the person next to you is being slow, 'clumsy', or walking very awkwardly?
- Do you assume impairments are visible and instinctively distrustful of mere spoken claims to disability, seeking further 'proof' of these claims, forcing what Couser (2009: 17) identifies as one of the social burdens of disability, 'the exposure to inspection, interrogation, and violation of privacy'?
- Lingsom (2008: 8) points to the flip side of concealment, which is important as one prepares to disclose one's invisible disabilities, and it is this: how do people with known but invisible impairments tactfully and effectively remind others of impairment effects?

Recommendations

Empathy, integrity and consideration: Each of us has a responsibility to treat others with respect. Take time to listen to others. Someone taking the lift one floor may be doing so because they simply cannot get up the stairs that day. Someone fiddling with a lock or security gate may be having the worst day, they are not slowing up your day intentionally. Take a moment to be kind to others, but do not unilaterally decide what would be helpful to the disabled community. Assumptions can be very damaging. An 'able' human does not know what the limitations of those less able are or how unique those limitations are. Do not presume to know. A well-intentioned assumption often has the reverse effect to its intention and forces disclosure that the disabled individual is very uncomfortable with.

Inclusive culture: Others in this book mention the legal obligations in relation to the Equality Act 2010 and health and safety at work legislation, or the responsibility to provide reasonable adjustments to accommodate employees with disabilities (see in this collection the chapters by Mann and Clift; Martin; Smith; Daddow; Janssen; Mounsey and Booth; and Farahar and Foster). I have reflected on the problems of the Disability Support Allowance that limit the abilities of institutions to tailor their response to students. A specific suggestion in light of these limitations is that disabled students should be invited to opt in to emails requesting volunteers for disability research, rather than the current uniformed consent. Johnson and Goldstein (2003) discuss the different impact of opt-in rather than opt-out strategies from a behavioural economics perspective. However, equally as individuals we can treat others around us with respect, empathy and thoughtfulness. In fostering a climate of respect, we, as a group, can form a network and collectivise support at a time when institutions are unwilling or unable to provide it.

Mentoring: As part of the support network I suggest an informal mentoring network would be valuable. I know I would have benefited a great deal from this support in the early days of my return to what I perceived as an ableist world with high stigma of disclosure. If I can support someone else through this process this paper will have achieved something.

Celebrating difference: 'Being human in this ableist community or society is not merely being, but being perfect and meeting specific criteria' (Brown & Leigh, 2018: 988). I am not perfect. I do not meet 'specific' criteria. The accident has profoundly changed how I am as a person. But in terms of my interactions with others this is often for the better. I am far more patient, empathetic and respectful of others. I willingly give people the gift of time, regardless of how busy I am. I am a better personal tutor for having been through this. When we can, we need to raise our voices and say this body many not be perfect, but I am *some* body, and I can and do contribute.

Acknowledgements
I thank all those people, medical, family, friends, colleagues and supervisors who mean I am here writing this today. I am in awe of all of you.

References
Beadle, E.J., Ownsworth, T., Fleming, J., & Shum, D. (2016). The impact of traumatic brain injury on self-identity: A systematic review of the evidence for self-concept changes. *Journal of Head Trauma Rehabilitation*, 31(2), E12–E25.

Brown, L.C. (2013). Stigma: An enigma demystified. In: Davis, L.J. (ed) *The Disability Studies Reader*. New York: Routledge, pp. 147–160.

Brown, N., & Leigh, J. (2018). Ableism in academia: Where are the disabled and ill academics? *Disability & Society*, 33(6), 985–989.

Collie, A. et al (2019). Patterns and predictors of return to work after major trauma: A prospective, population-based registry study, *Annals of Surgery*, 269(5), May, 972–978.

Couser, G.T. (2009). *Signifying Bodies. Disability in Contemporary Life Writing*. Ann Arbor, MI: University of Michigan Press.

Davis, A.N. (2005). Invisible disability, *Ethics*, 116(1), Symposium on Disability (October), 153–213.

Eckstein, S. (2013). A private life made public, *Life Writing*, 10(4), 459–470, doi: 10.1080/14484528.2013.819522

Frueh, B.C., Grubaugh, A., Elhai, J.D., & Ford, J.D. (2012). *Assessment and Treatment Planning for PTSD*. Hoboken, NJ: John Wiley & Sons.

Giddens, A. (1991). *Modernity and Self Identity*. Cambridge, Polity.

Golob, J.F & Como, J.J. (2015). Mechanisms and demographics. In: Smith, C.E. (ed) *Trauma Anesthesia*. Cambridge: Cambridge University Press. pp. 1–5.

Grimes, S., Southgate, E., Scevak, J. & Buchanan, R. (2019). University student perspectives on institutional non-disclosure of disability and learning challenges: Reasons for staying invisible, *International Journal of Inclusive Education*, 23(6), 639–655. doi: 10.1080/13603116.2018.1442507

Hannam-Swain, S. (2018). The additional labour of a disabled PhD student. *Disability & Society*, 33(1), 138–142. doi:10.1080/09687599.2017.1375698

Herman, J. (1992). *Trauma and Recovery*. New York: Basic.

Inckle, K. (2018). Unreasonable adjustments: The additional unpaid labour of academics with disabilities. *Disability & Society*, 33(8), 1372–1376. doi:10.1080/09687599.2018.1480263

Johnson, E.J., & Goldstein, D.G. (2003). Do defaults save lives? *Science*, 302(21 November), 1338–1339.

Kattari, S.K. (2017). *Development of the Ableist Microaggression Scale and Assessing the Relationship between Ableist Microaggressions and the Mental Health of Disabled Adults*. PhD, University of Denver.

Lingsom, S. (2008). Invisible impairments: Dilemmas of concealment and disclosure, *Scandinavian Journal of Disability Research*, 10(1), 2–16.

Mixer, L. (2017). If/Then. *Humboldt Journal of Social Relations*, 39, Special Issue: Diversity & Social Justice in Higher Education, 8–11.

Palmer, C. (2007). Major trauma and the Injury Severity Score: Where should we set the bar?, *Proceedings of the Association of Advancement of Automotive Medicine*, 51, 13–29.

Robbins, M. (2018). *Bring Your Whole Self to Work*. Carlsbad, CA: Hay House.

Watson, N. (2002). Well, I know this is going to sound very strange to you, but I don't see myself as a disabled person: Identity and disability. *Disability & Society*, 17(5), 509–527.

Conclusion:
Disability imaginary of the future

Nicole Brown

Ableism in academia and the lived experiences

On 23 March 2018, the Ableism in Academia conference took place at the UCL Institute of Education. The event was unique for the UK higher education landscape in several ways. First, the conference offered delegates a safe space to exchange ideas and theorise experiences not from the vantage point of being a typical, fully 'able-bodied and able-minded' academic, but from the very personal and intimate understanding of what it means to not fit the mould. The conference was not at all limited or restricted to academics with disabilities, chronic illnesses and/or neurodivergences, but the nature of the topic clearly affected and interested that group of scholars the most. I know that every single delegate had one form of need or another. Second, and related to the fact that every delegate had disclosed some need, the conference was the first of its kind by way of accessibility and inclusion. The event was organised in such a way that delegates could participate in and contribute to within the halls of the conference setting, but also remotely from home. The organisation had included ensuring the right foods would be available, people would be able to see and hear and to withdraw and relax whenever and whichever way they needed to (see Brown et al, 2018 for full details). And third, the conference stood out for its aim to have a lasting effect on conference speakers, delegates and the volunteers involved. The topic of ableism in academia, and the emotions of frustration, stress, embarrassment and failure, were just too important and raw for the conference to be a passing fad. I was determined that the conference would lead to tangible results, such as practical recommendations for the sector and a beginning network of colleagues and friends, who would recognise each other's strengths and struggles. In many ways, the conference did keep that promise with particular strategies and recommendations having been implemented across a number of universities. Research institutions, grant funders and learned societies are also increasingly focusing on issues of accessibility, equality and inclusion; and I know that, although we were not the only ones to speak up at the time, our voices had impact. If the impact is already felt, one may ask what then the point is of this particular edited book.

Although contributors and delegates at the conference developed specific recommendations for the higher education sector, one important element somehow got lost in the cacophony of voices on the day: despite the many unique and individual needs associated with all types of disabilities, chronic illnesses and/or neurodivergences, there are many experiences that are comparable, similar and alike.

Another key aspect that this book offers, which the conference could not, is more breadth of experiences and an increased depth of theorisations. All of the contributions at the conference and in this edited book are embedded in and arise from personal experiences and individuals making sense of the same. However, not all disciplines are used to or approve of autobiographical and autoethnographic approaches. Yet, as the chapters by Angharad Butler-Rees, Laura Ellingson, Jennifer Leigh and Sharon Smith highlight, it is that deep engagement with one's own narrative and embodiment that allows us to shed light on issues, such as discrimination and microaggressions, and to (re)negotiate one's own position in the grander narrative of human existence. Naturally, critiques of these approaches are abundant. Despite truly rational responses to critics (Ellis, 2009), there are still many who consider autoethnography as too self-centred and self-indulgent to be meaningful (Holt, 2003; Salzman, 2002; Sparkes, 2002). Similarly, despite the recognition that it is impossible to have an emotionless experience (Spencer, 1992), there are many who consider personal emotions an intrusion or risk to academic work (Fitzpatrick and Olson, 2015). In addition, categories and lenses are never defined in a clear-cut and unambiguous way, which means that the ways of working that Angharad Butler-Rees, Laura Ellingson, Jennifer Leigh and Sharon Smith have presented may not be equally accepted by and acceptable for everyone. Naturally, any research can be done badly; and that also goes for research using embodiment, autoethnography and/or emotions as a basic theoretical framework. Nevertheless, it is difficult to argue with the raw accounts and representations of experiences presented in Part II of the book.

Strategies for inclusion in higher education

Despite the multitude and wealth of experiences presented in this collection, there are similarities, and so most of the experiences can be 'treated' or 'dealt with' in similar ways, too. The aim of this book was not to offer a quick-fix solution. Actually, now, at the end of this book and after so many chapters of individual stories ending with personal recommendations from the authors, it becomes clear that there *is* no quick-fix solution. What is required is an attitudinal shift among everyone studying, working and living in academia in order to build a higher education sector that becomes inclusive and allows for all sorts of ways working. Jeanne Barczewska and Rosalind Janssen, for example, ask for increasing awareness for individuals' conditions or needs, with Nicole Brown, Chloe Farahar and Annette Foster and Oliver Daddow even suggesting professional development training and education.

For many contributors, awareness through education and training form the basis upon which can be built the understanding, empathy and compassion that, according to Oliver Daddow, Nicola Martin and Clare Lewis, are required to make academia more accessible. Another key thread is the development of a support network through online community, peer group support or mentoring schemes, which Robert Mann and Bryan Clift, Mikael Vejdemo-Johansson and Ian Gent, Clare Lewis, Nicola Martin, and Jennifer Hiscock and Jennifer Leigh highlight. Jennifer Hiscock and Jennifer Leigh as well as Chloe Farahar and Annette Foster, Emma Sheppard and Jo Sullivan also emphasise the need for a learning design that may make use of technology and tools in order to be inclusive for students, while Oliver Daddow emphasises that we should not ask individuals to rely entirely on technology. The point these authors make is that we should not only look to our own needs, but be active role models for others and embody the kind of empathy and compassion we would like to see from and in others.

The final strand that is particularly strongly developed in the chapters by Ben Lunn as well as Chris Mounsey and Stan Booth, but that is also present in others' contributions, such as those by Jo Sullivan and Sharon Smith, is the need for engaging disabled, chronically ill and/or neurodivergent members of staff in the narrative of disability in academia. At the same time, the contributions show some radical differences in how individuals define themselves. This is best exemplified by how Chloe Farahar and Annette Foster and Jo Sullivan approached the topic of autism, as well as in the chapter by Emma Sheppard, who deliberately avoided naming a medical diagnosis, and the chapter by Nicole Brown that specifically addresses individual's identities as hearing impaired, deaf or Deaf. Similarly, the fact that both Nicola Martin and Jeanne Barczewska felt uncomfortable with some of the support mechanisms that were arranged for them shows the individuality of illness trajectories.

To sum up, the 'quick-fix' that actually is not one means the following should be the strategies for inclusion in higher education: involving those who are affected by disabilities, chronic illnesses and/or neurodivergences in conversations around their experiences at work; truly listening to their stories and plight; and empathetically supporting them in the way they say that they would like to be supported.

Looking to the future

As I am finalising the manuscript of this edited book, I cannot help but be guided by a look to the future. When the journey towards the Ableism in Academia conference started out in 2017, the #MeToo and #TimesUp movements against sexual harassment were just gaining traction as a reaction to the exposure of unspeakable and reprehensible practices in the entertainment industry. I noticed at the time that for many individuals these two movements represented the beginning of a new era of emancipation and self-assurance. Where in the past, the marginalised would have stayed marginalised, would have remained silent and therefore unheard, after #MeToo and #TimesUp people voiced their views, highlighted their concerns and confidently raised awareness for their needs.

In 2018, by the time that the activist Greta Thunberg had mobilised masses of pupils and students across the world to take action against politicians failing to address issues of climate change, individuals with disabilities, chronic illnesses and/or neurodivergences had gained a steady voice. I cannot ever be sure whether Greta's own diagnoses of mental health issues, Asperger syndrome and selective mutism played a role in this or not. But I am certain that the confidence with which the disabled community resisted against vague plans to create car-free days to combat global warming was new and unrivalled.

Two years later, in March 2020, the world is experiencing another extraordinary, rather frightening event: the coronavirus pandemic (COVID-19). The virus is a highly contagious disease that attacks the human respiratory tract, which, in difficult cases, leads to pneumonia and multi-organ failure. As a result of COVID-19, entire countries have been ordered to comply with measures of social isolation and physical distancing associated with lockdowns. Being forced to stay at home and to not engage in any social events or outings has sent shockwaves through populations across the globe.

In response to the measures aimed at stemming the pandemic, employers have had to accept changes to ways of working. Within academia, we suddenly moved from in-person teaching, research and meetings to fully online deliveries across the board.

Where once requesting reasonable adjustments, such as flexible working hours or working from home, may have been seen as an unnecessary luxury, overnight this became the reality for one and all. Suddenly, practically overnight, individuals with disabilities, chronic illnesses and/or neurodivergences became professionals, as for many of these individuals staying in is the normal way of life and coping with sensory or information overloads and the resulting fatigue and physical crashes are their everyday routine.

Here I am now, by the end of the journey to this edited book, and I am truly hopeful and entirely optimistic. Already, it is difficult to trace and keep track of the masses of recommendations available to support individuals with their wellbeing and mental health alongside the guidelines for making working from home not only possible, but effective and productive. I am hopeful and optimistic that once this crisis is over, as a society we will not return to expectations around ways of working that were commonplace before COVID-19. Instead, we now have a strong precedent to build upon that enable working remotely and using supportive and assistive technologies as a matter of course rather than as a 'reasonable adjustment'. As a consequence, individuals with disabilities, chronic illnesses and/or neurodivergences will be more easily bound into and connected to the academic community and no longer be seen as 'difficult' individuals, whose special needs cause extra work and require additional finances. Instead, the disabled and ablebodied, chronically ill and healthy, neurodivergent and neurotypical will all work alongside one another with the heightened sense of community and empathy that the contributors to this edited book have been asking for. This is my disability imaginary of the future.

References

Brown, N., Thompson, P., & Leigh, J.S. (2018). Making academia more accessible. *Journal of Perspectives in Applied Academic Practice*, 6(2), 82–90.

Ellis, C. (2009). Fighting back or moving on: An autoethnographic response to critics. *International Review of Qualitative Research*, 2(3), 371–378.

Fitzpatrick, P., & Olson, R.E. (2015). A rough road map to reflexivity in qualitative research into emotions. *Emotion Review*, 7(1), 49–54.

Holt, N.L. (2003). Representation, legitimation, and autoethnography: An autoethnographic writing story. *International Journal of Qualitative Methods*, 2(1), 18–28.

Salzman, P.C. (2002). On reflexivity. *American Anthropologist*, 104(3), 805–811.

Sparkes, A.C. (2002). Autoethnography: Self-indulgence or something more. In: Bochner, A.P., & Ellis, C. (eds). *Ethnographically Speaking: Autoethnography, Literature, and Aesthetics, 9*. Lanham, MD: Rowman Altamira, 209–232.

Spencer, P. (1992). Automythologies and the reconstruction of ageing. In: Okely, J., & Callaway, H. (eds). *Anthropology and Autobiography*. London: Routledge, 61–74.

Index

The index follows the text in using capitalised and non-capitalised terms such as autism and Autism, deaf and Deaf, to mark when a specific identity is intended (see page 10, note 1).

Page numbers in *italic* refer to figures; those in **bold** refer to tables.

M

NHS Constitution 220–221, 223
Nielsen-Hayden, T. 278
noise-reduction headphones/
    earphones 204
non-disabled people 77, 182–183
North Korea 241
nursing, undergraduate
    education 9, 217–218
  autism perceptions in
    academia 218–220
  challenges of, and
    autism 220–224
  recommendations 225–228
  reflective questions 225
  value-based recruitment 218, 221,
    225–226
Nursing and Midwifery
    Council 221, 222, 224

O

objectivity, in social science
    research 44–45
OCR (optical character
    recognition) 175, 183
older women
  in the academy 164, 165–166,
    166–168
  and chronic illness 159, 164
  gender and ageism 164–165
online support networks 318
optical character recognition
    (OCR) 175, 183
'othering' 284
overwork 25, 255
Oxford English Dictionary 74

P

pain, chronic 307–308
Paralympic Games 83
Paraorchestra 238, 239
ParaOrchestra and Friends 244
Parental Bereavement (Leave and
    Pay) Act 2018 285
Parkes, C.M. 289
passing strategies 306–308,
    309, 310
peer support 47, 123, 208, 318
pension rights 39
perfectionism 206, 207
'person with a disability'
    terminology 76
personal front 115
PhD vivas

and Autism 204
and stammering 120–121
Phillipson, C. 164
planning, and Autism 207
Polanyi, M. 59
positionality 59
postgraduate students
  Autistic 20
  autoethnography 21
  disability disclosures 3, 4
  disabled 304–305
  mental health conditions 265
  see also students
post-positivism 15
post-traumatic stress disorder
    285–286, 290–291, 305
PowerPoint 100
practice, as research 59–60
Pratt, A. 38, 39
pregnancy, autoethnography of 21
presentation scenario,
    stammering 115–116, 118,
    119, 120
Price, M. 192
Prigerson, H.G. 289
primary school teachers' voice
    issues 127–128, 135–136
privatisation 37
productive difference, and
    stammering 123
professional development
    training 317
'professional voice users' 127–128
psychiatric disability,
    autoethnography of 21
Puar, J.K. 25
Public Health England 102, *103*

Q

qualitative research 15

R

racism 21
radical specificity 93
Read, B. 42
reasonable adjustments 75, 172,
    190, 192, 311, 320
  and Autism 201
  and cancer 285, 295
  and colour blindness 107–108
  and disability disclosures 3–4
  lived experiences of 179–181
  and stammering 123

UCU (University and College
   Union) 39
undergraduate students
   disability disclosures 3–4
   see also students
Universal Design for Learning 85,
   254, 261
University and College Union
   (UCU) 39
University of Southampton 254
University of St Andrews,
   Scotland 267
   see also Depressed Academics
   group blog
unmeant gestures 118
upward mobility 120

V

verbal communication skills 120
   see also stammering
visibility, of disability in
   teaching 185–194
   recommendations 194–195
   reflective questions 194
visual impairment 7, 37–38, 42–43
VLEs (Virtual Learning
   Environments) 100
voice 112, 117
   recommendations 137–138
   voice loss 8, 127–132, 137
      legal status of 130
      reflective questions 137
      voice development 132–136,
         135, *136*
      voice rest 128–129, 133
   see also stammering
voice to text software 174,
   175, 256

W

Wacquant, Loïc 60

Walker, N. 197–198
Walpole, Galfidus 171–172
Waterfield, B. 25, 27
Watson, D.R. 131, 137
Watson, N. 309
Wellard, Ian 58–59
wellbeing, in the workplace 286
White, C. 289, 290
White people 21, 59
   students 2
white sticks 174
Wiliams, J. 296
women
   empowerment of 88
   older women
      in the academy 164, 165–166,
         166–168
      and chronic illness 159, 164
      gender and ageism 164–165
   see also gender
word to text software 256
Worden, J.W. 289
working conditions, academic 2,
   4–5, 37, 38–41, 62–63, 255
   disabilities resulting from 26
   and disabled academics 42–43, 47
   working from home 320
work–life balance 121
World Health Organization
   on deafness 142–143, 146
   gender and ageism 164–165
written preparation of teaching
   material 257–258
written work, formatting
   of 186–187

Y

yoga 54–55, 62, 63, 251

Z

Zhitomirskiy, Ilya 267